# Contents

*Preface* **vii**

**Part 1**    **The Factors of Effective Communication**   **1**

Chapter 1    Introduction   **1**

Chapter 2    Implications of the Theory of Communication   **7**

Chapter 3    The Writing Process: Getting Started   **21**

                  Isolating the Purpose   **22**
                  Researching the Material   **23**
                  Planning the Organization   **23**
                  Writing the First Draft   **25**
                  Cooling the First Draft   **25**
                  Editing the First Draft   **26**
                  Submitting the Completed Communication   **26**

Chapter 4    The Relationship of Form to Content   **31**

                  Organization   **31**
                  Unity   **32**
                  Paragraph   **32**
                  Coherence   **40**

Chapter 5    The Sentence   **53**

                  Types of Verbs   **54**
                  Types of Sentences   **58**
                  The Relative Pronouns and Modification   **61**
                  Variety in the Sentence   **65**

**Part 2**    **The Editing Challenge: Revision is Quality Control at Its Best**   **69**

Chapter 6    Sentence Structure and Style   **69**

                  Unnecessary Shifts in Structure   **69**
                  Passive Voice   **73**
                  Point of View   **73**
                  Level of Usage   **75**
                  Parallelism   **77**
                  Other Concerns in Structuring Sentences   **83**

Chapter 7    Correction of Misconceptions   **99**

                  Use Language Assertively   **99**
                  Be Concrete   **103**
                  Avoid Wordiness   **104**
                  Avoid "Smoke" Talk   **107**
                  Be Aware of False Elegance   **108**
                  Recognize Tautology   **108**

|  |  |  |  |
|---|---|---|---|
|  | Avoid Meaningless Modifiers **109** | **Part 3** | **Application: Reporting the Message 193** |
|  | Watch Out for Euphemisms **109** | Chapter 11 | Professional Documents **193** |
|  | Take Out Malapropisms **110** |  | Paraphrasing **193** |
|  | Watch Out for Word Confusion **110** |  | Reaction Paper **194** |
|  | Remove Trite Phrases and Mixed Metaphors **111** |  | Definition Paper **195** Process Paper **196** |
|  | Eliminate Jargon **112** |  | Analysis **197** |
|  | Watch Out for "Snow" Jobs **113** |  | Proposal **199** Memorandums **200** |
|  | Eliminate Sexism **114** |  | Trip Report **201** |
| Chapter 8 | Grammatical Specifics **119** |  | Letter of Inquiry (for Information) **201** |
|  | The Noun **119** |  | Letter of Inquiry (for Position) **202** |
|  | The Pronoun **121** |  | Letter of Application **203** |
|  | The Verb **127** |  | Resumé **205** |
|  | The Adjective **135** | Chapter 12 | Formal Report **207** |
|  | The Adverb **136** |  |  |
|  | Comparison of Adjectives and Adverbs **137** |  | Structure of the Report **207** Letter of Transmittal **209** |
| Chapter 9 | Punctuation for Meaning **145** |  | Abstract **210** |
|  | Potential Ambiguity **145** |  | Executive Summary **214** |
|  | Basic Chunking **147** |  | Sample—Student's Formal Report **214** |
|  | Punctuation Specifics **149** | **Information Sources 221** |  |
| Chapter 10 | Editing Challenges: Word Usage—Diction **169** |  | Guide to On-Line Reference Data Bases **221** |
|  | Words that Sound Alike **169** |  | Indexes to Interdisciplinary Scholarly Journals **223** |
|  | The Problem of Dropped D's **177** |  | Subject Encyclopedias **224** |
|  | Common Mix-ups **177** |  | Subject Dictionaries **226** |
|  | One Word or Two? **184** |  | Scholarly Book Review Sources **227** |
|  | Words that Go Together **185** |  |  |
|  | Referring to Two or More **185** |  | Social Science Indexes **228** |
|  | Quantitative Differences **186** |  | Specific Subject Sources **229** |
|  | Singular or Plural **186** |  | General Book Review Sources **240** |
|  | Awkward Words and Phrases **188** |  |  |

# Pre-Professional Writing

**Dr. Bernadine Carlson-Carmichael**
**Dr. Bradley Hayden**
*Western Michigan University*

**KENDALL/HUNT PUBLISHING COMPANY**
2460 Kerper Boulevard   P.O. Box 539   Dubuque, Iowa 52004-0539

Copyright © 1991 by Kendall/Hunt Publishing Company

ISBN 0-8403-6350-8

All rights reserved. No part of this publication may be reproduced, stored in a retrieval system, or transmitted, in any form or by any means, electronic, mechanical, photocopying, recording, or otherwise, without the prior written permission of the copyright owner.

Printed in the United States of America

10  9  8  7  6  5  4  3  2  1

Indexes to General Interest
  Periodicals  **240**
Newspaper Indexes  **240**
Quotation Sources  **241**

Film Reviews and Film
  Review Indexes  **241**
Style Guides  **242**

**Index  243**

# Preface

***Objectives:*** *Pre-Professional Writing* is a text for undergraduate or graduate students committed to some professional goal and serious about their writing skills preparation. It introduces students to the importance of all aspects of communication to their professional specialization, provides important and relevant concepts in English language usage and skills, and offers opportunity for the practice and use of these skills.

It stresses the importance of effective communication to industry, science, business, engineering, or academic concentration; it specifically indicates the role and responsibility of the individual in achieving such communication. The emphasis is on the development of a straight forward expository style characterized by accuracy, precision, conciseness, specifics, concreteness, objectivity, clarity, integrity—but also readability and individuality.

***Philosophical concerns:*** Whether it is in business, technology, science, or any of the specialized academic areas, the purpose of any communication is to effect—that is to inform, persuade, sell, record, etc. Any communication situation involves Sender-Message-Receiver. Good communication implies getting the message to the receiver with a minimal loss of content. This means that senders must know what they want to send and also the best way to send it. Moreover, the tone, diction, and style must be appropriate to the purpose of the message and intended audience. If people have something important to say or report, it is only logical that it will be more important if they can say it well. Poor writing could be the outward and visible form of an inward confusion of thought.

Today, the increased diversification of business and industry makes good written communication an imperative. Since it is not unusual for a main office to be on one coast, its research facilities on another, and its production facilities at several spots in between if not in another part of the world, its management and professional teams must be capable of producing effective exposition. Our experience in conducting executive writing seminars throughout the United States has made us especially cognizant of the communication needs of business and industry. Company representatives attending these workshops, all involved in high level positions outside a university community, have always stressed their need and that of others within their companies to be able to write clear, concise, and effective communication.

*Approach:* The approach here is functional with its application of value for all communication across the curriculum. The materials have proved not only successful for the needs of business, scientific, and technical writers but also on campuses for other academically oriented writers.

*Pre-Professional Writing* also focuses on writing as a process and provides examples for different applications. Thus, the emphasis is on basic skills that provide students with a practical framework for any professional career.

**Part 1** *The Factors of Effective Communication*

# 1 Introduction

Have you ever heard anyone say "I know what I want to say but I don't know how to say it" or "How I say it isn't important, it's what I say that's important"? These near-maxims enjoy a wide and enviable degree of currency both in and out of the campus community and indicate facets of a communication fantasy. Is it possible that adherents of such clichés do not want to go to the bother of trying to say "it"? Instead they expect their listeners to accept them as great writers or thinkers on some kind of blind faith. Unfortunately, their apparent stress on "what" is said could be a mere license for carelessness or a glib cover-up for a lack of skill or industry. Isn't it more likely that if a writer has something to say, he or she is going to say it, and more importantly, say it well? If some concept is comprehensible to the writer and to a reader, the writer must have found a "good" way to say it—that is what makes it comprehensible.

The non-starters and the style apologists are not the only victims of a kind of fantasy. At another extreme are the unsure writers who equate "good writing" with the long, involved sentence. Achievement of their ideal means stuffing each sentence with a generous assortment of polysyllabic words or stretches of specialized jargon. Their desire to impress outweighs their need to express. Franklin D. Roosevelt once very forcibly reminded one of his writers about this tendency. The writer had included the following sentence in one of the "Fireside Chat" scripts: "We are endeavoring to construct a more inclusive society." President Roosevelt changed the line to read simply as "We're going to make a country in which no one is left out."

Whether in business, technology, science, or any of the many professional areas, the purpose of any communication is to effect; that is to inform, persuade, sell, record, entertain, influence. Successful communication implies being understood; it also implies not being misunderstood. Today, a message can travel around the world in seconds—a communication failure can travel just as fast.

Good writing means effective writing: it is a clear, concise, accurate, objective, and appropriate expression of a well-focused and audience-oriented message. Bad writing means ineffective writing: it has lapses in logic, sentence-structure makeup, grammatical usage, punctuation, and spelling. More unfortunately, it may also be the visible evidence of some inward confusion of thought. Clear and effective writing means clear thinking. It means making a piece of writing come "alive"—making it appealing and making it meaningful. If bad thought corrupts language, language can also corrupt thought.

Communication is crucial in this age of industrial expansion and decentralization. Writing has become the business of business. There is only more and more paper work and less and less time to write it and read it. Today, the firm handshake in some face-to-face encounter confirms few if any decisions. It is the written material that is important. Sometimes this written material may travel half way around the world and to somebody who needs a translator to understand it.

The growing decentralization in the world of business has brought about this tremendous increase in paper work—in writing. The executive offices, research facility, manufacturing plant, or sales rooms may be thousands of miles or even continents apart. This makes the written memorandum, letter, news release, report, or advertising copy the important or only means of contact within and without the structure of a company. Moreover, a major change, such as the development of a new product, adoption of a new process, or the expansion or deletion of a facility may involve many individuals, for it may have research, personnel, financial, production, and marketing implications. This means the report must be understandable to many audiences. It may need to be stripped of unnecessary jargon, ambiguous terms, archaic phrases, and obscure vocabulary. The investment of thousands or millions of dollars or hundreds of human work hours may depend on the results of a piece of research or a recommendation contained in a letter, report, or brief.

The efficiency and persuasive aspect of a piece of writing depends on the quality of the information, not on the quantity. It is the writer who must make sure the communication clearly provides the essential and pertinent materials. A writer needs always to be wary of the "you know" syndrome—the reader may not know and not think it important to ask for an explanation. The latest estimate on the cost of a one-page letter leaving a firm today is approximately eleven dollars. The figure represents the cost of time spent in composing, processing, and mailing the correspondence. Considering the number of letters put out each day by the many firms in just one city, to say nothing of the state, national, or international coverage, the financial implication of this cost is staggering—as are the communication implications of such massive paper weight.

In speech, a speaker has his or her whole body to reinforce what the words are saying—the face, the eyes, the stance, the hands. By closely observing, the audience can surmise whether the speaker is sincere, serious, or joking. They can even ascertain whether the speaker seems puzzled or confused. But in written communication, writers must depend only upon language—the choice of words and how to string such words together into meaningful sentences. Writers have to depend on the twenty-six letters of the alphabet plus a few punctuation aids to convey concepts that are important and concepts that are not.

The writer works very close to the source of both new and old information. Today, research is one of our largest industries but until the information gleaned from such research appears in some organized and understandable written communication and is available to the appropriate decision-making groups or individual, it may be of little value to a company or to society as whole.

For example, the important research in the middle of the last century into thermodynamics basic to the development of our synthetic rubber and plastics remained in obscurity until this century. It was the difficulty of the earlier scientists to write understandably about their important discovery that delayed its practical application for over fifty years. Scientists in this century found it easier to rediscover the synthetic process than to try to decipher some of the notes and written reports of the earlier researchers. The tremendous importance of synthetics today only further emphasizes the tragic consequences of the original discoverers' handicap of not being able to communicate well.

A long time ago, Lord Bacon stated that "knowledge is power." He also implied that such knowledge can be fully productive only if shared. John Stuart Mills very strongly concurred with this concept as the following quotation indicates:

> Hardly any original thoughts on mental or social subjects ever make their proper importance in the minds even of their inventors, until aptly selected words or phrases, as it were, nailed them down and held them fast.

Communication is still essentially a human affair. Computers and word processors can take tremendous masses of data and bring order out of them in seconds or less. But the information fed into the computer comes from materials received from the activity of the human mind that has worked over endless reports. What impact any computer data will have requires the services of the writer to use it in relevant and pertinent proposals, reports, memoranda, letters, and the like. Thus, the computer needs human services for both its input and use of its output—and both ends depend upon the accuracy and completeness of written researched material.

The commodities of industry are products and reports. The importance of written communication in putting a product on the market is evident in the simple cycle represented in Figure 1.1. As it shows, reports are essential for the original development and manufacture of a product, for marketing it, for improving it, for marketing the improved product, for replacing or changing its style or function, and for marketing the emerging new product.

The cycle is also relevant to business and professional services. Any new business venture or professional activity or program must begin with an idea and progress through related stages of development—from research to first proposal, to improvement, to expansion, to adaptation, perhaps to acceptance. Each stage results from a written report based on further study, research, or evaluation; each stage requires the persuasion of the involved groups to support or accept the procedure or program. Thus, communication not only precedes any innovation, change, or promotion but also precipitates the action. The larger the business or the more important the professional commitment, the more crucial is the communication.

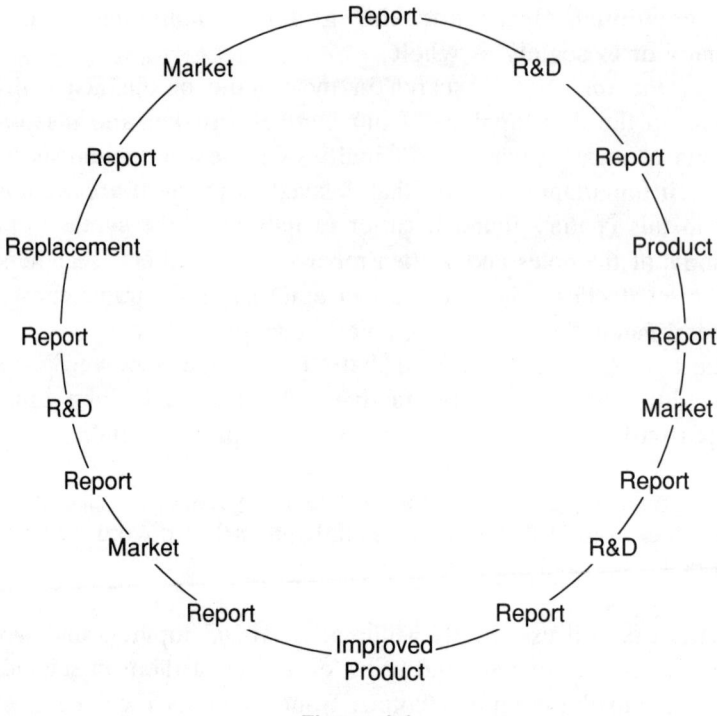

**Figure 1.1**

Writing is the principal means of transmitting scientific, technical, professional, and business information. New ideas, proposals, suggestions, or procedures, appearing in writing are available for critical study at another time and place or by other experts. It is the written word that ensures the protection for the individual, organization, supplier, labor group, competitor, stockholder, or anyone dependent on such information.

Writing is time consuming and often a lonely activity. There are no magic formulas or three easy steps for achieving good writing. To believe such means exist leads only to disillusionment. Fortunately, in any professional or executive capacity, writers are always working from strength. They write about familiar things or ideas learned through formal education, experience, or research. Thus, since such writers already have access to the essential knowledge and data, they are in a better position to concentrate on how to say it—that is provide organized, accurate, easy-to-read and understandable messages for the intended audience. Furthermore, writing stimulates thinking and often serves to bring ideas into clearer focus.

To be a pre-professional student implies looking toward management and executive positions. Management implies control and control means communication. The lowest levels of work may require little writing. A good knowledge of technical procedures is often adequate. But as the professional rises to the supervisory and managerial levels and in salary, the amount of writing increases accordingly. The top level responsibility is virtually all communication and thinking. Executives providing good suggestions at some high level conference are likely to be asked to put their thoughts in a memorandum or proposal for distribution in order to facilitate a more leisurely study and consideration of them. Individuals receiving this responsibility cannot request someone else to do this writing. It is the person who signs this type of report that will receive the credit for the idea and possibly the promotion that might follow because of its importance to the company. A first position may result from an individual's technical knowledge; but a next position may be more dependent on the level of his or her communication skills. The following statement of Peter F. Drucker makes this point very clear: "As soon as you move one step up from the bottom, your effectiveness depends on your ability to reach others through the spoken or written word." Thus, good writing is the channel for personal advancement as well as for company or corporate change and expansion.

## Questions

1. Summarize the circle graph (Figure 1). Use the following words for your introduction: "The circle graph suggests. . ."

2. How can you apply the theory of communication to your area of professional specialization?

3. How may your writing improve or detract from your professional growth?

4. List as many specialized terms as possible that are unique to your profession. Why is it important to be aware of such terms when reading, writing, and listening? Did you spell them correctly?

5. How does the following quotation apply to your situation? "A professional's success in today's job market is almost a direct function of being able to express ideas in writing and speaking."

6. Do you agree or reject the following ideas?
   a. Great scientists are always bad writers.

   b. Some technical, scientific, or business ideas are too complex to explain simply.

7. How is an individual's professional image reflected by his or her spoken or written communication?

8. Will you have a wide variety of clientele? Why is it important that you know about your clientele? What should you know about them?

9. Will your company or firm have a special format for memoranda, business letters, reports? Could you devise or revise one?

## Assignments

A. In an essay, answer the following questions:
   Do the media make the news or does the news make the media?
   What are some of the communication issues in our society?

B. If you were asked to determine the cost of a one-page letter sent by a firm, what factors would you have to consider? Multiplied by the amount of correspondence generated by offices in your city, or the United States in one day, how much are we investing in communication-related activity?

C. Talk to some professionals in the field of your interest. How much of their time involves communication activities? What kind of activity?

# 2 Implications of the Theory of Communication

We are now in the shadow of the twenty-first century, living in an age of atomic turmoil and prolific and instant communication. We have come a long way since the time of the solitary monk sitting on his hard, stone bench in a candle-lit lonely cell and endlessly copying the frugal words of a handful of writers for an almost equally small number of readers. Today, we depend upon our writing and speaking to furnish the means for our prodigious social and commercial expansion and progress; promote understanding among myriad diverse and self-serving groups; and protect us from technological mindlessness and the challenges of competitors, government agencies, labor groups, consumers, and clients. Our ability to communicate supported by its related activity of logical thinking may be our only skill saved from the encroaching competition of the robot.

Effective communication is crucial to business, industry, and the professions. It is basic to every aspect and activity of an enterprise. Business and the professional fields need creative talent, ideas, and capital to develop and provide essential services. Industry needs money, machines, raw materials, and workers to produce goods. The only way to secure these needs is through continuous communication activity.

The role of an executive is to create and develop ideas, manage people, and promote essential services. Proficient management depends on communication. An effective executive must be capable of sending messages to many different levels of receivers who have many varying interests and points of view. Personnel officers must communicate with prospective employees and with higher echelons of management. Research and development specialists must make known their needs for raw materials, equipment, and additional staff to the financial and procurement officers as well as explain the importance of their on-going research for marketing or sales. In turn the marketing and the sales contingency must assess the views and project the needs of the consumer or client if a company is to continue providing satisfactory products or services.

Figure 2.1 summarizes the essential and extensive role of communication in all phases of production and marketing. It also indicates the complicated information

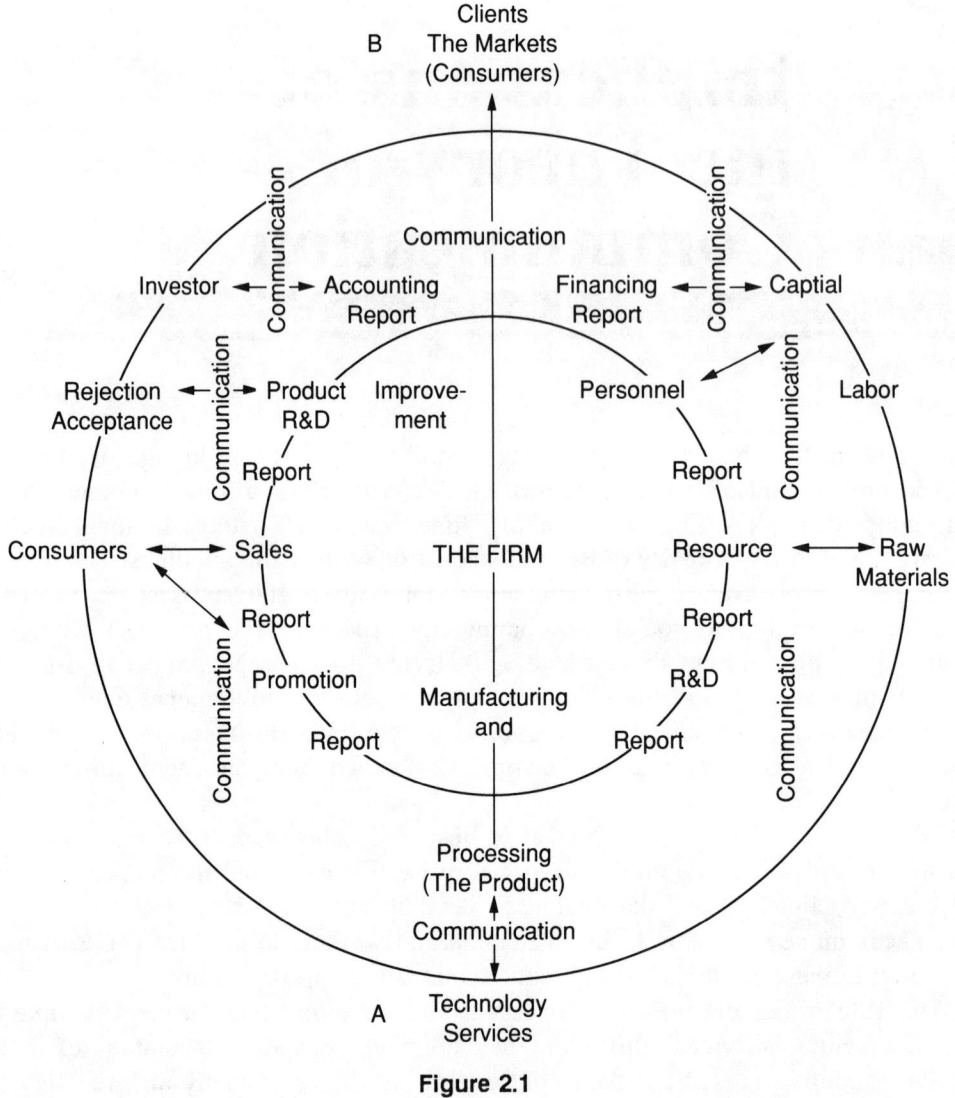

**Figure 2.1**

network inherent in professional activities. The vertical line *AB* extending from "Technology, through Manufacturing and Processing in the Firm to the Markets or Consumers or from Services provided by the Firm to Clients" is simplistically misleading in its apparent directness. The imposed circles provide the real clues to the many possible facets and levels of audience interdependency. The chart further suggests that communication is the pervasive activity linking individual specialties to an overall design. A misunderstanding occurring at any point in the process could lead to a serious breakdown in the flow of essential information.

The function of professional communication is to inform, report, record, and to persuade—often at the same time in different areas for different audiences: in development, production, promotion, sales, and evaluation. Any proposal, report, letter, or memorandum is the organized and timely presentation of relevant information directed to a particular individual or group to achieve a specific purpose. Each must be appropriate to the level of the reader and the type of information conveyed. To achieve their purpose, writers must be aware of the needs and influence of their readers, depending on logical and persuasive presentations of essential and controlled ideas. Good communication does not mean that the receiver must agree with the sender, only that he or she clearly understands the message sent.

Good writers, as do good speakers, appreciate and understand the basic relationships involved in the information exchange process—the Who, to Whom, the What, the When, and the Why. Just as they carefully collect and study the data for their messages, writers must also study their intended audience (the Whom)—their interests, knowledge level, attitudes, previous orientations, and needs.

Good writers also realize early that they must handle their messages differently for different audience interests and different audience levels. For example, a report written to top management probably would not contain all the technical procedures found in an analysis written for a technician or specialist. Material written for a financial vice president would properly emphasize more the roles of financial return and investment in the research project. The writer sending the same report to multiple levels of audience would have to identify with the least specialized receiver. This could entail including more background material and eliminating much of the specialized technical or scientific vocabulary or providing good definitions for any included. For instance, in explaining the process of chemical sludge activation to a chemically uninformed audience, the micro-organisms could become the "workers" and the chemical change their "duty" in the process.

It could also mean rearranging the order of the sections so that the discussions of the more technical data would appear last with the summary of the import of the project placed first. The writer could adapt the conventional formal scientific report pattern to the understanding and needs of the audience.

| General Ordering of a Scientific Report | |
|---|---|
| **For Expert** | **For General Knowledgeable Audience** |
| Introduction | Summary (Conclusions) |
| Materials and Methods | Introduction (Background Purpose) |
| Results | Results |
| Discussions | Materials and Procedures |

**Figure 2.2**

The following triangular diagram indicates the information needs by the various audiences in the hierarchy of institutions, businesses, plants, and firms. It also reveals the reading habits at each audience level.

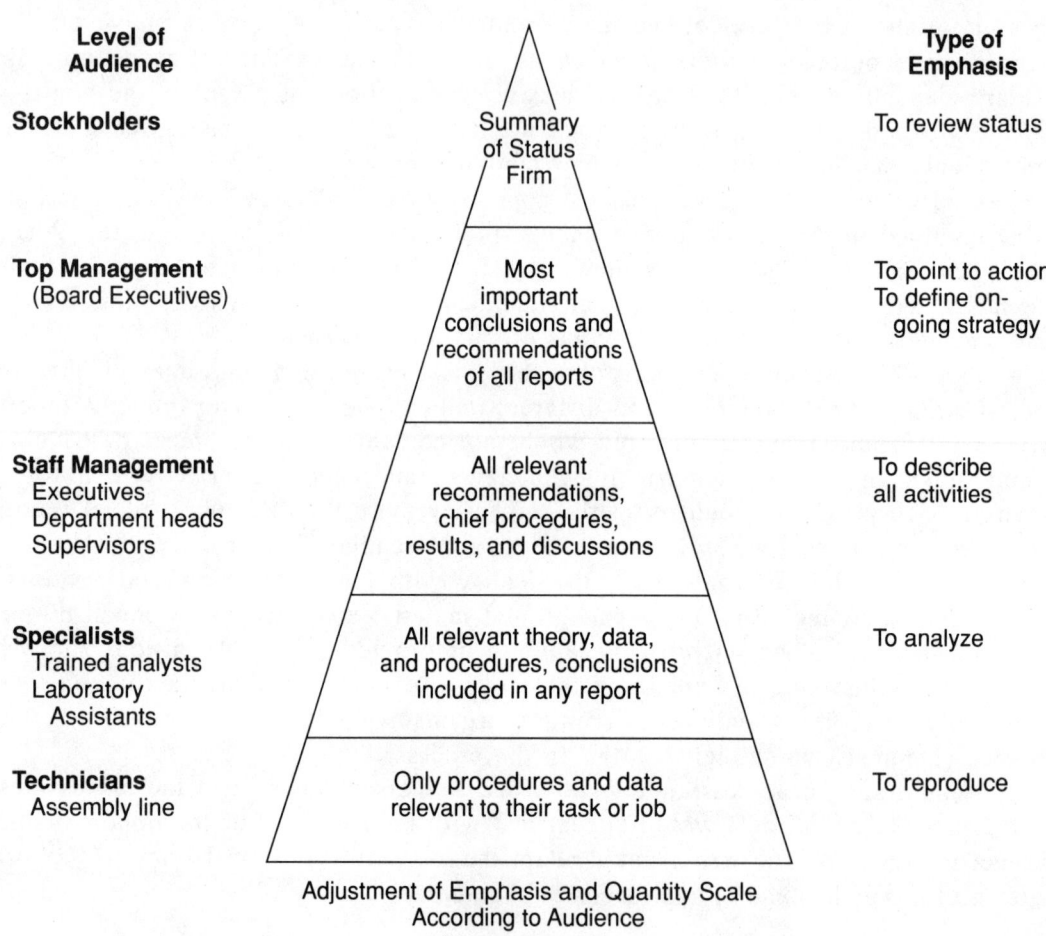

Adjustment of Emphasis and Quantity Scale
According to Audience

**Figure 2.3**

The schemata in Figure 2.4 below provides representative types and levels of senders and their possible varying levels of receivers.

| Sender (Who) | Words | Message (What) | Words | Receivers (whom) (Why) |
|---|---|---|---|---|
| | | Noise—Breakdown | | |
| | | *Point of Distortion Probability* | | |
| source | | | | audience |
| writer | | | | reader |
| speaker | | | | listener |
| encoder | | | | decoder |
| authority | | | | authority |
| subordinate | | | | subordinate |
| authority | | | | subordinate |
| subordinate | | | | authority |
| engineer, technician, scientist | | | | lay person |
| engineer, technician, scientist | | | | professional |
| professional | | | | client, patient consumer |

**Figure 2.4**

The sender, writer, or encoder hopes to have the message received by the audience, reader, or decoder as nearly like he or she sent it as possible; that is have the ideas similarly interpreted and understood. However, since an individual is the product of a unique environment, perfect communication is probably not ever possible as the background and attitudes of any sender or receiver will never exactly coincide. Too much deviation from the way the sender sends the message to the way the intended receiver interprets it could result in a communication "breakdown." This means some type of "noise" enters the message along the way. This noise could be the result of anything from careless mechanics and word usage to errors in judgment, inadequate information, or jumbled and wordy sentence structure.

The two sentences below appear innocent enough but each harbors a problem that could trigger a serious communication failure:

> He stated that his mother rented her house for a hundred dollars a week.

> Without oil transportation in this country as we know it would not be possible.

The first sentence contains an ambiguous word—rent. Does his mother receive the rent or pay out the rent? The second sentence needs a comma after oil before it can make much sense.

An audience, of course, can react in various ways: read the communication with interest and act on it, file it, pass it on to a colleague or another department for possible action, ignore it, or toss it out. If one or the other of the last two alternatives becomes the case, then the sender may somehow have misunderstood his or her role, mistaken the interest or mood of the receiver, failed to provide sufficient information, or been careless in the tone or manner and style of writing. Moreover, an audience can be hostile, skeptical, receptive, or supportive. The communication for the hostile and skeptical will require some additional persuasive efforts and some adjustment in tone and the number and type of facts provided. The receptive and supportive audience will be responsive to and satisfied with any clear, concise presentation of appropriate data.

Various factors can affect the influence and acceptability of a piece of communication. Important among these is the way the audience perceives the sender. If the receivers respect the writer as a well-informed, capable, and reliable information source, they will also give more credence to a proposal or report submitted to them. The sender can earn and enjoy this respect only if his or her messages consistently reflect good logic and indicate that the ideas or concepts are the result of careful research and attention to details. Dependence on superficial knowledge coupled with poor English usage skills will do little to inspire reader respect and confidence.

Closely related to this factor is the way the writer perceives his or her role in a communication situation. Senders who feel pressured to impress rather than express evidence a certain insecurity in their abilities and knowledge. This insecurity reflected in their writing can further detract from any respect or confidence hoped for from associates or superiors.

Writers must also consider how a company may use their material. Knowing this will provide them with further insight into the nature of their writing commitment. If a document is to enter a retrieval system or is to serve as an official record, the writer might assume an almost infinite potential audience for it. This would require definition of any technical or scientific terminology, large quantities of documentation, and careful analyses. Additional explanation would be crucial if lay clients or technical assistants were involved. However, a relatively informal memorandum sent to colleagues would not need to define all the jargon nor offer the same amount of documentation, definitions, and support.

Another consideration is the amount of time a reader might have to commit to the reading or study of any particular document. Often readers do not have time to read a document from cover to cover. If so, the writer must summarize the key points at the outset and preface the work with a good summary or abstract. This could be particularly important for readers that might not be knowledgeable in the subject but yet have some obligation and need to be familiar with its major ideas or proposals. Often the immediate audience will not be a colleague or the supervisor of the department. The document also could pass to many departments in a company for appraisal or be retained in retrieval disks or in files for years awaiting the action of a more distanced reader.

So far the discussion has centered about the obligations of the writer (Who) for preventing communications breakdowns. The stress has been on the responsibility of the sender for appropriate coding of well researched materials and good audience prediction. Communication, however, is really a two-way responsibility. The receivers (to Whom) must also be competent and accommodating decoders; that is they must be responsive and objective to all messages coming to their desks.

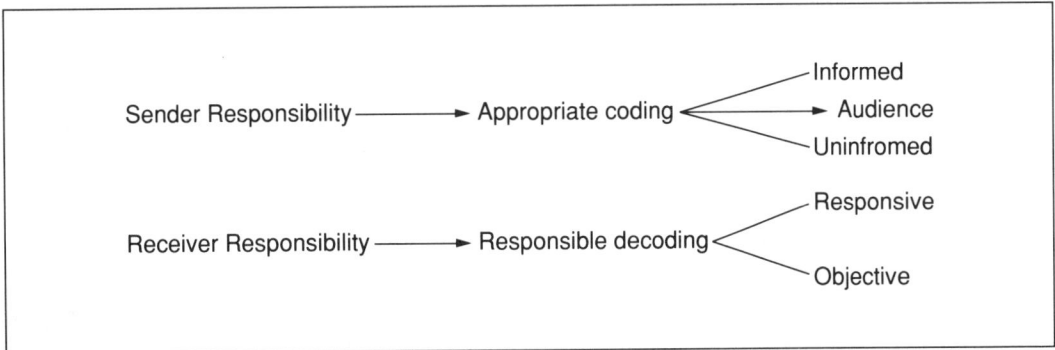

**Figure 2.5**

The third part of the communication schemata is the message (the What): the ideas, proposals, and information that the sender projects to the receiver. The message can be one word to a one-sentence directive, a paragraph to several paragraphs, or a book length report to a volume series. Gibbon uses several volumes to provide his picture of *The Rise and Fall of the Roman Empire* as does Winston Churchill for his *History of the English Speaking People*. A yearly report or proposal may be nearly book length, a letter may be little longer than one or two paragraphs, and a memorandum could contain only one or two sentences. Of course, some memoranda could be as long as a report.

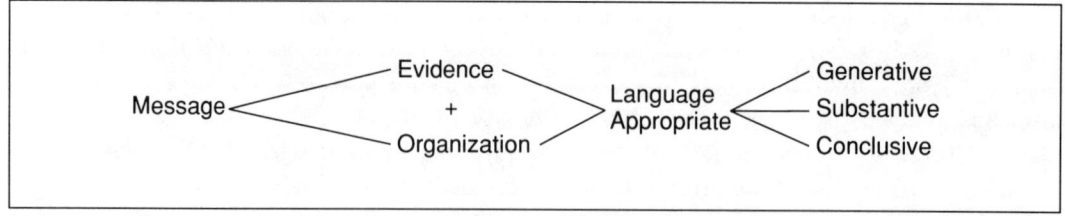

**Figure 2.6**

Evidence derives from investigation, testing, experimentation, and study. It represents the data, ideas, concepts, conclusions—the raw material of a report, letter, or memorandum. The organization is the appropriate sequencing of the ideas into sentences and paragraphs—the logical arrangement of the factual material to provide the specific emphasis for a specific audience.

A message is *generative* if it provides the basis for new construction, new programs, new products, or new direction. It is *substantive* if it answers inquiries, explains procedures, or summarizes current achievements and on-going activities. It is *conclusive* if it is the end product of some venture, research, experiment, or study.

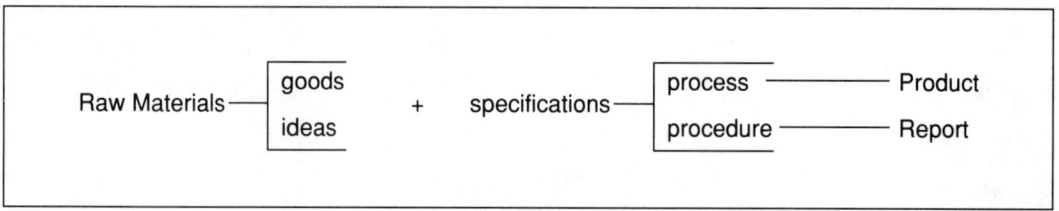

**Figure 2.7**

Just as products are processed from raw materials plus specifications, reports derive from information plus another type of specifications.

Graphs, charts, tables, and figures are supplements to writing and represent aspects of language in its broader sense. The tone and style of the message are the result of the type of language selected for the encoding. The use of specialized terminology, reliance on long and involved sentences, and presentation of large quantities of statistical material imply a more formal tone and a document for a more knowledgeable and specialized audience. A document simply written providing definitions and explanations for any "hard" terminology and using a minimal amount of statistics would indicate a more informal style.

Wordiness of the message does not mean substance. The quality of a message is far more important than the quantity. What a writer intended to say, what he or she wrote, and what the reader will read must be the same.

To say a message must meet the informational needs of an audience provides a somewhat oversimplification of the process. Figure 2.8 below shows that a firm has many audiences, many levels of audiences both inside and outside the firm.

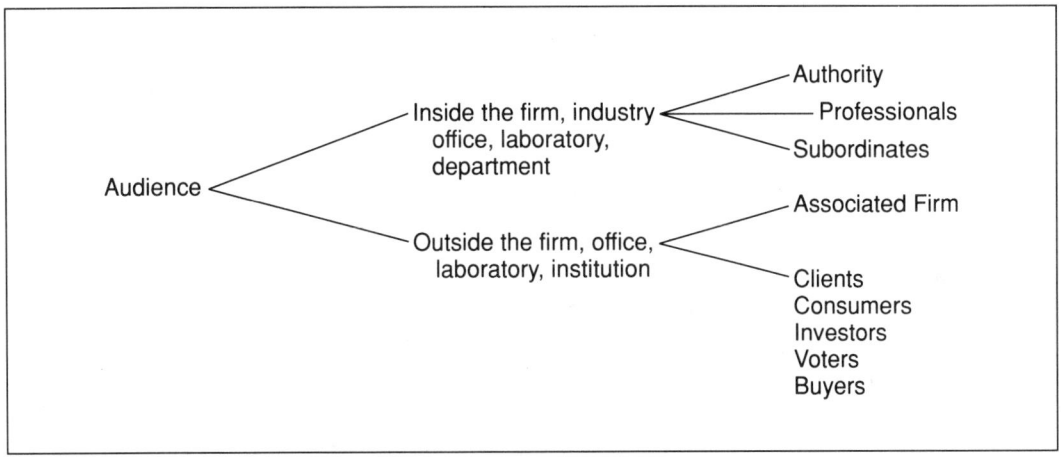

**Figure 2.8**

The virtual hierarchy inside a company or institution makes in-house relations as important as producer-consumer relations. Each level or position in this hierarchy not only shares certain experiences but also evidences considerable disparity—thus harboring a basis both for understanding as well as misunderstanding. The differences in perception at the various levels can be infinite.

Besides providing information for such audiences, each piece of communication also sends an image about the writer—his or her knowledge level, attitudes, and skill for communicating this knowledge. Each piece is a personal emissary. It is the tool of business when it is impossible for a firm representative to make a personal visit. It is also a permanent record.

Inside the firm, the message may be going to another informed professional, to an authority figure, to a subordinate, to another department, or to another area. Whether traveling to some destination inside or outside the firm, the message projects two images—the writer's capability or concern and the prestige and good will of the company. When a writer signs or initials a letter or memorandum, he or she is accepting the responsibility for its content. Thus, a letter must carry the right image of the writer and the firm with it. Companies are very jealous of their image. The good will and respect a good image reflects is essential for their continued financial success. The inadequate communication skills of an employee at any level could jeopardize a company's standing as well as limit any opportunities for his or her promotion. It could even lead to an employee's dismissal from the firm.

In any firm, business, or profession both horizontal and vertical lines of communication exist. Figure 2.9 indicates some of the possibilities for horizontal communication: engineer to engineer, scientist to scientist, authority to authority, subordinate to subordinate, service professional to other service professionals. However, a manager to an employee, an engineer to a lay person, or a service professional to a client or consumer represents vertical lines of communication.

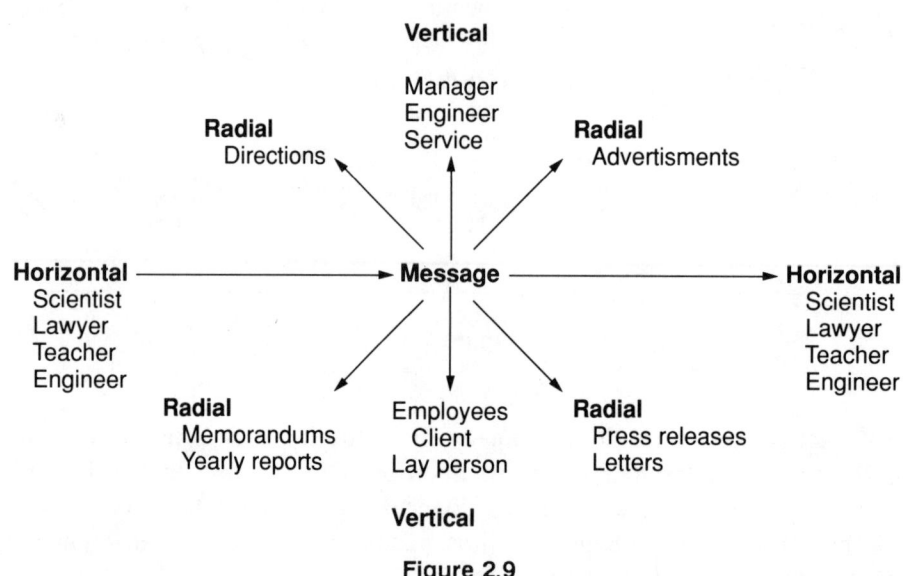

Figure 2.9

These lines seem very clear-cut; however, the process is much more complicated than it appears. For instance, the report of a Ph.D. on some phase of science about some five-year research project to other Ph.D.'s in the field would actually represent as much vertical as horizontal communication. True, the similar formal educational background and interest orientation of each should provide some basis for understanding; however, the five years the writer spent investigating or developing a theory or product would place him or her at a different knowledge level. To assure good communication could require the inclusion of some background for the material, explanation of new procedures and materials, and definition of new terms. Thus, a writer must be cautious in assuming sophisticated backgrounds even among colleagues. There is never a complete similarity of knowledge. Actually overspecialization and too much knowledge can be roadblocks to good communication even with informed audiences in the same profession.

Normally upper management executives would exemplify the best in horizontal communication. However, a vice president in charge of research in some scientific area of a company might have little in common with the vice president in stock-holder affairs. The research vice president might have a great deal more in common with the specialists working under him or her. Thus, in certain cases, these communication lines could represent both horizontal through knowledge level and vertical through line-of-command level.

Radial communication perhaps requires greater skill on the part of the senders (writers). These messages include press releases, advertisements, product directions, annual reports, letters, memorandums, notes, to name a few. All of these are for outside audiences diverse in interest, needs, and educational level.

Writers must always be sensitive to the requirements and interests of their readers who really determine the scope and format for any type of communication. Many factors, among them corporate direction and personality, affect the production of a piece of writing. Effective professional writers begin by cultivating correctness and acknowledging their limitations. They learn to match the function of their document with the appropriate format and their strategy with that of their audience.

How can writers know when their messages have too much "noise" and a break down in communications is imminent if not already the case? They can be very sure that such is the case when one of the following begins to occur: the communication receives no response or an unexpected response, requires continued correspondence or phone calls, indicates misinterpretations of some of the items, and evidences an obvious misunderstanding of the purpose.

How can writers then measure the success of their writing? The effectiveness, of course, depends upon satisfying the purpose of the communication. In company relations, some pertinent questions receiving "yes" answers would indicate a considerable degree of success: Did the company expand, replace outmoded equipment, adopt new safety measures, develop a new process, discover a new product? Similar questions for business would include the following: Did the firm show a profit for the year, find needed supplies, add new clients, consumers, customers, or enjoy continued good will both inside and outside the firm? On a personal basis, a writer could assess his or her success in other ways: Did he or she receive an increase in pay, the much desired promotion, or a more prestigious position?

# Questions

1. What causes a communication breakdown? Specifically what type of "noise" might occur in communications in your specialization?

2. What is your attitude toward the following letter? What images does this letter project?

Jan 17, 1990

To:

    In regards to your letter of Jan. 10, 1990. Your interest check on account #291-5-00000008 was mail out to you Dec. 31, 1989 cashiers' check #90098508. You should have it by now. If not, a stop payment needs to be placed. We need your account #291-5-00000008 and for you to say that you never received it, so to say you want a stop payment placed on it, along with your signature, than we can issue you a new check.

Bank of _____



Mary Smith




3. What does the following letter tell you about the writer—and the attitude? How would you respond to this letter?

November 10, 1989

Dear Customer

    As a result of an error in our Bill (Bank) Payment Plan processing, we deducted a lesser amount from your checking account than the amount reflected in the "Total Due" amount (which includes a Gas Supplier Refund) of your October service bill. This difference is equal to the amount of the Gas Supplier Refund and is due to the refund amount having been subtracted twice in determining the amount to deduct from your checking account.

    To correct this error, the "Total Due" amount of the service bill you will be receiving or have received for the November bill month contains a "Last Month's Account Balance" in addition to the current month's charges. The "Total Due" amount on your November bill will be deducted from your checking account on the stated due date. If you have any questions concerning this situation, please contact the Company office at the telephone number shown at the bottom of your service bill. We apologize for any inconvenience this error may have caused.

Thank you.


Bill Caspers
Moon Power Company




4. How do you know when you have a communication breakdown? Must your audience agree with you in order for communication to take place?




5. How are people influenced by communication? Manipulated?




6. Does knowledge increase a writer's capability? Why or why not? Give specific examples from your experiences.

7. Explain the importance of these concepts:

        breakdown                message
        noise                       jargon
        purpose                  verbosity
        appropriateness     cliché
        straight English      audience

8. What communication breakdown might occur in your "on-the-job situation"? Analyze it as a problem of prediction.

9. How is communication important at all levels and between all levels in a business, industry, or profession.

## Assignments

In an essay, discuss one of the following: 500 words

1. Explain how communication will affect you in your professional field?
2. Describe three factors which could lead to communication breakdown. Support your points with examples taken from your present experiences.

# 3 The Writing Process: Getting Started

Good writing always demands hard work, but through an understanding of the composing process, a writer can reduce the stress or tension that might accompany an important writing assignment. Many writers seeking professional careers have not learned the logistics of effective composing and often stumble when confronted with the need to communicate. At times, the result can be a much wasted effort, ending in the acquisition of a genuine writing phobia or anxiety. Weak writers often work without a specific plan, relying almost solely on the vagaries of inspiration. Good writers cultivate good methods. They control their composition through a structured working approach.

The amount of time required for any piece of writing, of course, depends on its purpose, its importance, and its length. But regardless of these factors, a clear, concise, and effective piece of communication is more likely to emerge if from the outset a writer perceives the task as a progression through some very specific stages. The seven steps outlined below are crucial to any written communication. Following these steps can provide the incentive for getting started and increase a writer's insight into the various aspects of the subject matter.

Isolating the Purpose—Defining the Audience
　　Researching the Material—Collecting the Data and Ideas
　　　　Planning the Organization—Providing a Logical Structure
　　　　　　Writing the First Draft—Composing
　　　　　　　　Cooling the First Draft—Distancing
　　　　　　　　　　Editing the First Draft—Revising, Revising, Revising
　　　　　　　　　　　　Submitting the Completed Communication—Circulating the Finished Product

Figure 3.1

# Isolating the Purpose—Defining the Audience

One thing that may make professional writing easier is that each piece of communication whether a memo, letter, long proposal, or summary of some research work has a clearly defined purpose from the outset. A manager, business executive, researcher or technician knows what the subject is and why the piece of written communication is necessary. This writing must be creative but in a different sense than that of a poet or novelist. It can have only one interpretation. A poem, play, or novel may permit many interpretations, the more usually the better the critical review. But in the process of providing an account or description of some investigation, development, treatment, or in answer to some inquiry from a consumer or client, the message must be objective, accurate, complete, and clear.

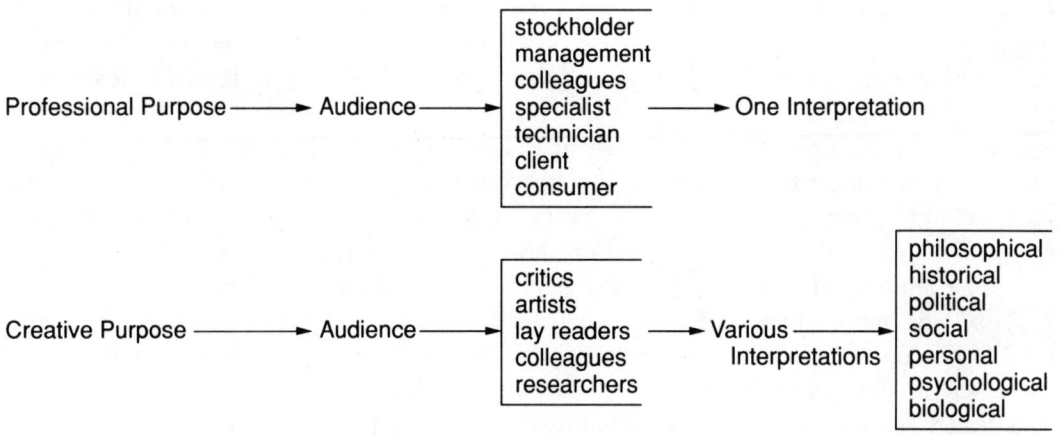

**Figure 3.2**

Writers must possess a very clear perception of the purpose from the beginning. What to say and how to say it depend upon a clear concept of the need and use of the communication.

One of the key failures in professional communication occurs if writers are uncertain of the specific nature of the writing assignment and audience. Without a thorough knowledge of the purpose behind the communication, writers cannot create a proper and effective focus for their work. In most cases, they can correct this problem by discussing the proposed document with the office making the assignment. Writers may also learn much by referring to similar kinds of documents in files; however, they should be wary of unthinking emulation. This could lead them to duplicating archaic, mediocre, or poor work.

# Researching—Collecting the Ideas

Good writing begins with solid research, learning all the facts necessary for communication to occur. Writers cannot express what they have not learned and do not know. Good writers must first be good researchers. Their answers to any inquiries or the support for any proposal depends on it. Through research the writer procures the information and data to develop, expand, or clarify some point of view or answer for some question. This could include gathering materials in the library, performing laboratory experiments, studying and recording the intricacies of some process, conducting surveys, or talking to some knowledgeable authority. Fortunately, today the relatively inexpensive on-line computer searches can provide researchers with rapid and easy access to large quantities of bibliography and information.

Good writers need to cultivate good research skills and acquaint themselves with standard journals and indices of their profession. Successful writers also cultivate good contacts within their profession, for their colleagues can be important sources for information. Regardless of the project, it is usually impossible to write without notes of some kind—usually the more copious the notes the better. Working from some notes is essential even if only dictating an answer to some enquiry or writing up a one-page memorandum or short proposal.

There are many ways to collect information. Some writers, such as scientific researchers, work from notebooks filled with the supporting data. Others write from notes recorded on notecards or material stored in a retrieval system on tapes or disks. Many keep enormous files of such information, some of which may be usable for many other projects. Professional writers learn early not to throw anything away.

The amount and type of material required depend upon the nature of the assignment and the anticipated audience or audiences. Formal reports to specialists in the field require much supporting data and special documentation of the sources. Scientists or technicians may depend upon their notebooks, disks, or tapes to document their procedures and results. Thus, they need to include the particulars of their research in their files and keep them up to date and active. Writers must always give credit to the work or contributions of others and should understand and use the basic documentation style of their specialty. (See Information Sources)

# Planning the Organization—Providing a Logical Structure

The researching should now be complete and the information, data, or support material ready for organizing, the first stage of the composing process. The writer should review the accumulated material quickly, sort it into seemingly relevant piles, and then try to compose a "working title." This is a good way to define the scope and determine the main focus early. For a longer work, the writer might even go so far as to write a one-paragraph "working summary" which would include the purpose, the main support items, and the conclusion. These two steps are just what their titles imply—

"working" aids to guide the writer and keep the writing going toward the main purpose. In the final draft of a letter or short memorandum, the "working title" will appear at the beginning on the line following "Subject," "Concerning," or "Re."

The next step in planning is organizing the material in accordance to the main focus expressed in the "working title." Literally, this means arranging the materials in the order they may appear in the final draft. This can mean developing a formal outline to serve as a basis for writing each major part or a simple informal jotting down of major ideas, putting any background or historical materials first and the conclusion last. In between these parts will come the main ideas (proof) and divisions and the supporting information.

A long report may require graphs, tables, or charts. If so, these need to be designed during the early planning stage. The first draft of these may be crude but they will serve as good patterns later for experts to redraw. Since the tables and illustrations often contain the evidence for the basic thrust of a paper, developing them early can help with presenting the ideas, show any gaps in the evidence, and indicate whether more material, observations, or reading is necessary.

Planning has two other considerations: scheduling time to work on the assignment and finding the right place to work. Good writers do not leave their writing to the last minute. Successful professionals are also skillful organizers of time. They understand practical time tables and take into account the circumstances of their environment and abilities. Obviously, much more work must go into a formal report being submitted to a corporate board than to informal proposals, letters, or memorandums going to colleagues. Moreover, when beginning any written project, the writer must realistically confront the problem of how much time will be necessary to complete the project. No matter what kind of assignment the pre-professional undertakes, selecting the appropriate approach to finishing the work on time is crucial.

The amount of time required is also closely related to the environment in which the writing must take place. The writer working in a quiet office without distractions faces an entirely different set of obstacles to good composition than does a harried professional trying to write in a busy modular office situation with desks separated only by thin, partial partitions. The probability of any distraction in the office can be a reason for allowing more time.

Few successful people have the luxury of working on only one project at a time. This means they must budget their time among various commitments. It also makes the planning and organizing of the research materials for each project that much more important. Having a good "working title" or "summary" will be invaluable to the writer who must keep returning to a long writing project after many hours or days of interruptions.

# Writing the First Draft—Composing

At this stage, the writer should have a very clear idea of the skeleton of the paper—the purpose, the kinds of support, and the conclusion. The next step is to write the first draft as rapidly as possible, preferably at one sitting. Of course, extensive proposals will require considerably more time with perhaps only one section accomplished at a writing session. However, on returning to the task, the writer should begin writing immediately and not go back to edit any previously completed part of the draft. This pressing forward with the composing is a very important step.

Too many writers spend hours trying to get the first paragraph perfect. They not only waste hours of time but also reams of paper in the process. At the end of a writing session they may find themselves with only a wastebasket full of crumpled, discarded sheets and no real start on their assignment. They will also be exhausted and greatly exasperated with themselves and with the task that still lies ahead. This "to perfect" syndrome is a real hazard and serves only to make the writing more difficult. Usually, if writers push on and do not make the fatal mistake of "trying to perfect," they will find that the ideas begin to flow and the writing improves and takes on a clearer and more organized focus. Expressing thoughts also can create thoughts.

No professional writer expects to come up with a perfect piece of writing on the first draft. James Michener who has written thousands of words once said, "I am not a good writer first time around but am one of the world's great rewriters." He also stated, "I write everything almost three times and would never dream of sending out the first draft of an important letter." Once the basic ideas are down on paper, a writer will find it easier to go back and add to them, reorganize them, correct any lapses in logic, and attack any glaring slips in usage skills—punctuation, spelling, grammar, or sentence structure. The first draft is the time to write out in more detail the ideas previously gathered only in notes. Whether the writer composes the first draft at the typewriter, at the word processor, or with the time-honored method of pen and paper, the important thing is to get the material down as quickly as possible—regardless of quality or even of logic.

# Cooling the First Draft—Distancing

Once a piece of writing is in first draft, the next stage is to hide it away for a few hours or days depending on its scheduled deadline. In other words, it should have time to "cool." Even a short letter or memorandum should have a little "breathing" time before closing the envelope. A writer attempting to write, correct, and polish an important piece of communication all in one sitting will not only read what is on the paper but also what is still left in the head. Unfortunately, the audience will have access only to what is on the paper. Consequently, the reader may be deprived of important points and have a document leaving many unanswered questions. Few, if any writers, ever have an easy or natural style in the first draft and most often not even a clear one.

## Editing the First Draft—Revising, Revising, Revising

Once a first draft becomes sufficiently "cold," the next stage in the composing process is the editing or polishing. This may include considerable rewriting: adding support material, such as more statistics or more concrete examples; substituting more precise vocabulary; moving sentences or paragraphs to other pages; deleting repetition or unnecessary materials; or checking for the usual English grammatical and usage errors. This may also be the point to adjust the "working title" to represent the focus of the final draft better.

Some first drafts may require several editing sessions. These may also entail criticism from a colleague, a supervisor, or someone from the professional writing staff if the company is large enough to have such experts available. The finished product should be one that the writer is willing to have the whole world see. Similar to the check of products for blemishes as they toll off the production line, the editing of a manuscript is quality control at its best.

## Submitting the Completed Communication— Circulating the Finished Product

The final stage is submitting the edited finished report to the proper receiver—department chairperson, vice president, member of the board, or whoever commissioned the communication in the first place. If it is a long report, it will need a letter of transmittal to accompany it—a formal means of concluding and handing over a completed requisitioned study or report. A letter or memorandum, however, will go directly to a client, consumer, another colleague, or another company. At this point a communication becomes public property with the writer's name clearly appended.

If from the beginning a writer knows a piece of communication will probably appear in some national publication, such as a journal, he or she should become acquainted with the format preferred by the targeted journal and study its audience. Many publications are quite specific about the form they expect a writer to follow and about the subjects they will accept. Their instructions can include such things as the type of print, size of the paper, width of the margins, spacing of the lines, or number of words to the page. Many have their own method for footnoting or bibliographical citation. Some journals may accept only manuscripts on a specified subject for a particular issue or for some centennial year. For writers to be aware of the acceptable form or any such subject limitations can save them time and perhaps disappointments.

Publishers usually print their specifications for submission at least once a year in one of their issues. Some have them in the back of each issue. If not, they will send such materials on request.

When writers submit documents, they should be careful to avoid a fault that occurs when the introduction includes irrelevant background information instead of focusing immediately on the main issue. The result is often a flood of superfluous information.

This problem of focus, sometimes called "the writer's fallacy," refers to a writer beginning a report with the facts in the order researched rather than emphasizing what is most important. The following passage illustrates this problem, in this case the overuse of historical details:

> The Richland plant built in 1979 installed Production Line #30 in 1980 for the manufacture of wall panels #92. The original units manufactured by Bromer and Co. were similar. . . .

This introduction leaves the reader wondering why such historical background is relevant at this point. The writer should recast the paragraph to state the main issue immediately and then proceed to present various ramifications:

> A six-month cost study indicates that unless we modernize Richland Plant Production Line #30 now, the profit margin on wall panel production #92 will disappear. The Production Control Committee recommends replacing unit #30 with Unit #8 manufactured by the Franklin Corporation. The current research indicates this production shift will increase productivity by 32% for a possible pay back of 3.9. years.

In the revised version, the writer emphasizes an appropriate and readily identifiably thesis and provides for a concise and effective introduction. The words contain specific references and convey appropriate information.

Any memorandum, letter, or any other piece of writing should begin by stating the main issue or topic as soon as possible regardless of whether that information has already appeared in a title or "subject" line. Not repeating this information is a fundamental error of many inexperienced writers. Good writers never assume that the reader will automatically transfer the topic from the title or heading to the opening paragraph—and thus begin in mid-stream. However, as in the following example, immature writers are not always aware of this necessity:

> **Title:** State Will Issue Bonds
>
> **Poor first sentence:** *They* can be a primary source of funds for renovation projects in our city . . .
>
> **Improved first sentence:** *Tax-free bonds* are a primary source of funding for renovation projects in our city . . .

Titles and subject lines announce only the topic. Should the title become separated, it would make no difference to an understanding of the message. A good test is for the writer to see whether he or she has developed the topic enough to ensure understanding without the heading, title, or subject line. If so, the writer has done a credible job. This is evident in the following introduction to an informal report from a large pharmaceutical house in the Midwest:

December 13, 1985

**TO:** Dixie Smith

**FROM:** Dana Cadwallader

**RE:** The *Compensation Management System*

Background

    The *survey module* of the *Compensation Management Information System* provides a valuable tool for the Office of Corporation Compensation (CC). Using this *system,* CC personnel are able to summarize, analyze, and present information gathered via the Salary Information Retrieval System Survey. Once compiled, the information exists primarily in the form of easy-to-analyze graphs and supporting tables.

    By using the *Survey Module,* CC is now able to compare salary lines between companies or groups of companies during any given six-month period. *The system* allows researchers from CC to conduct meaningful analyses of the structure and efficacy of salaries and compensation. A detailed description of how the *system* works follows.

This paragraph is easy to understand because the writer has been explicit in stating the topic and its means of development. The writer explains issues logically and, thus, informs the reader. The result is an effective piece of corporate communication.

Figure 3.1 indicates that of the seven stages involved in the writing of a piece of communication, the first and last—the purpose and submission—are uniquely tied together. The other five are related to the process of the actual composing. What makes the difference between mediocre writing and quality communication is the writer who clearly understands the purpose of his or her task and submits the completed document with organized, relevant support and appropriate information for the proper audience. This insight into the communication theory allows good writers to fine tune their work and to transfer precise information in the most efficient and economical manner.

# Questions

1. Explain how "The Writing Process" can be relevant to you in your future profession.

2. If you were going to propose a change in a policy or a procedure, how would following the seven steps be valuable in generating the document, such as change in parking or registration procedures, safety regulations, etc.

3. How is creativity relevant to good professional communication?

## Assignments

Outline a topic of your choice. Then write your paper following the seven steps of the writing process.

# 4 Relationship of Form and Content

"Getting Started" outlined the important steps in the writing procedure—from the inception of the sender's idea to its final submission to a receiver. These steps in writing are as applicable to a one-paragraph letter or memorandum as to a multi-page report or proposal.

A good piece of writing is clear, concise, and effective. It answers questions for the reader and its subject matter is appropriate in tone, language usage, and difficulty for the knowledge and skill level of the audience. That companies are aware of the importance of these factors and the need for their employees to realize their importance and their ultimate effect is evident in the variety of slogans found on the walls or desks in various offices: "Our letters are our silent salesmen, "Better letters make for better business," "Your reports are our ambassadors of good will," and "Keep the quality up."

Besides the manner of encoding words, other format considerations are important, also. First, any piece of communication should have a meaningful title or if a letter or memorandum a "Subject," "Concerning," or "Re" line; that is, one that informs the receiver exactly about the concerns of the document. Second, it should provide proper identification of the sender and his or her position in the firm and relationship to the document. Third, it should be neat and in good condition if it is to make a good impression on its arrival whether inside or outside a firm. And fourth, if it is a long communication, even a quick flip of the pages should convey the impression of a thorough piece of work with its parts and any charts or graphs clearly identified and inserted in relevant places.

## Organization

For the reader to be able to understand and follow the writer's thinking, the message needs an organization—an organizing pattern that provides for a careful sequencing of the ideas. The following figure indicates a usual overall structure for almost any professional communication: Introduction, Body (support ideas), and

Conclusion. Its contour not only depicts the place of each part but also its relative length in any type of message.

The **Introduction** provides a preview of the subject and the purpose, thus revealing the basis and scope of the writing. In other words, it informs the reader about what to expect in the following communication. The **Body,** the largest segment as the diagram indicates, includes the facts, arguments, statistics, and concepts that explain and verify what the introduction implied was to be the subject. The **Conclusion** usually reemphasizes the main points and the importance of the message.

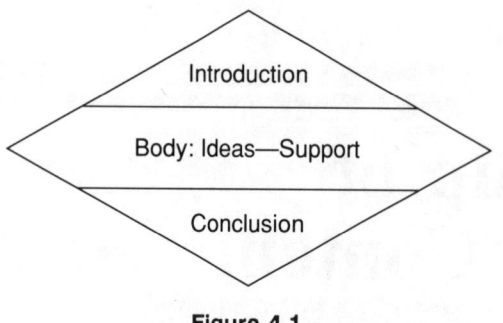

**Figure 4.1**

## Unity

A good piece of communication whether a memorandum, letter, article, report, or proposal must have **unity.** That is, it is a logical and patterned sequence of paragraphs and sentences within the paragraphs from the introduction to the conclusion. To say it is patterned means that the writer has *consciously* decided on a plan for presenting the ideas in response to or for a specific situation. Each of the paragraphs must pertain to the subject—all must further explain and develop the announced topic whether indicated by the title if some type of article or proposal or as noted above by such a word as "Subject," Concerning," or "Re" line for memoranda or letters. Thus, every sentence and every paragraph must contribute to the development of the core idea.

## Paragraph

A **paragraph** is a group of sentences that focus on and provide support for a single idea. The function of the paragraph is to break up the larger concept into meaningful chunks of information. The function of its sentences is to expand upon the main idea stated in the **topic** sentence—the key to the development and the subject of the paragraph.

Besides being the key to the ideas expressed, the topic sentence can provide the clew to the organization or means of relating the ideas. The following topic sentences taken from articles of various publications exemplify different types of organization:

| | |
|---|---|
| **Statement—Support: Deductive** | "Illiteracy in United States is indeed a problem." |
| | "The inequities of the European class system was an influential stimulus to migration to the new world." |
| **Analogy—Comparison:** | "Chemical equations, symbolic representations of chemical reaction, are like kitchen recipes in that both identify ingredients that react to form a finished product." |
| | "My son is like a Formula I Racer." |
| | "In expounding the philosophy of highway safety, the bureau likes to use the analogy of sending a teacup by mail." |
| | "The easiest way to visualize DNA is as an immensely long rope ladder, twisted around and around into a corkscrew shape." |
| **Definition:** | "The word 'modern' has no well-defined limits; its limitations depend upon the thing it modifies." |
| | "Although the word 'symbiosis' is sometimes restricted to intimate reciprocal relationships, here it is used in a very broad sense to cover all close relationships between two different kinds of organisms." |
| **Contrast:** | "In contrast to nature's materials like wood and metal, plastics are man-made materials." |
| **Analysis and Division:** | "Three basic steps involved in case analysis are defining the problem, formulating the alternatives, and recommending the best alternative." |
| | "Participation in dramatics is beneficial to a person's general development in two major ways." |
| **Chronological Arrangement:** | "The new earth, freshly torn from its parent sun, *was* a ball of whirling gases, intensely hot, rushing through the black spaces of the |

universe on a path at a speed controlled by immense forces; *gradually* cooling then began to occur.

**Question—Answer:** "When genetic engineering is perfected, what kind of body will be fashionable?"

"Does an economy need a constant infusion of new industries to remain healthy?"

Usually the topic sentence is the first sentence in the paragraph, thus early announcing the main idea of the paragraph loud and clear for the reader. This is a particularly good placement for unsure writers as the topic sentence can serve as an excellent guide for the selection of the supporting ideas and as an aid to paragraph unity. Figure 4.2 below indicates the basic structure of a paragraph—the position of its topic sentence and its supporting sentences.

---

*Topic Sentence*

    Supporting Sentence
    Supporting Sentence ——— Concepts,
    Supporting Sentence         Statistics,
                                  examples, etc.

    Summary (final Sentence)

---

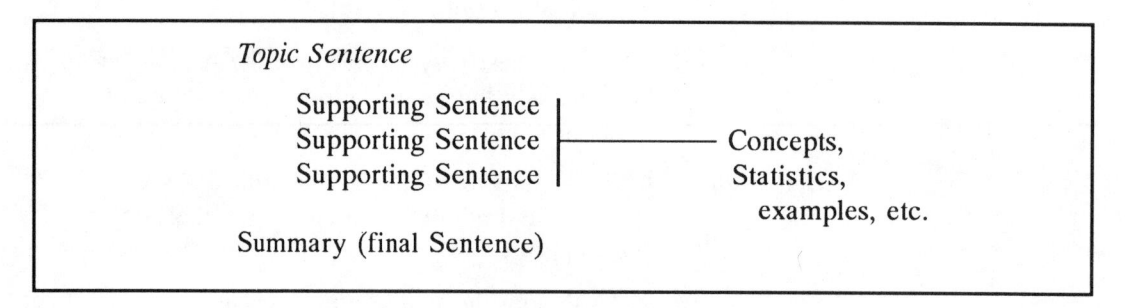

**Figure 4.2**

The following examples, A, B, and C, show the close relationship between the first (topic) and last sentences of these paragraphs:

Example A: *We especially need technologies that might serve to restructure our older industries.* They are now the major offenders against the environment because their own processes are rapidly growing obsolescent. The wheel-on-steel railroad dates basically from 1800; the steam power plants based on the Carnot cycle, from 1824; the automobile, based on the four-cycle Otto engine, from 1876. *Thus, we need an entirely new level of technology if we are to meet the needs of the late twentieth century and those of the twenty-first century.*

Example B: *Another matter of concern—and one that troubles the auto industry—is reliability.* Terribly uptight these days about product-liability suits, the auto makers are haunted by visions of air bags going off when they shouldn't or failing to go off when they should. Airbag systems, sensors and all, will have to be reliable after traveling in cars for years and for tens of thousands of miles. Only *extensive real-world field testing and engineering can provide this reassurance of reliability.*

Example C: *Language is a living thing.* It also is fossilized poetry. As words change their form and transmute their meanings, they preserve for the keen and loving observer the rich history embedded in them, revealing how their ever-evolving use reflects their users' changing perception of the universe. As perception changes, so does language and its meanings, *thus creating miraculous changes in language.*

The final sentence in the paragraph although often a very brief summary can also serve as a bridge into the paragraph to follow. This is very evident with Example A. The reader would expect this writer in the following paragraphs to discuss some possible new levels of technology. In Example B, the words of the topic sentence—*another matter of concern*—serve as a transition from a preceding paragraph. This alerts the reader that the writer has discussed at least one other matter of concern in a previous paragraph.

A topic sentence, however, can appear in other places in the paragraph to provide for emphasis or variety in the writing style.

In an *inductive* paragraph, it may be the last sentence with the preceding sentences providing the ideas, statistics, or examples pointing to a logical conclusion. The following paragraph is a good example of this technique.

The Fortune 500 Company corporate executive directs a company whose sales in 1975 averaged almost $1.75 billion, whose assets totaled $1.33 billion, and which provided employment for almost 29,000 people. This executive directs the firm in a manner that allows it to earn an 11.6 percent return on its total investment. Such a rate of return is not guaranteed simply because a corporation is large. The opportunities to lose money are many; the management of 28 of the 500 largest industrial corporations managed to show a loss in the recovery year of 1975. It is possible, moreover, to lose big: Singer reported a loss of $451.9 million in that year, and Chrysler $259.5 million. A chief executive who heads a management team that can avoid such losses and constantly succeed in earning a profit is obviously not only very valuable to the employers but also to other corporations; thus his own firm pays him handsomely to retain his services.

—*Robert Thomas*
"Is Corporate Executive Compensation Excessive?"

Occasionally a paragraph may seem to have no apparent topic sentence. Instead its sentences add up to an obvious and encompassing meaning. Some mature writers use this style once in a while; however, the topic sentence placed at the beginning of the paragraph probably will produce the clearest communication. The following paragraph is a good example of the "idea" technique.

> One day during the Second World War, I was called down to Washington to see Vannevar Bush. He told me that Harold Urey, of Columbia, wanted to see me in connection with a diffusion problem that had to do with the separation of uranium isotopes. We were already aware that uranium isotopes might play an important part in the transmutation of elements and even in the possible construction of an atomic bomb, for the earlier stages of this work had come before the war and had not been made in the United States.
>
> Norbert Wiener<br>I Am a Mathematician

## A Complete Communication

Figure 4.3 below provides a paradigm of a five-paragraph message: introductory paragraph, three support paragraphs (body), and a summary paragraph. A long piece of writing, however, could have any number of support paragraphs just as a long paragraph could have any number of supporting sentences; that is, any number necessary to explain the subject fully.

```
                         TITLE
Paragraph I:       Introduction—Topic Sentence
Paragraph II:      Topic Sentence      ⎤
Paragraph III:     Topic Sentence      ├─ Body (Support Material)
Paragraph IV:      Topic Sentence      ⎦
Paragraph V:       Summary (Conclusion)
```

**Figure 4.3**

The following examples of writing not only indicate specifically the close relationship between the title or memorandum "subject" line and the various paragraphs but also how placing the topic sentence first immediately indicates to the reader the basic concept of each paragraph.

**✎ Example**    The Eternal Triangle in Personnel Affairs
(Title)

**Paragraph I:** Introduction

Topic Sentence   Three general philosophies of personnel management are organizational theory, industrial engineering, and behavioral science.

**Paragraph II:**

Topic Sentence   The organizational theorist believes that human needs are so irrational or so varied and adjustable to specific situations that the major function of personnel management is to be as pragmatic as the occasion demands.

**Paragraph III:**

Topic Sentence   The industrial engineer holds that man is mechanistically oriented and economically motivated and his needs are best met by attuning the individual to the most efficient work process.

**Paragraph IV:**

Topic Sentence   The behavioral scientist focuses on group sentiments, attitudes of individual employees, and the organization's social and psychological climate.

**Paragraph V:** Summary

Topic Sentence   Since there is always a lively debate as to the overall effectiveness of the approaches, the three philosophies can be depicted as a triangle with each one claiming the apex angle.

In this example, the introductory paragraph informs the reader that the article will discuss three philosophies of personnel management. In keeping the same order for the philosophies as introduced, the topic sentences of paragraphs II, III, and IV signal the main idea for their supporting sentences. The summary again mentions that the discussion has concerned three philosophies and with the words "eternal triangle" refers back to the title. Thus, this unity in form and concepts provides the reader with an understandable piece of communication. This analyzing or dividing a topic into parts and then developing each part as indicated in the above example is one means of organizing subject matter and clearly and effectively communicating the ideas to an audience.

## ✎ Example 2 — Why Men Came to America
(Title)

**Paragraph I:** Introduction

The impulse of migration may be described, negatively, as an impulse of escape, for the Americans fled from a Europe where they could find no satisfying fulfillment of their energies and confronted conflicts and dilemmas that had no easy solution.

**Paragraph II:** Of the various factors that caused men to come to America, the economic was no doubt the most important.

**Paragraph III:** An almost equally influential stimulus to migration was the European class system.

**Paragraph IV:** Privation and inequality weighed upon all underprivileged persons in Europe but did not cause all of them to come to America.

**Paragraph V:** Summary

The settlement of American then was a selective process that attracted those with the appropriate bent and disposition appealing not necessarily to the ablest nor to the strongest but usually to the most enterprising.

Again, from the Title to the Summary, this article reflects the close unity of the writing. This introduction does not specifically mention "three causes" as the introduction of the previous article stated "three philosophies." Instead, the writer chose to begin with a more historical approach in the opening paragraph and then develop the background of two specific factors—the economic factors and the inequality of opportunity.

The conclusion notes that even the strong impetus provided by these factors did not encourage all people to leave their homeland, usually only the enterprising. Although the writer uses a different means of setting forth the premise (main idea), the unity of the concepts presented provides the reader with easy access to the meaning of the message.

## ✎ Example 3

The following example is the full text of a memorandum sent in response to a request for the writer to recommend the purchase of a film for use in an effective writing class for adults.

January 15, 19--

To:

From:

Subject: Review of Film Preview of "Strictly Speaking" for possible class use.

The material for the film "Strictly Speaking" comes directly from two books by Edwin Newman—*Strictly Speaking* and *Civil Tongue*. The film catches American communicators at their redundant, pompous, and euphemistic worst. It stresses that much that passes for so-called good communication is little more than a serious case of political, scientific, and social gobbledygook.

Through a series of sketches presented by a professional acting group, the film seriously but quite humorously demonstrates the stereotypes, clichés, and jargon that abounds in present-day English communication. The sketches poke fun at the vague but important-sounding communication of the educator, scientist, politician, corporation executive, pollster, and sportscaster. The examples used in these sketches come from articles in magazines and newspapers as well as from speeches by some of American's most "profound" leaders.

The film shows how far our everyday communication has strayed from a clear, concise, concrete, creative, and correct style. It focuses on the declining state of English communication brought on by overuse of words, misuse of words, and the growing tendency of "izing" (finalizing, prioritizing) or "wising" (consumerwise, economicwise) everything in sight. It exposes the redundancy of such phrases as "young juveniles, free gifts, shot fatally three times, and face reality as it is." It also deplores the free wheeling of such expressions as "nitty gritty, bottom line, out of sight, and game plans."

The film catches the important message in the books and does it in an interesting and entertaining manner. "Strictly Speaking" would be very appropriate for use in management and personnel training classes as well as in English or communication classes. Its material is relevant for any writer and any group. A second viewing would be helpful for catching the many ideas and suggestions presented.

The "Subject" line here serves as the title for this memorandum just as a "subject" line does for a letter. The receiver of this memorandum will know immediately the purpose of the communication. Paragraph I, the introduction, provides the essential background for the film; Paragraph II and III present specifies of the film—the method of presentation and specific examples; Paragraph IV not only affirmatively evaluates the film but also recommends it as relevant for any audience.

# Coherence

Besides unity and organization, a piece of writing must also have **coherence.** This means the careful relating of the sequence of ideas. To cohere means to stick together and that is exactly what each sentence must do to the next sentence, each paragraph to the next paragraph, and each part to the next part. Good writers take their readers by the hand and literally lead them down the page—almost imperceptably. Henry David Thoreau once said, "good writing is art without the appearance of artifice."

A writer achieves this coherence through the use of various transition devices. One way of defining a transition is to think of it as a two-way indicator—a signal or link between what the writer said and what he or she is going to say. It is a means of closely relating ideas. Transitional expressions provide for smoothness in the flow of ideas.

The following transition techniques or means for achieving coherence are essential to and very evident in any type of writing.

## 1. Sentence Connectives

Certain words or phrases are inherently transitional and serve as guide posts to the reader. They also provide specific relevancy in indicating the relationships of the ideas. A representative list of such connectives would include the following with each group providing its own meaning concepts.

| | |
|---|---|
| **Cause and Effect** | thus, consequently, nevertheless, besides, therefore, accordingly, however, certainly, instead, as a result, on the other hand |
| **Comparison** | for instance, in such cases, similarly, equally, comparable, in other words |
| **Enumeration** | one, two, three... |
| **Sequence** | first, second, third... ; last, finally, also, as follows, as above |
| **Example** | for example, in addition, such as, that is |
| **Time** | now, then, earlier, later, meanwhile, often, gradually, frequently, seldom, previously, currently, today, tomorrow, last week, next week, at this time, in that age |
| **Place** | here, there, as noted above, as appears below, at that point, in that place |

The following italicized words and phrases indicate the sentence connectives used to relate the ideas more fully.

> We did not have a quorum at our meeting last night; *therefore,* we could not vote on our next year's budget proposal.

> At this time, we are unable to complete our evaluation of your credentials; *consequently,* we must postpone our decision on your appointment until next week.

> *For example,* two principles, *especially,* guided him in his writing. The *first* principle might be called intuition made articulate, and the *second* principle was to be vital and write with gusto.

> *For instance,* the jurors had no option but to find the prisoner guilty as the law decreed.

## 2. Repetition of a key word or idea of the preceding sentence or paragraph

The repetition of a key word means the use of an echo word. The use of "they see" in the following paragraph exemplifies this technique.

> When the auto makers look ahead a few years, they do not like what *they see. They see* emission standards badly impairing engine performance. *They see* bumper standards increasing length, weight, and price. Far from the least, *they see* safety regulations relentlessly *adding* costs without *adding* any commensurate consumer satisfactions.

Other examples of the echo technique are evident in the following sentences:

> Certainly, rational therapeutics consists of the selection of the *right* drug for the *right* patient in the *right* amounts at the *right* time.

> An investor in any electric power company must earn an adequate return on his money; *otherwise,* there will be *no* investment capital, *no* construction, and *no* new power supply to meet the increasing demand.

The following sentences illustrate the repetition of a key idea but by a different word with a similar meaning:

> The impulse of migration may be described negatively as an impulse of *escape.* The American *fled* from a Europe where he could find no satisfying fulfillment of his energies and was confronted by conflicts and dilemmas that had no easy solution.

> To continue providing customers with reliable electric power, electric companies have *to build new generating plants and other facilities.* This *construction* requires enormous amounts of money.

The overuse of a key word (echo word) can present a problem, however. A writer must decide when such repetition provides good emphasis and when it is just careless or monotonous writing. For instance, some readers might think Example 1 contains too many "they see's." Thus, the line between what is skillful emphasis and what is distracting repetitions can be very fine.

## 3. Use of Parallel Thoughts in Parallel Constructions

This technique often can eliminate the repetition from the overuse of echo words. The following rewrite indicates how to eliminate "they see' twice but without sacrificing any unity and coherence of the ideas.

> When the auto makers look ahead a few years, they do not like what *they see. They see emission standards* badly impairing engine performance; *bumper standards* increasing length, weight, and price; and far from the least, *safety regulations* relentlessly adding costs without adding any commensurate consumer satisfactions.

Parallelism within the sentence means that if two or more words or phrases are doing the same thing, that is serving in the same part of the sentence, they must have the same grammatical form: all be nouns, adjectives, verbs, or verbals, etc. In the above example, "emission standards, bumper standards and safety regulations" are all noun phrases serving as the object of the phrase "they see." Even by omitting their subject and verb, they retain their same grammatical form and become parallel forms in a more shortened version.

The following examples indicate another form of parallelism, one which adds emphasis and balance to the ideas between sentences. They also reflect an effective use of the echo technique.

> *We do not need ever more* new improved consumer novelties.
> *We do need* especially technologies that might attract new customers.

> *It is clear enough* that no massive new spending programs are in the cards;
> *it is also clear* that the face of technological change is ever increasing.

> Once they have developed these two qualities, students of dramatics *will have gone a long way in equipping themselves* for work in a most exacting art.
> Also, *they will have gone a long way toward equipping themselves in the art of living.*

## 4. Clear Pronoun Reference

Substituting a pronoun for a noun used in a preceding phrase or sentence is a good means of showing relationships, avoiding repetition, and providing coherence within a sentence, between sentences, or between paragraphs.

> Any *word* that a worker might not understand requires definition the first time *it* is used. Otherwise, the writer must replace *it.*

> A *critical review* is both a discovery and an evaluation. *It* may evaluate any artistic work, but *it* usually deals with books or, more recently, films. In evaluating, of course, *it* describes.

The committee feels that the *present distribution system* has two disadvantages: *it* provides for duplication of work and creates unnecessary delays in the production of several departments.

The *American* fled from a Europe where *he or she* could find no satisfying fulfillment of *his or her* energies and no easy solutions for *his or her* conflicts.

In general, the *groups* who came to all parts of the New World were *those* who were most acutely discontented with *their status* in European society and who had the least hope of being able to improve *it*.

*Human behavior* is conditioned by economic and social factors in the sense that *these* establish the problems to be solved; however, *it* is not determined by *them*.

As these examples indicate, clear pronoun reference requires that the pronoun agree with its antecedent—the person or thing it refers back to or replaces—in both number and gender. In the above sentences, *word, system,* and *behavior* are all singular nouns referring to a thing and require the *it* to refer back to them. *American* is also singular referring to a masculine or feminine person and in this case requires *he or his* (or *she or her*) as the pronoun. *Groups* is plural and needs both *those* and *their* to satisfy the reference. *Factors* in the last sentence is also plural and must have the plural demonstrative pronoun *these. Human behavior* is a thing and requires the *it*.

## 5. Subordination of One Part of the Sentence to Another Part

This technique depends on certain words (subordinators) that indicate a relationship between ideas and at the same time make one sentence dependent on another for providing the full meaning of the concept. These subordinators also indicate the relationship between important and less important ideas, thus giving the proper perspective to the support material. They provide the cause-effect element between ideas and show tight, logical sequencing of the points. A representative list of such words would include the following.

| as, as soon as | even though | when |
| although | if | where, wherever |
| because | since | whereas |
| before | while | unless |
| after | until | |

These sentences illustrate how such words provide relationships between what otherwise could seem like unrelated statements.

 a. *Without subordination:*

  We did not vote on next year's budget proposal.
  We did not have a quorum at our annual meeting.

*Revised with subordination:*

*Since we did not have a quorum at our annual meeting last night,* we did not vote on next year's budget proposal.

We did not vote on next year's budget proposal last night *because we did not have a quorum at our meeting.*

**b.** *Without subordination:*

We were anticipating trouble from the ice buildup.
We did not anticipate a power failure of that duration.

*Revised with subordination:*

*Although we were anticipating trouble from the ice buildup,* we did not anticipate a power failure of that duration.

We did not anticipate a power failure of that duration *even though we were anticipating trouble from the ice buildup.*

**c.** *Wordy and unstructured statement:*

He is my partner and we have a suite of offices together. We seldom see each other.

*Revised with subordination:*

*Although he is my partner and we have a suite of offices together,* we seldom see each other.

We seldom see each other *even though he is my partner and we have a suite of offices together.*

**d.** *Without subordination:*

We finished reading the books. The librarian returned them to the proper shelves.

*Revised with subordination:*

*After we had finished reading the books,* the librarian returned them to the proper shelves.

The librarian returned the books to the proper shelves *after we had finished* reading them.

*When we had finished reading the books,* the librarian returned them to the proper shelves.
The librarian returned the books to the proper shelves *when we had finished reading them.*

*Since we had finished reading the books,* the librarian returned them to the proper shelves.

The librarian returned the books to the proper shelves *since we had finished reading them.*

Each of these subordinates also implies a certain meaning and provides for a certain relationship between the ideas. In the above examples, *since, although, even though, and because* indicate a cause-effect relationship—one in which something did or did not happen in response to something else. *After and when* indicate a time relationship to the happening. Thus, choosing the right subordinator is important for a writer who wants to present a special meaning for a situation.

Structurally words that the subordinator precedes become a fragment or dependent clause. In other words, the subordinator does exactly what its name implies—it turns the sentence it precedes into a nonsentence (fragment).

**Complete Sentence**      **Complete Sentence**

We did not go to the beach yesterday.      It rained all day.
We finished our packing.      We were waiting for the package.

### Addition of subordinator

a. We did not go to the beach yesterday *since* it rained all day.
   We finished our packing *while* we were waiting for the package.

**Complete Sentence + Subordinator +** complete sentence

b. *Since* it rained all day, we did not go to the beach yesterday.
   *While* we were waiting for the package, we finished our packing.

**Subordinator +** complete sentence **+ Complete Sentence**

Thus, the addition of a subordinator turns *it rained all day* and *we were waiting for the package* into fragments—groups of words that cannot stand alone. As is evident also below, such structures signal only part of the meaning and seem incomplete to the reader.

*because* Bill is not coming

*although* the weather is bad

*even though* her grade point average was very high

*before* he left for Europe yesterday

*unless* the prosecution has more evidence in the case

*while* the committee debated that question

However, without a subordinator preceding them, the same groups of words become sentences or independent clauses:

Bill is not coming.

The weather is bad.

Her grade point average was very high.

He left for Europe yesterday.

The prosecution has more evidence in the case.

The committee debated that question.

The subordinated part of the sentence can appear either at the beginning or end of the total structure. If it comes at the beginning with the main idea at the end, it signals a *periodic* sentence—one with the complete sentence at the end just before the period.

> **Since** it indicated no specific charge against him, *the warrant for his arrest was invalid.*

If it comes at the end with the main idea at the beginning, it signals a *loose* sentence.

> *The warrant for his arrest was invalid* since it indicated no specific charge against him.

Of course, both types of sentences are structurally and stylistically correct. Which one a writer might use would depend upon which form would provide the best emphasis or coherence value in a specific situation or paragraph.

The contrast in the "before and after" versions of the following memorandum indicates how a clear topic sentence and relevant subordination structures not only eliminate some repetition but also clarify and strengthen the message of the paragraph.

### Original memorandum

Excessive noise in the office has become a problem. We need to solve this problem now. The problem exists because the only blockage of sound between desks is a small partition. Another reason is because there is now heavier traffic in and out of the office. One way to alleviate the problem would be to put in larger office-like partitions to fully enclose the desks. A second way would be to make a reception area for visitors to wait and not disrupt employees. Such changes would greatly help the problem.

### Rewritten memorandum

Excessive noise in our office has become a problem for two reasons: the use of small, low partitions as the only blockage of noise between desks and the increased heavier traffic in and out of the office. If our company would install larger office-like partitions to enclose the desks fully, the noise factor certainly would be considerably less. Moreover, if the company would also provide a reception area where visitors could conveniently wait for their appointments, the employees would have fewer disruptions while working. These minimal changes would create a much improved office atmosphere.

## Sentence Connectives—Subordinators

Two of the transition devices discussed here can provide for a cause-effect relationship between two independent clauses: sentence connectives and subordinators. Although the meaning may remain the same, the resulting structures will differ considerably.

    a. The technicians stayed on in the laboratory during lunch; *however,* the nurses attended the lecture.

    He wanted to take tennis lessons at noon; *therefore,* he cancelled all his luncheon appointments.

    Mary had no desire to take that trip; *consequently,* she did not send in her deposit on time.

    b. *Although* the technicians stayed on in the laboratory during lunch, the nurses attended the lecture.

    *Since* he wanted to take tennis lessons at noon, he cancelled all his luncheon appointments.

    *As* Mary had no desire to take that trip, she did not send in her deposit on time.

In the Group **a** sentences, the connectives *however, therefore,* and *consequently* relate two ideas, but in each case the two sentences involved retain their independent structures.

| **Complete sentence;** | + | **however,** | + | **complete sentence.** |
|---|---|---|---|---|
| Independent; | | **therefore,** | | Independent |
| | | **consequently,** | | |

In the Group **b** sentences, the subordinators *although, since,* and *as* also relate the two ideas but reduce the sentences that they precede to dependent structures—ones that can not stand alone.

| **Subordinator** | + | **complete sentence,** | + | **complete sentence.** |
|---|---|---|---|---|
| | | dependent | | independent |
| **Although** | | , | | |
| **Since** | | , | | |
| **As** | | , | | |

## Sentence Subordinators as Prepositions

Some of the subordinators can also function as prepositions:

    **a.** We went home immediately *after* dinner.
    **b.** We went home immediately *after* we had eaten dinner.
    **a.** He left the dinner *before* the lecture.
    **b.** He left the dinner *before* the lecture had started.

In the **a** sentences *after* and *before* are serving as prepositions preceding noun phrases and indicating time. In the **b** sentences, *after* and *before* are subordinators, each preceding a complete (dependent) sentence not just a noun.

This change in the function of such words may appear confusing on first thought; however, it really indicates the great versatility and flexibility of the English language. By understanding and using the many options available, writers are able to communicate their ideas more clearly, specifically, and effectively.

The following adapted paragraphs of "The Phenomenon of Bird Migration" is a good example of how these transition techniques actually work together to provide unity and a coherent picture in a piece of writing. The lines drawn to the various parts of the article and the underlined words and phrases should make clear the subtle but essential interconnections between the title, paragraphs, and sentences of this well-written and unified piece of writing—not only the paragraphs follow each other logically and clearly but also the sentences within them.

### The Phenomenon of Bird Migration*

[1] *Two-thirds* of the species of songbirds that breed in the Northern U.S. travel south for the winter. The distances of migration typically range from 600 to 1,800 miles, but *some birds* make one-way trips of up to 4,000 miles. *Moreover,* the adult birds return with amazing precision to the same northern breeding grounds the following spring. *How* do *such birds* select the appropriate flight directions and if off course make the appropriate corrections? *How* do *they* know when *they* have arrived at the proper latitude?

[2] The *phenomenon of bird migration* has long intrigued biologists. Today, many *scientists* around the world are involved in studying questions of animal navigation. Thousands of migrant birds are being marked with a leg band so that field *investigators* can determine *their* migratory paths by plotting *their* recapture locations. In the laboratory, *other workers* are testing the ability of birds to detect different directional *cues* and are examining how *they use such cues*. *Ornithologists* are tracking "unseen" migrating birds with radar and following individual migrants by small radio transmitters attached to *them*.

[3] *One cue system*—orientation by the stars—has been under intensive study recently and appears to be of major importance to night-migrating birds. *These researchers* believe that there are *two ways* these birds can determine direction by the stars. *One way* is for a bird to locate a critical star (or a group of stars) and then guide *itself* by flying at a particular angle with respect to it. The position of a star, *however,* is not constant for it shifts from east to west with the rotation of the earth. *Thus,* in order to maintain a given compass direction, the *bird* must alter *its* angle of flight so as to compensate for the apparent motion of the star. *Its* mechanism to do this must be analogous to that of a day-time bird migrant that has to compensate for the daily movement of the sun across the sky. *A second way* would be for a bird to use patterns of stars, such as the Big Dipper, to determine

---

*Adapted from Stephen T. Emlen, "The Stellar-Orientation System of a Migratory Bird," *Scientific American,* (August, 1975), pp. 102–111.

directional reference points. *Although patterns of stars also move across the sky,* their shape remains constant and *each* preserves a distinct geometric relation to the North Star. *Thus, by this way,* the *bird* could determine *its* direction from the geometric patterns of the stars independently of any internal time sense or "biological clock."

⁴Tests with the *North American Indigo* bunting (nocturnal migrator) have shown that buntings kept in captivity but exposed to all *the night sky patterns were able to orient themselves* to either north or south patterns of migration immediately upon release. *Other buntings* kept in captivity and not exposed to night-sky patterns were not able to achieve north or south orientation at first. *This suggests that a bird's navigational and meteorological skill is perhaps more than mere instinct.*

⁵However informative *these star orientation tests* appear, *they* do not answer all the questions in the migratory success story. *Bird navigation is not a simple affair. It is also not dependent on any single cue or sensory system,* obviously. Probably, bird navigation relates to *many cue systems. Our scientists* have still much work and study ahead of them.

Paragraph one introduces the subject and suggests the basis for the discussion to follow. It represents the top level or "introduction" of the earlier diamond diagram (Figure 4.1) contouring a piece of writing. Its topic sentence indicates to the reader immediately the author's real interest is with bird "travel" or migration:

> ¹Two-thirds of the species of songbirds that breed in the northern U.S. travel south for the winters.

Paragraphs two, three, and four represent the "body" or support material with each developing the topic a little further and providing more specifics and details. Their topic sentences introduce the points covered in the respective paragraphs:

> ²The phenomenon of bird migration has long intrigued biologists. Today, many scientists around the world are involved in studying questions of animal navigation.

> ³One cue system—orientation by the stars—has been under intensive study recently and appears to be of major importance to night-migrating birds.

> ⁴Tests with the North American Indigo bunting (nocturnal migrator) have shown that buntings kept in captivity but exposed to all the night sky patterns were able to orient themselves to either north or south patterns. . . .

Paragraph five serves as the "summary" and represents the lower part of the earlier diagram. It is involved with bird migration but also indicates the need for further on-going study if scientists are to find real answers to the questions posed in the introduction.

> ⁵However informative these star orientation tests appear, they do not answer all the questions in the migratory success story.

Deeper probing into this writing indicates that besides the topic sentences providing coherence and continuity to the concepts, one or more of the various transition techniques also closely tie the sentences within the paragraphs together. Paragraph 1 contains at least four of the six transition techniques: echo word—"adult birds," "some birds," and "such birds"; the sentence connective—"moreover"; two uses of the pronoun "they," referring back to such birds; and parallel constructions with the two questions introduced by "How do."

The opening words of paragraph two specifically echo the title. The word "phenomenon" also relates to the last two questions in the preceding paragraph. The words "scientists around the world" and "other workers" in the laboratory identify the intrigued biologists.

Moreover, the use of the pronoun in such phrases as "their migratory paths," "their recapture locations," "how they use such cues" and "transmitters attached to them" illustrate the substitution of a pronoun to show relationships yet avoid the overuse of the noun "birds." These plural pronouns also agree with their plural antecedent "birds" (the noun they carefully refer back to) and serve as guideposts in the paragraph for the reader.

The words, "one cue system," introducing the topic sentence of paragraph three directly echoes the word "cues" in the preceding paragraph, thus tying these two paragraphs closely together. The use of "these researchers" to refer back to the "ornithologists" in paragraph 2 exemplifies the use of a different word but with the same meaning to provide the same idea, thus avoiding the use of an echo expression. These researchers note two ways they believe the birds determine the direction of the stars. The words *one way* and a *second way* logically and clearly sequences the ideas. Such sentence connectives as "however, thus, and thus, by this way" provide further coherence to the sentences and concepts expressed. The "although preceding *patterns of stars also move across the sky* illustrates subordination of one sentence to another and provides good cause and effect relationship of the ideas—although something happens, something else remains constant:

"Although     +     patterns of stars also move across the sky,

Subordinator  +    complete sentence       +

   their shape remains constant and each preserves a distinct geometric relation to the North Star."

**complete sentence**

Subordinator + complete sentence, + **complete sentence**

Paragraph 4 analyzes *tests* with North American Indigo buntings known as *nocturnal migrators*. This paragraph offers specific examples of birds for reading geometric patterns of the stars as proposed in the preceding paragraph. *Other buntings* expands the example and provides additional evidence for the birds' use of the stars. *This,* introducing the last sentence, refers to the contrasting ideas in the paragraph and leads to the conclusion that more than instinct is really at work.

Finally, in paragraph 5, the *however informative these star orientation tests appear* summarizes the general flow of ideas in the previous paragraphs. *They* (pronoun) in sentence one clearly refers back to these *tests*. The following two sentences are good examples of paralleling structures for emphasis and summary:

> Bird navigation is not a simple affair.
> *It* is also not dependent on any single cue of sensory system.

The *it* refers quite specifically to *bird navigation* in the preceding sentence, thus serving as a very close transition clue. The repetition of *cue* relates back to the earlier cue discussions. *Our scientists* in the final sentence refers to those mentioned earlier as involved in the exploration and research into bird migration.

All the concepts and details in these paragraphs further explain and relate directly to the title. No where is any other subject except bird migration and its possible amazing means introduced. Through careful attention to the use of transition devices, the writer provides the readers with a clearly marked roadmap to assist them in understanding the thesis and the supporting arguments

## Questions

1. Find examples from relevant textbooks or journals to illustrate effective paragraph development. Underline the devices. Remember! Good writing is good writing in any field.

2. Find examples of paragraphs developed by the following types of organization. Does the topic sentence clearly indicate the type? Why did the authors choose a particular form?
   Analogy, Enumeration, Comparison, Contrast, Division, Definition

3. Do you consider the following paragraphs well written? Why or why not? Can you rewrite them easily?
   Example A:  I am opposed to the use of a card for paying for groceries for two important reasons. I buy groceries every week by check. I dislike the increase in prices because the store accepts bad checks. The store must be responsible for their own actions and not put the added cost onto the consumer. However, a card is an easy way for the supermarket and consumer to pay for

groceries. The card, in my opinion, could cause over spending just as a non-sufficient-fund check could. The only way to stop bad checks and bad cards is by some other means than the above approach.

Example B: Many older students have difficulty for awhile in their courses in college. Having been out of school for several years, they have lost the habit of study and the power to concentrate. Formulas in chemistry and mathematics, which are recited readily by students fresh from high school, are only dim memories to them. Their age and the greater sense of responsibility most older students have is an advantage to them. Many of them have held responsible jobs or positions in the armed services and now many of them have families dependent on them. Consequently, they are serious about getting an education.

4. How many transition devices have the authors used in this chapter? Specifically identify fifteen of them.

5. How could subordination improve this sentence?
   He is my friend and he lives in Chicago and we seldom see each other.

6. Does your writing reflect a repetition in the use of transitional devices? Do you use "however, therefore, thus, as you know" too many times?

# Assignment

1. Choose some topic from your field of specialization and write topic sentences illustrating each of the development types discussed in this chapter.
2. Develop one of these topic sentences into a good paragraph—use as many of the transition devices as you can to achieve unity.

# 5 The Sentence

Students asked to define a sentence usually respond in one of the following ways: "A sentence is a group of words expressing a complete thought." "A sentence is a group of words containing a subject and a predicate." Both definitions, of course, are correct as far as they go; however, both presume a certain level of knowledge on the part of the listeners or readers.

An expression of a "complete thought" can and usually does entail more than a mere one sentence summary. Several closely related sentence or even paragraphs may be necessary to accomplish this. The second definition may provide more confusion as both *dependent* and *independent* clauses contain a noun and a verb. Students who can recognize nouns and verbs usually find the subject and predicate in the dependent clause also and then mistake it for a sentence. A group of words containing only a subject, only a predicate, or only a subordinated dependent clause is a *fragment* or nonsentence. A complete sentence or independent clause has both a subject and a predicate and needs no further words to complete its meaning. Mistaking a fragment for a sentence also leads to problems in punctuation.

Fragment: *Since* Bill hadn't called (. ;) ?
Complete: Since Bill hadn't called, we did not know what to do.

Fragment: *Although* we were expecting a large crowd at the lecture (. ;)?
Complete: Although we were expecting a large crowd at the lecture, we had no idea about its real popularity.

Fragment: What Bill really wanted us to do (. ;) ?
Complete: What Bill really wanted us to do was a real mystery.

Fragment: The tires stacked high at the station (. ;) ?
Complete: The tires stacked high at the station were a danger to the customers.

Fragment: When driving past the fire zone (. ;) ?
Complete: When driving past the fire zone, he was careful to stay in his own lane.

The words introduced by the adverbial subordinators *since* and *although* are not sentences but dependent adverbial clauses expressing a reason. "What Bill really wanted us to do" is a dependent noun clause, one replacing the subject of that sentence. "The tires stacked high at the station" is a complete subject having a noun and its modifying structure (stacked high at the station) but no predicate and thus not able to stand as an independent clause. The same is true of the participial phrase "when driving past the fire zone."

Knowing the English language requires much more than being able to pick out or identify the correct number of nouns, verbs, adjectives, or adverbs in a passage even though these word types account for most of the English vocabulary. The important thing is understanding how they combine to convey meaning. In other words, "a language lives in its system, rather than in its vocabulary." If a catastrophe were to wipe out the structure of the English sentence, there would be no English language even though all of the vocabulary items remained. However, if a catastrophe were to wipe out all the vocabulary, the English language would remain because its basic system could function even with words made up or borrowed from many other languages. Lewis Carroll in the "Jabberwocky" illustrates this very well"

> Twas brillig, and the slithy toves
> did gyre and gimble in the wabe;
> All mimsy were the borogroves
> And the nome raths outgrabe.

As Alice listened she thought the nonsense words had meaning, yet she didn't know what each of the vocabulary items meant. "Brillig, slithy, and mimsy" seem to be adjectives because of their endings and position in the sentence; "toves and borogroves," plural nouns because of the "s" inflectional ending marking the plural; and "gyre and gimble," verbs because they are preceded by the modal *did* in a compound predicate describing the action of the "toves." Thus, reading is not just correctly pronouncing words picked at random from all parts of a page. Reading and comprehending and writing mean understanding words in a phrase and how they work together to convey ideas and concepts.

## Types of Verbs

The basic sentence has one subject phrase and one verb phrase. The subject consists mainly of nouns or pronouns which determine whether the verb will be singular or plural, for the verb must agree in number with its subject. The verb denotes the action of the subject, the action of something else on the subject, or the state of being of the subject. The four main types of verbs provide for seven patterns of verb phrases.

1. **The Transitive Verb** requires a direct object (another noun or noun substitute) to complete its meaning.

The *crew* cleaned the *roads* this morning.
    Noun¹         Noun²
  subject     direct object

The transitive verb also can undergo the passive transformation: the subject of the original sentence and the object exchange positions.

The *roads* were cleaned by the *crew* this morning.
  Noun²              Noun¹

The subject is no longer the actor but one receiving the action. The verb phrase includes a form of the *be* verb (were) and the past participle of *clean* (cleaned). *Crew,* the former subject, becomes the object of the preposition *by.*

Active:  The *children* read the *books* left on the table.
Passive:  The *books* left on the table were read by the *children.*
Active:  His *ideas* about the tree removal surprised the *mayor.*
Passive:  The *mayor* was surprised by his *ideas* about the tree removal.

The verb *have* (has, had, having) is similar to the transitive verb in that the noun in its subject and the noun in its direct object position refer to two different persons or things,

*The boys* have a good *clubhouse.*
 Noun¹         Noun²

The *men* have several *rugs* for sale.
The *girl* has two *tests* today.

The verb *have* differs from the transitive verb in that its sentences never convert to passive structures. At least native speakers of the English language would never use it in this way.

**Passive:**  A good *clubhouse is had by* the boys. (?)
           Several rugs for sale *were had by* the men. (?)
           Two *tests were had by* the girl. (?)

2. **The Intransitive Verb** has a subject but its verb phrase requires no direct object. Instead some type of adverbial phrase may follow it directly providing answers to when, where, how, or for what reason. The adverbial phrases may be one word, a prepositional phrase, or a subordinated dependent clause.

*The children ran* to school because they had overslept.
               Intransitive verb

*The book lies* on the desk now.
 subject verb  where   when

*The pump will run* for two hours today because we released that gear.
   subject     verb    how long   when    why, for what reason

*She lectured* at the conference yesterday.
              where        when

3. **The Verb-Be** *(to be)* requires one of three kinds of complements: a noun phrase, an adjective phrase, or an adverbial phrase of place.

*John* is the *president* of his class.
Noun[1]   =   noun[1]

The complement here is *president* referring also to *John*. The two nouns refer to the same person and equal each other: John = president, the second noun more specifically identifies *John.*

*John* is *intelligent.*
Noun[1]   Adjective phrase

*Intelligent* is an adjective and the complement in this sentence. It *describes* John rather than identifies him.

*John* is in Florida at school.
Noun   where   where

The complement here consists of two adverbial phrases specifying *where* John is at the present time.

4. **The Linking Verb** also links the subject to its complement which can be either a noun or adjective phrase.

*John* became *the president* last month.
Noun[1]        Noun[1]

*He* became *her hero* immediately.
*His home* became *his sanctuary.*
*Whatever she said* became *law.*

In all of these sentences, the subject and complement refer to the same person or thing: John = president; home = sanctuary; and Whatever she said = law.

The complement of a linking verb can also be an adjective which describes the Noun[1] (subject) in the sentence.

*John* seems *intelligent.*
*Noun*[1]   Adjective

This pattern describes John more fully. Other verbs, such as *appear, become, look,* and *grow,* are equivalent in function when followed by an adjective describing the subject (noun[1]).

The child appears sad. (The sad child)
The man became unhappy with his position. (The unhappy man)
The house looks good to me. (The good house)
The corn grew tall. (The tall corn)

Verbs referring to the senses, such as *smell, taste, feel,* and *sound,* belong to the linking verb classification when their complement describes the subject.

The soup *smells good.*
The bread tasted fresh.
The apple tastes good.
The music sounds good.
Her voice sounds husky this morning.
The children felt bad about the accident of the dog.
He feels good this morning,

To use adverbs in the place of the adjectives in the first two examples would attribute the ability of the soup to smell itself or the bread to taste itself. Probably the soup would not be able to muster a very good sniff on its own? The writer is describing the aroma of the soup and the taste of the bread and apple and, therefore, needs an adjective to complete the concept. Moreover, the sentence about the children is describing a feeling within them not indicating something they are doing to something which would require a transitive verb and its object, as does the sentence below:

The children *felt the fuzzy material* on their stuffed animals.

         Transitive   Object
           verb

Somewhat confusing, however, is the use of *well* rather than *good* when describing physical health.

She feels unusually *well* now following her illness.

*Well* although usually an adverb becomes an adjective in referring to health situations.

In contrast, adverbs describe verbs.

He *ran well* in the last race. (how he ran)
He *works happily* all day. (how he works)
He always *eats quickly* before his class. (how he eats)

Some of the sense words can also function as transitive verbs. In each of the following sentences, the subject is doing something to something else not describing some reaction.

He smelled the soup.
Noun[1]    Noun[2]

He sounded the alarm
The group tasted the bread.

## Types of Sentences

English has four types of sentences: the simple (basic), the compound, the complex, and the compound-complex. Experienced writers use all four of these patterns, choosing whichever one best conveys their concept at the time. Long sentences merely consist of combinations of these types.

1. **The Simple Sentence** has one subject and one predicate (verb plus the object or complement). The *simple* subject is just the noun or pronoun that the verb must agree with in number.

Computers have a mind of their own.
  Subject    Predicate
   Plural     have (plural)

The rulebook  is  explicit on that point.
   Subject    Predicate
   singular    is (singular)

The judge  provided the references for that point of law.
  Subject   Predicate

A subject in a simple sentence may have some modifiers or contain more than one word. Understanding the difference between the *basic* and the *complete subject* is of particular importance in deciding subject-verb agreement. The verb always agrees with the *basic* subject not the *complete* subject.

| | |
|---|---|
| Basic Subject: | The first two *explorers* to reach the South Pole *were* Roald Amundsen and Robert F. Scott. |
| Complete Subject: | *The first two explorers to reach the South Pole were* Roald Amundsen and Robert F. Scott. |
| Basic Subject: | The *decision* of the courts on such matters *has* deterred companies from engaging in such practices. |
| Complete Subject: | *The decision of the courts on such matters has* deterred companies from engaging in such practices. |

The basic subjects here are *explorers* and *decision*. Since explorers is plural, the verb must also be plural or *were*. Since decision is singular, the verb must also be singular or *has*. The complete subject includes the basic subject and words that complete its meaning or modify it.

Even in a simple sentence, the subject may include more than one person or thing or even a series of persons or things.

> *John and Mary* washed their shoes after their hike.
> *John, Mary, and Bill* competed in several of the races yesterday.
>
> The *promise and the peril* of Antarctica *have* enticed many adventurers to its exploration.
> The slides, microscope, and textbook *were* on the table by the door yesterday.

The predicate may also include more than one verb phrase; that is, be a *compound predicate*. The verbs or series of verbs, however, will relate to only one subject phrase.

> *The children visited* the hospital yesterday *and entertained* some of their young friends with some songs.
>
> *The children visited* the hospital yesterday, *read* stories to some of their young friends, *and entertained* everyone by singing several familiar songs.

In certain transformed or stylistic sentences, the subject may not appear before the verb phrase.

> *It is* the teacher's prerogative to decide on the day's course of study.
> The teacher's prerogative is to decide on the day's course of study.
>
> *There are* three small creeks feeding into that basin.
> *Three small creeks* feed into that small basin.

*It and there* are not the subjects of these sentences even though they occupy the subject position. They operate as placeholders for the noun (subject) that is to follow. This pattern, a stylistic variation for writers, can lead to wordiness by its wordy delaying of the subject.

A simple sentence can also be one or two words. The following imperative or command sentences have their subject "you" understood.

> Run.
> Don't stop the car.
> Wash your hands at once.

Indicative sentences make a statement or comment about something; interrogative sentences ask a question.

> Bill has just produced his seventh play.
>
> Have you seen Bill's last play?

2. **The Compound Sentence** consists of two or more independent clauses (sentences) joined by one of the coordinating conjunctions *and, but, for, or,* and *nor* indicating a close relationship between the two ideas.

> The technicians stayed on in the laboratory, *and* the nurses attended the lecture.
>
> The technicians stayed on in the laboratory, *for* the nurses attended the lecture.
>
> We were expecting an ice storm, *but* we didn't anticipate a power failure of that duration.
>
> Flexibility is the result of creativity, *and* productivity is the result of both.

Thus, the compound sentence has the following structure:

| Complete sentence | + | ,and | + | Complete sentence |
|---|---|---|---|---|
|  |  | ,but |  |  |
| Subject + Predicate |  | ,for |  | Subject + Predicate |
|  |  | ,or |  |  |
|  |  | ,nor |  |  |

3. **The Complex Sentence** consists of an independent clause and at least one dependent clause. Often it is a substitute for the compound sentence but providing better cause-effect relationship between the concepts.

> The technicians stayed on in the laboratory *since* the nurses attended the lecture.
> *because*
> *even though*
> *as*
>
> We were expecting an ice storm *although* we didn't anticipate a power failure of that duration.

*Since the nurses attended the lecture* and *although we didn't anticipate a power failure of that duration* are no longer independent clauses or complete sentences. Such words as *since, because, even though, although, as,* and *if* subordinate the words following them into a dependent structure. The subordinated structure may also appear at the beginning of the sentence possibly to provide better cause-effect emphasis or variety in the style pattern.

> *Since* the nurses attended the lecture, the technicians stayed on in the laboratory.
>
> *Although* we didn't anticipate a power failure of that duration, we were expecting an ice storm.

The Complex sentence has the following structure in contrast to that of the Simple or Compound structure.

        Complete Sentence    +    subordinator——complete sentence
or

Subordinator——complete sentence, + complete sentence

**4. The Compound-Complex** sentence consists of at least two independent clauses (sentences)—the compound part—and at least one subordinated structure.

> The technicians stayed on in the laboratory, *and* the nurses attended the lecture *even though* they were behind in their experiments.

or

> *Even though* they were behind in their experiments, the nurses attended the lecture, *and* the technicians stayed on in the laboratory.

> I become very nervous whenever I hear a siren, *for* I know something serious has happened.

or

> Whenever I hear a siren, I become very nervous, *for* I know something serious has happened.

The compound-complex sentence reflects the following basic structure:

<u>Complete    + ,and    + complete</u>  + subordinator—complete
<u>Sentence      ,for         sentence</u>                     sentence
         Compound Sentence

## The Relative Pronouns and Modification

The above complex and compound-complex sentences included only dependent clauses introduced by adverbial transition subordinators. They provided answers to the when, where, why, how, for what purpose, and cause and effect relationships within the sentence. Other types of dependent clauses result from words that relate structures to nouns and pronouns. These words—which, that, who, whom—are the relative pronouns.

**Which** clauses are explanatory and nonrestrictive and relate dependent clauses only to things or ideas.

> Our bank, *which* Bill manages, has just raised its interest rates.

> Her latest book, *which* arrived yesterday from the publisher, distorts the concept of democracy in the world today.

> His suggestion about moving the books, *which* seemed absurd at the time, has proved to be our best solution to our overcrowding.

In each of these dependent clauses, *which* replaces the word it modifies:

> Our bank, Bill manages *our bank*

> Her latest book, her *latest book* arrived yesterday

> His suggestion, his suggestion seemed absurd.

The *which* clause provides good information but not essential information. Deleting the clause from the sentence would not change the main import of the meaning.

>   Our bank has just raised its interest rates.

>   Her latest book distorts the concept of democracy in the world today.

>   His suggestion has proved to be our best solution to our overcrowding.

Nonessential clauses then are set off from the rest of the sentence with commas.

>   *That* as a relative pronoun can relate dependent clauses to either things or people. *That* clauses define and restrict and do not require any punctuation around them.

>   Any bus *that emits such a profusion of fumes* should be banned from all city streets.

>   The man *that phoned yesterday* has made an offer for our house.

>   The word processor *that you were using yesterday* is our latest model.

As was true with which, *that* substitutes for the word its clause is modifying.

>   Any bus *any bus emits such a profusion of fumes that*

>   The man *the man phoned yesterday that*

>   The word processor *the word processor you were using yesterday that*

**That** clauses are essential to the total meaning of the sentence. Deletion of the clause would result in ambiguity or quite another interpretation for such sentences:

>   The bus should be banned from all city streets.

>   The man has made an offer for our house.

>   The word processor is our latest model.

*Who* and *whom*, the other two relative pronouns also appear in complex or compound-complex sentences. Whether to use who or whom can be a dilemma for many writers. In speech, many people are careless in making the distinction. However, conscientious writers do use these words correctly. Once on the page, the word is available to the critical scrutiny of all readers.

*Who* appears as a subject or a complement in the dependent clause:

>   Who:   The man *who* rents my house wants to buy it.
>   The man wants to buy it.
>   *the man* rents my house.

>   Who:   Bill who writes well is our associate editor.
>   Bill is our associate editor.
>   *Bill* writes well.

Whoever: The college will award the grant to *whoever has the* greatest need.
*whoever* has the greatest need

Thus, in the first two sentences *who* is replacing either the *man* or *Bill* and is serving as the subject of the dependent adjective clauses. In the third sentence, *whoever* is the subject of the verb *has* in the dependent noun clause *whoever has the greatest need*. This entire clause is the object of the preposition *to* not just whoever.

*Who* is also the correct choice when replacing the complement in a dependent relative clause.

Who: I know *who* the winner will be.

Complement: the winner will be *who*.

Who: It is difficult to decide just *who* your best workers are.

Complement: your best workers are *who*.

In these sentences, the verb phrases in the relative clauses are *will be* and *are*. Both are part of the Verb-Be that requires a complement but not a direct object.

One construction requiring *who* can cause considerable confusion for any writer. Intervening phrases, such as *I believe, I think, they say,* or *I feel* between the *who* and the rest of its clause, do not affect the case of the pronoun who.

Bill Marrow is the candidate for City Treasurer who *we feel* has the best qualifications for the office.

Bill Marrow is the candidate for City Treasurer
*Bill has* the best qualifications for the office.

*Who* is the correct usage in the above sentence. The phrase *we feel* could appear at another place in the sentence just as easily and thus eliminate the confusion.

*We feel* that Bill Marrow is the candidate for City Treasurer *who has* the best qualifications for the office.

The following example also indicates how an intervening phrase might provide for some confusion or doubt about whether to use *who or whom*.

The writer who *the editors believe* has the most on-the-job experience should receive the study grant.

The writer should receive the study grant
The writer has the most on-the-job experience.

*The editors believe* that the writer *who has* the most on-the-job experience should receive the study grant.

Obviously, such phrases pose problems for any writer forgetting the intervening phrase rule.

*Whom* serves as the object or the object of a preposition in the dependent clause.

  Whom: Mr. Beam *whom we knew in college* has just joined our firm.
      Mr. Beam has just joined our firm.
  Object: We knew *Mr. Beam* in college.

  Whom: The man *whom we met yesterday* wants to borrow our maps.
      The man wants to borrow our maps.
  Object: We met *the man* yesterday.

  Whom: I will award the scholarship to *whomever the committee chooses*.
      I will award the scholarship to (someone).
  Object: The committee chooses someone (whomever).

In the first two sentences, *whom* is the direct object of knew and met, verbs in the dependent clauses. *Whomever* is the object of *chooses* in the dependent clause which serves as the object of the preposition *to*.

 *Whom* also serves as the object of a preposition in its dependent clause.

  The man *to whom* I rented my house wants to buy it now.
    The man wants to buy it now.
  Object of Preposition: I rented my house *to the man* (to whom).

  I did not know *whom* they were talking to.
    I did not know something.
  Object of Preposition: They were talking to *whom*.

All of the complex sentences above indicate that *who* and *whom* always have specific places in the dependent clauses. Both replace the noun to which they are relating their clause. Noting that complex sentences always involve two sentences and observing which part of the dependent clause *who* or *whom* is replacing is essential in deciding the one to use.

*Who* or *whom* used in *interrogative* sentences may also cause writers to think through their constructions carefully. However, the same rules apply for this usage as constructions involving two sentences: *who* still serves as the subject or complement and *whom* still serves as the object of the verb or object of the preposition.

  Who: *Who* is the leader of this group?
     Subject

  Who: *Who* will the winner be?
     The winner will be *who?*
       Complement

Whom: Whom did you see at the lecture?
You did see *whom* at the lecture?
Object of Verb

Whom: To *whom* did you give your donation?
You gave your donation *to whom?*
Object of Preposition

## Variety in the Sentence

As illustrated under "Types of Sentences" above, a sentence is a patterned sequence of words but having the potential for a variety of rhetorical structures. Thus, writers have many ways of expressing their ideas without sounding simplistic or resorting to repetition. The *loose* sentence, the *periodic* sentence, and the *balanced* sentence are three terms also used to indicate variety of sentence patterns.

The *loose* sentence has the main concept occurring first with the addition of unlimited minor items or subordinated structures coming at the end just before the period.

> The *control* of nitrogen oxides *requires* an entirely different *technology,* one that is still largely undeveloped and that might end up costing the utilities something like $2.3 billion in capital outlays in the next five years to control emissions from existing boilers.

The *periodic* sentence suspends the grammatical completion until nearly the last word or just before the period—thus its name.

> Unless it is brought under control by the end of the century, the *emission* of sulphur oxides *will nearly quadruple.*

The *balanced* sentence contains clauses similar in length and movement and expressed in parallel constructions.

> Our management people *had authority* but now they *have responsibility* as well.

All three sentence patterns are correct. They lend variety in writing and in some cases, one or the other might provide for a clearer expression of an idea or for better emphasis. Further variety in sentence patterning also derives from the many alternate beginnings available for sentences. A representative list of the various types would include the following:

The Noun: *The company* cut the amount of excess air in the burners and resorted to two-stage combustion.

Coordinating Conjunction: *Neither low-sulphur fuels nor devices* to scrub sulphur dioxide do much to reduce emissions of the nitrogen oxides.

| | |
|---|---|
| Prepositional Phrase: | *Among the traditional functions of middle management* are expediting, work planning, control of inventory, and monitoring of mechanical drawing systems. |
| Clause: | *Since the cost of computing is being reduced ten times every decade,* it may not be long before the cost of operating a computer terminal in one's home will be very common. |
| Adverb: | *Consequently,* we must find new and better teaching principles. *Today,* any project of a similar magnitude would be too costly. |
| Transforms: | *There are* several reasons why the company can not afford more staff at this time.<br>*To make* a profit on every item is to be unusually lucky.<br>*That the lawyer would state* so early in the case that his client had no chance shocked even the reporters.<br>*What he wanted to do* did not tally with the facts of the case. |

## Questions

1. Write two sentences for each of the four types of verbs.

2. Write two sentences for each of the four types of sentences.

3. In your reading, find two examples in which the authors have used the four relative pronouns: which, that, who, whom.

4. Have the authors used them in essential (restrictive) or nonessential (nonrestrictive) clauses? Explain your answer.

## Assignment

Select one of your previously written papers and note the type of verbs and the type and variety of sentences you have used the most. Have you let one type of verb or sentence pattern dominate your writing?

Part 2  *The Editing Challenge: Revision is Quality Control at its Best*

# 6 Sentence Structure and Style

The stress here has been that a good piece of writing (of any length) must be clear, concise, and effective. The writing must be appropriate to the status of the writer, the type of subject matter, and the needs and position of the audience. The organization must be logical and the key ideas stated correctly, concretely, and objectively.

These statements summarize the basic theory of good communication. However, as in all imperfect worlds, stating and restating the theory does not lead easily nor immediately to a perfected finished product. Good writing requires time and commitment. It requires an understanding and an awareness of some of the sentence structure problems or lapses in style—ambiguities, vagueness, wordiness—that lead to loss of emphasis or failed communication.

The sentence structure problems and lapses in style discussed here are those that writers are most likely to confront in their last-hour revision excursions. The usual cry is "I know this sentence doesn't sound right, but I don't know exactly what's the matter." A knowledge of various shifts in structure and possible sentence meandering can be of assistance in solving this problem.

## Unnecessary Shifts in Structure

Shifts are changes in pattern. They are not always wrong, but they can distract and confuse the reader. They can indicate an off-course veering in the flow of the writing. A shift from active to passive, in point of view, in level of usage, and in mood can be roadblocks in a manuscript and not only reveal a lapse of thinking by the writer but also careless revision habits.

### Active-Passive Voice Problem

One problem that can arise from the transitive verb pattern is the overuse of the passive voice—the most overt stylistic problem in all types of writing. Some writers may use the passive voice almost entirely or clutter their messages by shifting from active verb forms to passive verb forms in the same sentence or in the same paragraph. Some scholarly and scientific writers insist that they must write in the passive voice in order to sound objective. In a few cases, this might be true. In most instances, the use of the passive voice is merely a bad habit or the result of speedy revision.

Today, the consistent use of the active verb pattern is essential for clear and concise communication. The passive voice robs a sentence of its inherent thrust and leads to vagueness, wordiness, and often omission of important information.

| | | | | | | |
|---|---|---|---|---|---|---|
| Active: | The Committee | + | chose | + | Jim | |
| | Noun phrase 1 | + | verb | + | Noun phrase 2 | |
| Passive: | Jim | + | was chosen | + | by the committee. | |
| | Noun Phrase 2 | + | verb | + | noun phrase 1 | |

Active: The *crew cleaned* the roads at dawn.
At dawn, the crew *cleaned* the roads.

Passive: The roads *were cleaned* by the crew at dawn.
At dawn, the roads *were cleaned* by the crew.

Active: The sales *manager will administer* the program.
Passive: The program *will be administered by* the sales manager.

Active: The company *paid the bill* on March 5, 1990.
Passive: The bill *was paid by* the company on March 5, 1990.

As these examples illustrate, the passive voice changes the order of the sentence by moving the doer of the action to the end of the sentence. With the active voice, the responsible group or person is the subject; with the passive voice, the emphasis is on *Jim,* the *roads,* the *program,* and the *bill.* The two nouns (subject and object) have just exchanged positions in the sentences:

| | | | |
|---|---|---|---|
| Active Voice: | Noun 1 (subject) | verb | Noun 2 (object) |
| Passive Voice: | Noun 2 (object) | verb | Noun 1 (subject) |

Moreover, the passive voice requires more words to deliver the same information. One way to identify the passive voice is to look for a form of the *Be* verb (is, are, was, were, being, been) followed by a past participle—*was chosen by, was cleaned by, will be administered by,* and *was paid by.*

Sometimes, the use of passive voice may cause the reader to suspect that the writer is trying to hide responsibility for the action as in such bureaucratic uses as "Your complaint will be looked into" or "Your registration has been lost." Other passive voice sentences may provide no key to the group or individuals responsible for the action. This may not be essential information and its omission of no importance; however, the actor (s) may not appear because the writer purposely prefers to be vague about who or what is responsible.

> The roads *were cleaned* at dawn.
> The water gauge *will be checked* at eight tomorrow.
> The game *was lost* because of over confidence.
> The mistake on your bill *will be checked* tomorrow.

The passive in the following sentences *causes* vagueness and leaves both sentences with a dangling modifier as an introductory phrase.

> Opening the safe door, the jewelry was immediately seen.
> By working overtime, the investigation was completed in a week.

Did the jewelry open the safe door? Did the investigation work overtime? The reader would know this was not the case, but the writer's responsibility is to write clearly and not enter the reader into a guessing game. The reader might think it important to know exactly who or what was responsible.

> Opening the safe door, the *police saw* the jewelry immediately.
> By working overtime, *we completed* the investigation in a week.

These active verb versions clear up any vagueness and specifically inform about the subjects—the *police* and *we*.

Another problem exists when the writer uses both active and passive verbs in the same sentence:

> Opening the safe door, the jewelry *was* immediately *seen,* and *we breathed* a sigh of relief.
>
> The *staff worked* late last night, and all phases of the experiment *were* finally *completed.*

Corrected these sentences are clearer and much more concise.

> Opening the safe door, *we* immediately *saw* the jewelry and *breathed* a sigh of relief.
>
> The staff *worked* late last night and finally *completed* all phases of the experiment.

Careless writers sometimes find themselves caught in sentences like this one:

> The committee *feels* that the present system has three disadvantages: it *causes* delay in the distribution of incoming mail, *duplicates* work, and unnecessary delays *are created* in the routine of several other areas.

The first two parts of this sentence exhibit good parallel structure and are correct—it *causes* and it *duplicates*. However, the "delays are created" indicates a shift to the passive voice providing for wordiness and upsetting the parallelism of *causes* and *duplicates*. Corrected the sentence reads much more smoothly and clearly:

> *It causes delay* in the distribution of incoming mail,
> *duplicates work,* and
> *creates* unnecessary delays in the routine of several other areas.

The following paragraph is a good example of how the shift from active to passive to active voice can be confusing to readers, provide for wordiness, and indicate some careless or even garbled thinking on the part of the writer.

> [1]There are several steps that a teacher must follow in order to shape up or *teach* a given response to an organism. [2]First, a list of potential reinforcers for the organism must be made up by the teacher. [3]Second, any behavior emitted by the organism that slightly resembles the target behavior must be rewarded by the teacher. [4]Thirdly, the teacher must only acknowledge behavior that closer and closer resembles the target behavior. [5]Finally, only the target behavior emitted by the organism must be accepted by the teacher.

The arrows indicate that the writer did not have a very clear concept of what he or she wanted to say: Sentence [1] is in the active voice, sentence [2] in the passive, sentence[3] in the passive, sentence[4] in the active, and sentence[5] in the passive. This alternating between active and passive voice not only confuses the role of the teacher but also weakens the natural flow of the passage.

The following revision more clearly and concisely states the four steps that the teacher must follow. Not only does it remove the passive but also the repetition of the word *teacher* and the unnecessary use of first, second, etc. The word *four* in the opening statement alerts the reader immediately to the number of steps stated in four parallel phrases. The consistent use of active verbs creates balance and force.

> A teacher must follow four steps in order to shape up or teach a given response to an organism: *make up* a list of potential reinforcers, *reward* any behavior emitted by the organism that slightly resembles the target behavior, *acknowledge* behavior that closer and closer resembles the target behavior, and finally, *accept* only the target behavior emitted by the organism.

The wordiness and the obtuseness of an overuse of the passive voice is also very evident in the following instructions about treating a burn. In such a crisis situation, any person having to handle the patient would want the instructions stated as clearly and concisely as possible. The consistent use of the passive voice does not answer this need.

> The following action *must be taken* when a serious burn *is treated.* Any loose clothing on or near the burn *is removed.* The injury *is covered* with a clean dressing, and the area around the burn *is washed.* Then the dressing *is secured* with tape. Burned fingers or toes *are separated* with gauze or cloth so that they *are prevented* from sticking together. Medication *is not applied* unless it is prescribed by a doctor.

In the following rewrite, the listed instructions about how to handle such a crucial situation are clear and easy for the reader to understand and follow.

Treatment of a serious burn requires the following action:

> Remove any loose clothing on or near the burn.
> Wash the area around the burn.
> Cover the injury with a clean dressing.
> Secure the dressing with tape.
> Separate burned fingers or toes with gauze or cloth to prevent them from sticking together.
> Apply only doctor prescribed medication.

The first word of each step, an imperative verb form, informs the person in charge about exactly what to do and when. Also, this active version omits the wordiness, has conciseness, and provides the proper emphasis.

## Proper Use of Passive Voice

Using the passive voice, however, is appropriate when the doer of the action (or responsible person) is not important and the writer really wants to stress the thing or person acted upon.

> The dogs *must be injected* morning and evening if this study is to be valid.
>
> Lethal dosage *was determined* by injecting the drug into 100 laboratory mice.
>
> The horses *must be exercised* twice a day to be in good shape for the race on Saturday.

Certainly the dogs being injected is more important to the outcome of the study than the one who is to do the injecting. In the other two sentences, the doer of the action is also not important; it is the "dosage that must be determined" and "the horses that must be exercised" that need the emphasis.

## Point of View Shift Problem

*Written* communication is always more clear and less confusing if writers maintain a consistent point of view; that is stay in the same "person" to relate their ideas. To understand this statement requires an awareness of the following paradigm—one also essential for conjugating verbs and selecting pronouns.

| Person | Singular    | Person | Plural |
|--------|-------------|--------|--------|
| 1      | I           | 1      | we     |
| 2      | you         | 2      | you    |
| 3      | he, she, it | 3      | they   |

Shifting point of view simply means a writer could begin writing in the first person singular (I) and gradually slip into second person singular (you)—one of the most common shifts in expository writing. The following short memorandum exemplifies this problem very well:

> If *I* am selected for this seminar, *I* would be an eager and enthusiastic participant in all aspects of the program. *I* firmly believe *you* must be willing to utilize every opportunity that presents itself to challenge and explore *yourself* and to broaden *your* knowledge of *your* career.

The writer begins with "if I am," "I would be" and "I firmly believe" but then shifts to "you" "yourself," and "your"—all second person singular subject—although the context implies the writer is still talking about *I*.

The following paragraph has even more inconsistencies in "person." The writer begins with *he* (third person singular) then uses "you" (second person singular) then "they" (third person plural) and ends with an imperative verb form whose subject is an understood "you."

> To a first year *student* in a machine woodworking class, the table saw is a thing of majestic beauty; *he or she* must learn to treat it with the respect of a tiger. To use it successfully, *you* must first learn the nomenclature and safety precautionary measures of the saw before *you* can learn the many different cuts *you* can make with it. *I* will try in words to relate to *you* how to cross cut boards on the table. The *students* must always remember the table saw will bite off fingers as quickly as a tiger, so *be careful*.

The following rewrite corrects this "point of view problem" and presents the ideas logically using third person plural (they) consistently. Using the plural pronoun avoids an inevitable over use of *he or she*.

> To first year *students* in machine woodworking class, the table saw is a thing of majestic beauty; however, *they* must learn to treat it with the respect of a tiger. To use it successfully, *they* must first learn the nomenclature and safety precautionary measures of the table saw before *they* can learn the many different cuts *they* can make with it. Cross-cutting boards with the saw is easy. . . . The *students* must always remember the table saw will bite off fingers as quickly as a tiger; so *they* must be careful.

Astute readers should be suspicious of the writer's motives after receiving the following memorandum written by a department supervisor and involving the question of proper image in a department. The editorial "we" tucked in here and there among the "you's" is probably used to make the underlying criticism of members of the department a little more palatable.

> A few words on a big subject. *We* all find *ourselves* with opinions that are not shared by others and become embroiled in disputes. How *you* handle *yourself* in these differences of opinion is very important to *your* job satisfac-

tion and *your* performance (and that of the division) It also can affect *our* public image if the dispute or discussion happens to be with a fisherman or a group of fishermen.

Respect the rights of others to disagree with *you* and try to confine disputes to the issues. When people don't agree with *you,* don't question their character or motives or intelligence. Don't be overbearing and keep your cool. *We* can't expect to be right all the time. It's a good plan to gracefully lose a few arguments if *we* expect to get along with people *we* work with. *We* all have a unique character. *We* must accept these differences and make allowances for them as *we* focus on the important things.

A shift in point of view can also occur in just one sentence in some larger unit of writing:

If a *person* enjoys a lifetime sport, such as swimming or bowling, the chances are *they* will continue the activity throughout adult life.

Before a *person* decides whether a job is really as glamorous as it sounds, *you* should study all aspects of it thoroughly.

In the first sentence the writer replaces the third person singular person (he or she) with the third person plural *they.* This not only indicates a shift in point of view but also shows incorrect pronoun reference. In the second sentence, the writer makes the very common shift to the indefinite *you*—a shift from third person singular (person) to second person plural (you).

The writer's responsibility in expository prose is to stick to a point of view and not thoughtlessly or carelessly skip from one "person" to another. Such shifting exposes some confusion in thinking on the part of the writer. Although the change in person may not always cause a serious communication breakdown, it could bring into question the writer's communication capability.

## Shift in Level of Usage Problems

What is good usage is related to the question of what is good English. The best definition of good English is that it is appropriate English. That is appropriate for the speaker or writer, for the subject under discussion, for the situation, and for the person receiving the message. Chapter 10 discusses some specific areas of usage and fine points of diction. Although there may be some disagreement about the correctness or acceptability or unacceptability of certain words or structures, the information whether pro or con is essential for successful writing in any professional career. In serious expository prose, a writer must maintain a consistent level of usage. One sentence in the following paragraph has an obvious shift to a lower level of expression, thus detracting from the major emphasis of the writing.

> Various Congressmen are suggesting that there will be a need to increase revenues, possibly resulting in higher taxes for most people. Both the White House and Congress are exploring means to do this. With his hope for a balanced budget somewhat in jeopardy, the President is proposing additional spending cuts to meet the goal. Several self-interest groups are *screaming* because their projects are not receiving *large fat appropriations*. Thus, Congress is considering the possibility of tax hikes to meet budgetary needs.

The descriptive phrases "groups are screaming" and "fat appropriations" are not on the same level of writing as the other sentences or word choices. This shift tends to affect negatively the importance of the subject matter and the seriousness of the author. Language too pompous is just as unfortunate as language too casual when more formality might be appropriate.

The obvious triteness of some of the phrases and cliché crutches in the following sentence are hardly consistent with the importance of the subject matter.

> The time is *now or never* for this company to *grab the bull by the horns* and aggressively pursue *all roads and by-roads* leading to increased profits through sale-oriented procedures and culminating in increased consumer satisfaction.

Perhaps a better version of this sentence might be similar to the following:

> It is time for our company to begin aggressively pursuing all means leading to increased profits through sale-oriented procedures and culminating in increased consumer satisfaction.

A trite phrase is a tired phrase—one that has had too much use through too many years and lost its original meaning. Speakers sometimes depend on such language just to keep the flow of conversation from sagging too much or too long. This is a questionable rationalization for using such phrases even in speech. Trite phrases and clichés are still trite as the following exemplify:

| | |
|---|---|
| each and every one | it goes without saying |
| one and only | the bottom line |
| slowly but surely | don't rock the boat |
| all in all | a figure in the ball park |
| better late than never | in the final analysis |
| easier said than done | my crystal ball shows |
| few and far between | where ignorance is bliss |

Writers of serious prose have little need for such language expressions as they have time to search for the concrete and precise words necessary for composing a communication.

## Shifts in Mood Problems

Mood refers to the manner of speaking or writing. English has three moods: the *indicative* that states a fact or asks a question, the *imperative* that expresses a request or command and has an understood "you" as the subject, and the *subjunctive* that expresses conditional, provisional, or wishful ideas in subordinate clauses, such as "if he were here." The problem occurring in writing is not with the mood per se but rather with unnecessary shifts from one mood to another, producing awkward, wordy, and unbalanced sentences as the following:

> Be sure to come often, and the management hopes you will recommend our services to your company.

This awkward sentence begins with the imperative—(you) be sure to come often—and ends in the indicative—the management hopes you will recommend. . . .

> Mr. Bates said that it was nearly time for him to speak and would I please adjust the volume of the microphone.

> He stated that his department would buy that software and would the company then demonstrate it for him.

In these two sentences the shifting back and forth between a statement of fact and a type of question-command requires the reader to do some quick interpretation. Rewritten the sentences become clearer and more concise.

> Mr. Bates said that it was nearly time for him to speak and asked me to adjust the volume of the microphone.

> He stated that his department would buy that soft ware if our company would demonstrate its use for him.

## Parallelism Problems

### Parallelism

Parallelism means that two or more words or structures in a sentence performing the same function must have the same form: all nouns, all adjectives, all verbs, all participles, all infinities, all clauses. A lack of parallelism produces unbalanced, awkward, and off-key sounding sentences. It can lead to serious misinterpretations. It is the mark of an amateur and careless writer. An understanding of parallelism is essential for good writing:

### *Parallelism with Nouns*

> The psychopath is *a menace, and one who is* dangerous to society.

|  | |
|---|---|
| corrected: | The psychopath is *a menace and a danger* to society. |
|  | Differential equations is another mathematical concept applicable to such things as the *bacteria growth* in a pond, the *population growth* of a city, and *producing equations*. |
| corrected: | Differential equations is another mathematical concept applicable to such things as the bacteria *growth*, the population *growth*, and the *production* of equations. |
|  | His work reflects research, thought, and is *imaginative*. |
| corrected: | His work reflects *research, thought,* and *imagination*. |
|  | In the next fifty years, we can expect greater space achievements, and *great urban centers will develop*. |
| corrected: | In the next fifty years, we can expect *greater space achievements* and *greater urban center development*. |

## Parallelism with Adjectives

|  | |
|---|---|
|  | The system is large and convenient and *it does not cost very much*. |
| corrected: | The system is *large, convenient,* and *economical*. |
|  | The majority of people have *honesty, are clean, and display decency*. |
| corrected: | The majority of people are *honest, clean,* and *decent*. |
|  | The project was of *value, interesting* and *provided education* for all participants. |
| corrected: | The project was *valuable, interesting,* and *educational*. |

## Parallelism with Participles

|  | |
|---|---|
|  | It is much better *to be* happy with your situation than *wearing* yourself out in vain ambition for wealth and social success. |
| corrected: | It is much better *being* happy with your situation than *wearing* yourself out in vain ambition for wealth and social success. |
|  | The final process is *to replace* all of the metal fixtures and *pulling off* the masking tape. |
| corrected: | The final process is *replacing* all of the metal fixtures and *pulling* off the masking tape. |
|  | His work consisted mainly of *writing letters* and *to check* the new drug listings. |

corrected: His work consisted mainly of *writing* letters and *checking* the new drug listings.

## Parallelism with Infinitives

Many older people are returning to college because they wish to improve themselves, to get a better job, or *because they have increased leisure time.*

corrected: Many older people are returning to college because they wish *to improve* themselves, *to get* a better job, or *to use* their leisure time better.

The manager demanded *to see* the accountant and *that he be allowed to investigate* all the books and orders.

corrected: The manager demanded *to see* the accountant and *to investigate* all the books and orders.

He tried *to separate* the components rather than *testing* the combination.

corrected: He tried *to separate* the components rather than *to test* the combination.

## Parallelism with Clauses

The business man today operates under many kinds of restrictions that tell him exactly *what he must do, how to prepare his records,* and even *what his employees can be paid.*

corrected: The business man today operates under many kinds of restrictions that tell him exactly *what he must do, how he must prepare his records,* and *what he must pay his employees.*

or The business man today operates under many kinds of restrictions that tell him exactly *what to do, how to prepare his records,* and *what to pay his employees.*

The later migration from the European countries were people who were looking for adventure, *also land hungry.*

corrected: The later immigrants from the European countries were people who were looking for adventure *and also more land.*

## Parallelism with Adverbs

They accused the technician of having acted hastily and *on impulse.*

corrected: They accused the technician of having acted *hastily and impulsively*.

The secretary answered the letter of enquiry *promptly* and with *courtesy*.
corrected: The secretary answered the letter of enquiry *promptly and courteously*.

## Parallelism with Prepositions

Writers must always be sure they have used all of the necessary prepositions. Some words for semantic reasons require a special preposition to complete their meaning and also to provide good balance to the items.

The remedial program is not compatible and is contrary to our curriculum objectives.
corrected: The remedial program is not *compatible with* and is *contrary to* our curriculum objectives.

compatible + ?
and
contrary to

Compatible requires *with*—that is *compatible with* something not *compatible to* something.

The President of the Council told the new members about their responsibility and that the council was starting its fund drive.
corrected: The President of the Council told the new members *about their responsibility* and *about the start of its fund drive*.

## Parallelism and Coordination

Parallelism also means proper balance and logical coordination. The same rules apply for the correlative conjunctions used in pairs as with any other type of parallel structuring: if a noun follows the first conjunction, then a noun must follow the second element; if an adjective follows the first part of the pair, then an adjective must follow the second part; etc. Following are some of the more common correlatives:

either—or           whether—or
neither—nor         not—but
both—and            not only—but also

*Either* the *accountant or treasurer* will have to fill the vacancy when Mr. Anton moves to Europe.

The young giraffe was *neither fearful nor clumsy* as it ran in the herd along side its mother.

*Both the actors and their understudies* resented the demands made on them by the manager.

He trusts the board *both in their sincerity and in their dedication* to the cause.

In his speech, he noted that *both walking and jogging* were excellent exercises.

Regardless of *whether Congress votes* a tax increase *or substantially cuts* certain appropriation, they will not have unanimous support for their action.

Probably *not only—but also* is the one correlative conjunction pair that causes the most problems. Often their close relationship escapes the writer as the parts may have several words separating them—hence, the omission of the *also* after the *but*.

|  | The purpose of this letter is *not only to* congratulate you *but to* notify you as quickly as possible of your promotion. |
|---|---|
| corrected: | The purpose of this letter is *not only to congratulate you but also to notify* you as quickly as possible of your promotion. |

|  | Truman turned out to be *not only* a capable president *but he* also had a sense of humility about the office. |
|---|---|
| corrected: | Truman turned out *not only to be a capable president but also to have a sense of humility* about the office. |

|  | We were able *not only* to rent a tractor-grader *but* borrow an operator for the park grading as well. |
|---|---|
| corrected: | We were able *not only to rent* a tractor-grader *but also to borrow* an operator for the park grading as well. |

|  | In the collaborative relationship the client and psychologist not only agree on the goals to be sought after, *but* how these goals are to be achieved. |
|---|---|
| corrected: | In the collaborative relationship, the client and psychologist *not only agree* on the goals *but also on ways* to achieve them. |

|  | In the collaborative relationship, the client and psychologist *not only agree* on the goals *but also agree* on ways to achieve them. |

In this last sentence, *agree* is understood in the phrase following *but also* in the first correction. A writer may omit it from the surface structure *if* it is clearly understood, thus avoiding some unnecessary repetition.

## *Parallelism in Listing*

Sometimes, instead of embedding a series of phrases in a sentence or paragraph, writers will list the items on separate lines. This format may give better emphasis and provide greater clarity to the concepts. The listed items must be in parallel form: that is the first word of each line must be the same part of speech and each line the same type of phrase. One line cannot be just a prepositional phrase and the next line a sentence. The following example indicates one form of proper paralleling of ideas.

The next step in the committee's proceedings was to list its objectives:

1. to create an awareness of the work opportunities in the industry.
2. to enlighten guidance counselors of the importance of the industry to the city.
3. to offer the opportunity for seminars and direct exposure to people already in the industry.
4. to render possible financial aid to needy students.
5. to provide an opportunity for summer work or job training.

This list could also be parallel by changing each of the beginning infinitives to participles: creating, enlightening, offering, rendering, or providing. However, mixing these two forms in the same listing would upset the necessary balance.

In contrast, the following items indicate a rather careless if not chaotic listing of the advantages of the sectional electric drive:

1. savings on power acquisition
2. handling of the machine is greatly simplified.
3. less strain is transmitted to the machine when starting up.
4. the back side of the machine is made accessible.
5. a saving in floor space.

The lack of smoothness resulting from such writing could very easily alienate a reader—perhaps lose him or her altogether. Corrected these items offer some very good advantages for this machine:

1. save on power
2. simplify greatly the handling of the machine
3. transmit less strain to the machine when starting up
4. make the back side of the machine accessible
5. save on floor space.

This use of only phrases introduced by verbs provides a smoothness and logical continuity to the ideas.

## Sentence Balance—Be-Verb + The Noun Phrase

The Be-verb plus the noun phrase can also cause writers some problems if they do not think through what they want to say carefully. Probably the reader can understand what the writer means, but the sentence still will not have the appropriate balance.

> I think my college *experience was the place* where I mentally matured.

Obviously an *experience* is not a *place;* the two nouns cannot equal each other.

> I think *college was the place* where I mentally matured.

This edited sentence does have balance for college can be a place.

> The greatest *discovery* in Alaska in the last fifty years *was the petroleum industry.*

*Discovery* and *industry* do not equal each other. However, changes in the wording provide the balance and the proper and intended concept.

> The greatest *event* in Alaska in the last fifty years *was* the *discovery* of petroleum.

Writers can stumble into such sentences very easily. To avoid leaving them in a manuscript or letter requires alert editing.

# Other Sentence Structure Problems

## Misplaced Modifiers

A modification structure placed too far away from a word or phrase it is supposed to modify (tells more about) can mislead the reader or provide some interesting humor. To correct such structure problems, the writer will need to recast the sentence.

> There are three kinds of animals that have been discovered by researchers *in this environment.*

The writer is probably talking about *animals in this environment* rather than researchers. Thus, the phrase must appear next to animals, the word it is to modify.

> corrected: There are three kinds of *animals in this environment* that have been discovered by researchers.

> In earlier times, *people* were oppressed by royal families *all over the world.*
>
> corrected: In earlier times, *people all over the world* were oppressed by royal families.

> *Being old and rotten, the landscape crew* removed the hedge with a minimum of effort.
>
> corrected: The landscape crew removed the *old, rotten hedge* with a minimum of effort
>
> Today, everyone knows and is quite cognizant of the fact that a woman needs an education *as well as a man.*
>
> corrected: Today, everyone knows that a *woman as well as a man* needs an education.

The last two sentences obviously need recasting. The reader would have no trouble deciphering their real meaning but would find considerable humor in the way the author had constructed them. Keeping descriptive words and phrases as close as possible to the words they describe avoids ambiguity as in the following example:

> Researchers gave the drug to *the dogs in the capsules.*
> Researchers gave *the drug in the capsules* to the dogs.

Of course, the drug—not the dogs—was in a capsule, thus the descriptive phrase should sit next to what it describes.

Putting a clause or phrase out of place in the beginning of a sentence leads to what grammarians call a "dangling modifier," such as *"Tails wagging, researchers* fed the dogs." Of course, researchers were probably not the ones with the wagging tails. Thus, correcting and editing the sentence is a matter of placing the descriptive phrase next to the appropriate word: "Researchers fed the *dogs, which wagged their tails."*

## Dangling Participial Phrases

A dangling modifier is exactly what its name implies. It is a structure waiting for rescue. It has lost its own subject and seemingly attached itself to the noun in the sentence following.

> *Looking back, the house* seemed grim and forbidding in the fog.

As it stands, it sounds as though the house is looking back which is not the case, of course.

> As *we looked* back, the house seemed grim and forbidding in the fog.
>
> Wandering slowly down the street, the cries and confusion were difficult to locate.
>
> corrected: As *we wandered* slowly down the street, we had trouble locating the cries and confusion.

>  Opening the office door, the fire-charred contents were appalling.
>
> corrected: As *we opened the office door,* we saw the appalling mess of the fire-charred contents.
>
> Looking back, the swarm of hornets was charging directly toward me.
>
> corrected: As *I looked back, the* swarm of hornets was charging directly toward me.

All opening participial phrases are not dangling modifiers. The dangling depends on whether they are to modify the noun in the sentence following. If they are, then the proper modification is there. The last two examples could also read correctly as follows:

> *Opening the office door, we saw* the appalling mess of the fire-charred contents.
>
> *Looking back, I saw* the swarm of hornets charging directly toward me.

In the following two sentences *he* is the one surveying and working; therefore, the initial participial phrases are not dangling.

> *Surveying the sodden mess inside, he* was appalled at the amount of flood damage.
>
> *Working late into the night, he* was able to complete the project on time.

## Squinting Modifiers

A "squinting modifier" is a descriptive clause, phrase, or a word that comes between two words seemingly relating to both at the same time: "She said *when the meeting was over* that she would return." Did she *say* this when the meeting was over? Or is she planning to *return* when the meeting is over? To make the meaning clear, the writer needs to move the clause to one end of the sentence or the other:

> *When the meeting was over,* she said she would return.
>
> She said she would return *when the meeting was over.*

Thus, this type of modifier is not waiting for something to modify; it already has too many things it could modify. The result is a vague sentence and one open to misinterpretation.

> What the voters believe *profoundly* affects their ability to evaluate issues fairly.

Does this sentence mean "what the voters *profoundly believe* affects their ability to evaluate" or does it mean "what the voters believe *affects profoundly* their ability to evaluate"? Literally the word *profoundly* "squints" in two directions. Both interpretations are possible. Framing profoundly with commas would be of no value in deciding the right interpretation either.

> The study indicated that the children who did not watch television, *as a general rule,* were less aggressive in their relationships with other children.

The same ambiguity exists with the phrase *as a general rule* as with *profoundly*. It could refer to "children not watching television as a general rule" or to "children being less aggressive as a general rule." The commas do nothing toward clarifying the meaning.

## Misplaced Which Clauses

A *which clause* left loosely attached to the end of a sentence provides for ambiguity and misinterpretation of the concepts and indicates fuzzy thinking on the part of the writer.

> Our state universities are financed mainly by funds allocated by the state legislature *which could prove a real problem.*

It is impossible to know whether it is the appropriations of the state legislature that could prove the real problem or the fact that the university financing comes from the state in the first place.

> An advanced degree is required for speech pathology *which doesn't appeal to me at all.*

A similar mixup in meaning is evident in this sentence. It is difficult to know whether it is speech pathology itself that the writer dislikes or the fact that it require another year of classwork.

> Before replacing the distributor cap on the housing, it is important that it be dust free *which might cause it to malfunction.*

This which clause makes little sense at all, for it seems to imply that being dust free could cause the problem. The writer is probably saying that if the cap is not dust free, it could cause the distributor to malfunction. However, the responsibility of the writer is to edit such ambiguities out of his or her writing.

Of course, all which clauses at the end of the sentence do not promote such a problem—only those that are not closely attached to a noun they really modify.

> I did not like his new pictures, *all of which* were too gaudy and overdecorated for my taste.

> I recommend that the Biological Center purchase ten additional word *processors which* can take care of the increased workshop group.

## Comparison Problems

Formal written English requires logic and precision in expressing comparisons sometimes not evident in informal speech or in some informal writing. Careful writers, however, do watch the form of their comparisons to prevent any misinterpretation or misunderstanding about what they wish to convey.

Three types of faulty comparison structures can plague writers: the incomplete, the illogical, and the ambiguous. Correcting any one of them can also be difficult, for while editing the copy, a writer may mentally supply the words that should be on the page. Unfortunately, the reader can not do this. Thus, writers need to be sure that they are comparing the exact words they intend to compare.

## *Incomplete Comparisons*

> His experiences in college and graduate school may differ from a lot of people.
>
> The temperature of subject A is the same as subject B.
>
> The frustration tolerance in the neurotic, as you might suspect, is lower than the average person.

These comparisons are incomplete. The writer means to compare the *experiences* of one group to the *experiences* of another group. Omitting the word *experience* or the word *those* which could replace it, marks the incompleteness.

> His experiences in college and graduate school may differ from *those* of a lot of people.

The second example needs the words *temperature of* or *that of* inserted before *subject B,* and the third, the word *tolerance* or *that* before *the average person.*

> The temperature of Subject A is the same as *that of* subject B.
> The frustration tolerance in the neurotic, as you might suspect, is lower than the *frustration tolerance of* the average person.

## *Illogical Comparisons*

> Our new filters are better than any filters received this month.
>
> Today, Chicago has more diverse ethnic groups within the city proper than any city in the United States.
>
> William Banes is a better writer and speaker than anyone in the English Department.

The first two sentences illogically state that the "new filters are better than the new filters" and Chicago has more ethnic population than Chicago." The third sentence excludes William Banes from the English Department. Thus, when comparing something or someone to another of the same group, it is essential to insert *other* after *than* and *else* after anyone.

> Our new filters are better than *any other* filters received this month.

> Today, Chicago has more diverse ethnic groups within the city proper than any *other* city in the United States.
>
> William Banes is a better writer and speaker than anyone *else* in the English Department.

## Ambiguous Comparisons

In such comparisons, the writer fails to clarify exactly what he or she is comparing. Without clarification, many of the statements can have two meanings—an interpretation problem for the reader.

> The technician condemned his supervisor more than his assistant.
>
> While he was in town, I saw more of him than Mary.
>
> I was closer to the stage than Henry.

All three of these sentences have at least two quite different interpretations—enough difference for a communication breakdown.

> The technician condemned his supervisor more than his assistant *did.*
> or The technician condemned his supervisor more than *he did his assistant.*
>
> I saw more of him than *Mary did.*
> or I saw more of him *than I did of Mary.*
>
> I was closer to the stage *than Henry was.*
> or I was closer to the stage *than I was to Henry.*

Which one of these versions is correct? The reader would have no way of knowing. It is the writer's responsibility to phrase the ideas into clearly stated sentences that leave no doubt in the reader's mind concerning the true meaning.

## Sentence Vagueness

Sentence vagueness may be very difficult for writers to find, for they know what they want to say and in their editing may read more than is really on the paper. Also, they may not be aware of a potential semantic trap or of a problem with some pronoun reference structures. The following two sentences conceal a problem with the meaning of words.

> He said his mother rented her condominium in Florida for a thousand dollars a month.
>
> The insurance executive told our group that Marian was his oldest employee.

The words *rented* and *oldest* in these sentences have two interpretations:
His mother could *pay* one thousand dollars a month for the condominium, or his mother could *receive* one thousand dollars a month rent for the condominium. Marian

could be the oldest in *age,* or she could have been with the company longer than any other employee. These relatively simple sentences do not provide a specific meaning for the reader.

In the following two sentences, the writer has been careless in using the pronouns *he* and *his.*

> Our supervisor told the plant manager that *he* did not understand the situation well enough to make a decision.

> The personnel director informed the union official that it was not *his* place to assess the dues.

*He* in the first sentence and *his* in the second do not identify clearly which person they are referring to. Either the supervisor or the plant manager could lack the understanding to make the decision, or either the director or the union official should be the one to assess the dues.

> Our supervisor said to the plant manager, "you do not understand the situation well enough to make a decision."

or Our supervisor said to the plant manager, "I do not understand the situation well enough to make a decision."

> The personnel director informed the union official that it is not your place to assess the dues.

or The personnel director informed the union official that it is not my place to assess the dues.

Which of the two corrected versions is the intended one? Only the writer can make such statements understandable and meaningful to the reader.

## Split-Verb Phrase Problem

The split-verb phrase problem refers to the practice of placing a transition adverb between the auxiliary and its verb as the following sentences indicate.

> This series of compounds *did, consequently, have* a moderate to high activity in the Phase 2 Assay.

> The laboratory assistant in that department *did not, however, understand* the question.

> Since we cannot handle concerns such as yours, *I am, therefore, forwarding* your letter to our supervisor in Chicago.

The place for transition adverbs, such as *consequently, however, therefore,* etc., is at the beginning of the sentence, immediately following the subject, or at the end of the sentence. The above interruption of the verb phrase detracts from the flow of the sentence. The following corrected sentences provide for clearer sentences and better reading

> Consequently, this series of compounds *did have* a moderate to high activity in the Phase 2 Assay.
>
> The laboratory assistant in that department, however, *did not understand* the question.
>
> We cannot handle concerns such as yours; therefore, *I am forwarding* your letter to our supervisor in Chicago.

## Split Infinitive Controversy

An infinitive is a *to plus a verb form,* such as *to go, to see, to indicate, to believe,* etc. A split infinitive occurs when an adverb comes between the two parts: to *quickly* go, to *actually* see, to *clearly* indicate, to *definitely* believe, etc. Today, the split infinitive is not one of the major sins of writing as in an earlier era. Its use, however, can still stir up considerable controversy in usage circles. Probably, most careful writers try to avoid leaving split infinitives in their writing. However, if removing the intervening adverb would result in a convoluted or stilted sentence, the wisest thing to do would be to leave the split infinitive.

> We project that we will have *to further scale* back our programs if instate registration monies are all that is available.
>
> corrected: We project that we will have *to scale* back our programs *further* if instate registration monies are all that is available.
>
> The government unit that is going *to actually put* the process in motion and directly benefit from the final product does not always supply the main funding.
>
> corrected: The government unit that is going *to put* the process in motion and directly benefit from the final product *actually* does not always supply the main funding.
>
> *To adequately solve* the problem of late registrations will require considerable cooperation of both the administration and the faculty.
>
> corrected: *To solve* the problem of late registrations *adequately* will require the cooperation of both the administration and the faculty.

Most split structures of this type are easy to change and often provide better emphasis to an idea.

## Excessive Noun Use as Adjectives

Although English has always used nouns in adjectival positions, the present-day stringing together of several nouns as adjectives preceding a noun has become a habit-forming activity. The practice not only increases the feeling of wordiness but also complicates the interpretation and understanding of the communication.

> The most apparent weakness in past modeling efforts has been our inability to reflect the changes of the *Lake Erie walleye population size increases.*

Improved  The most apparent weakness in modeling efforts has been our inability to reflect accurately the changes of the *increased walleye population of Lake Erie*

> *Your staffing level authorization reassessment plan* should result in a major improvement for your hospital.

Improved:  The *authorization of your plan for reassessing the various staff levels* should result in a major improvement for your hospital.

> A five-member board manages our *Home Ownership Savings Department Trust Fund.*

Improved:  A five-member board manages the *trust fund of our Home Ownership Savings Department.*

## Problem Words: Only, While, Where

### *Only*

*Only* is one of the problem adverbs probably misplaced in sentences as often or more than any other word. Its correct place is immediately preceding the word or phrase it is to limit. In the following sentences, the position of *only* could be correct, depending on the meaning the writer wishes to convey.

> *Only* the technicians reported the problems to the supervisor.
> The technicians *only* reported the problems to the supervisor.
> The technicians reported *only* the problems to the supervisor.
> The technicians reported the problems *only* to the supervisor.

Thus, changing the placement of *only* in a sentence also alters the meaning of the sentence. An *only* in the wrong place could reduce the needed emphasis of a specific word or phrase. The following examples indicate some of the problems:

> The doctor instructed each patient only to take the prescribed medications.

corrected:  The doctor instructed each patient to take *only the prescribed medications.*

|               | We agreed that the excessive rowdiness occurring in state parks could only be solved by collective effort. |
| corrected:    | We agreed that the excessive rowdiness occurring in state parks could be solved *only by collective* effort. |
|               | We can only accomplish this efficiently through long range planning. |
| corrected:    | We can accomplish this efficiently *only* through long range planning. |

## While

*While* means during and refers to time. It is not a substitute for a coordinator or a type of subordinator.

|                              |                                                                                                   |
| ---------------------------- | ------------------------------------------------------------------------------------------------- |
|                              | John Barry is regional sales manager *while* Joe Thomas is in charge of research.                 |
| corrected (coordinator):     | John Barry is regional sales manager, *and* Joe Thomas is in charge of research.                  |
|                              | *While* barely making ends meet, the manager continued to staff his small corner store.           |
| corrected (subordinator):    | Even *though* barely making ends meet, the manager continued to staff his small corner store.     |
|                              | *While* it may be questionable that the liquid wastes disposed of are toxic, there is no question about the violation accompanying the action. |
| corrected (subordinator):    | Although it may be questionable that the liquid wastes disposed of are toxic, there is no question about the violation accompanying the action. |

In the first example, *while* is really replacing one of the coordinators, either *and* or *but*. In the next two sentences, while is replacing a subordinator, such as *although, even though,* etc.

In the following sentence, the use of *while* is correct; here *while* really means *during the time* something was happening something else happened.

> *While* Barry was checking on his research references, I scanned the book shelves for some reading for myself.

## Where

*Where* refers to a place and is not a substitute for *that* to introduce a clause. When used in this type of context, the resulting structure is unbalanced and the meaning unclear.

|            | I read in the *Journal where* modules will become a part of your process. |
|---|---|
| corrected: | I read in the *Journal that* modules will become a part of your process. |

|            | She read in his *letter where* he planned to move his plant to Chicago. |
|---|---|
| corrected: | She read in his *letter that* he planned to move his plant to Chicago. |

In the following sentence, the use of *where* is correct; it refers to a specific place—he planned to locate his plant where (Chicago?).

She stated that she knew *where* he planned to locate his plant.

## Negative-Positive Problems

### Double Negative Positives

Casting positive statements with *not plus negative prefixes* can create sentences that are difficult to interpret. In fact, a cursory reading of them could lead to misinterpretation and misunderstandings.

|            | Documentation that is *not in*accessible is essential to the paper. |
|---|---|
| corrected: | Documentation that is *accessible* is essential to the paper. |
| or         | Accessible documentation is essential to the paper. |

|            | He does *not dis*trust the coordinator of the project. |
|---|---|
| corrected: | He *trusts* the coordinator of the project. |

|            | He does *not mis*trust the motives of the committee. |
|---|---|
| corrected: | He trusts the motives of the committee. |

|            | He did *not mis*interpret the second clause of the document. |
|---|---|
| corrected: | He interpreted the second clause of the document correctly. |

### Denotation-Connotation

The *denotation* of a word is its dictionary meaning. The *connotation* of a word refers to its social interpretation and the emotional or attitudinal meaning that may accompany it. Words having negative connotations can also interfere with communication. The underlined words in the following sentence negatively characterize the person involved.

> During the *interrogation*, he *admitted* that he had been *wrong* some of the time in his stock choices but for the most part had made quite a few *lucky gambles*.

The following version provides quite a different tone to the writing and quite a different image of the person involved.

When *asked*, he *said* that he had made some *mistakes* in his stock choices but for the most part his *investments* had been quite *successful*.

How a writer says it—the selection of words or structures—influences the reader's interpretation of the message. Thus, the writer's responsibility to communicate objectively is tremendous.

## Questions

Part I     Correct the unnecessary shifts in structure in the following sentences. Explain your corrections.

1. After I had spent four hard years on campus, college was completed and the exciting field of journalism entered.

2. Mr. Greer finished the experiment after his notes had been located.

3. Favorable comment on the company's buying practices has already been made in this report.

4. It was intended that the program be administered by the sales manager.

5. In order for the effectiveness of the new procedure to be properly evaluated, the help of our customers will be needed.

6. Relocation reimbursement must be approved by company officials.

7. It was felt by the committee that James Lewis should represent the department at the conference in Chicago.

8. Not only can a person see all these things on television, but the quality is better than you could find in any other one place in the world.

9. We may seem captives of the whims of politicians, but you do have the right to vote and could throw them out of office at the next election.

10. Any further occurrences of this nature could land you in the county "free holding" area; the next disciplinary action could include suspension and even termination of your services and loss of your pension advantages.

Part II  Correct the lack of parallelism in the following sentences. Explain your corrections.

1. He admitted that his favorite hobbies were making pottery, shooting baskets, and to sail his small sloop on Lake Michigan.

2. The system is large and convenient, and it does not cost very much.

3. Plea bargaining undermines the adversary system, diverts the rule of law, risk is involved, ignorance and also secrecy.

4. Many factors inside houses and factories affect the humidity in the winter as well as the summer months.

5. The patients received two injections on the first day, six on the third day, and on the fourth day they were discharged.

6. His first thought was to resign; his second thought was that he ought to resist.

7. Four characteristics of a good salesman are neat appearance; capable of meeting the public; well informed on such subjects as sports, and a firm believer in the products he is selling.

8. In his book, the author fails to make clear that social adjustment means cooperating, obedience, and making decisions.

9. There are many professions that provide higher salaries, work fewer hours, and have less tension than teaching.

Part III   Correct the sentence structure problems in the following sentences. Identify the specific problem by name.

1. While a narrative is optional since you have my prior application on file, I would again like to state my interest in attending the Academy in 1990.

2. They raced to catch a plane at the airport, which, unfortunately, had just left.

3. Having studied for hours, the test was easy to pass.

4. He explained in January that he was going to retire.

5. Our antibiotic clinic trial formulation efforts have focused on supporting local studies.

6. I need to better understand human characteristics and inter-personal relationships.

7. He spent the evening talking about the reports he had read with the librarian.

8. A broadband antenna is where certain characteristics of radiation pattern or impedance are retained.

9. Deliver the equipment to the Antibiotic Unit as soon as properly inspected.

10. After the Board decided that the work must be completed by Thursday, in spite of other commitments, it adjourned immediately.

11. Those control procedures would take 2.0 man years to bring the system in line, while the computerized system would only require 0.6 man years.

12. Please remove the data from the computer and throw it away.

13. Injected daily with this drug, the researcher was able to train the animals in two days instead of two months.

14. Our solution has, however, provided a certain amount of control and prevented other factions from becoming too powerful.

15. The breaking point in such groups is much harder to predict than the freshmen in college.

Part IV    The writer of the following paragraph has carelessly shifted back and forth between active and passive voice. Revise the paragraph putting all the verb phrases into the active voice.

Many departments *are involved* when a new item *is* introduced to a company's product line before it meets final acceptance. First, the Research Department draws an idea on paper that follows a designer's rough sketch or verbal description. A mold or die *must be designed and built* to form the item after the Board of Directors approves the idea. The production Department, under Engineering's approval, makes a test run after the mold or die *is completed.* The tool room handles any changes of tooling. Quality Control receives, measures, and tests the sample parts from Engineering. Quality Control, Research, and Engineering approve the sample parts. If approval *is not given,* then the original design or tooling *must be altered,* and the procedure *must be started* again. Testing must continue until satisfactory parts *are manufactured.*

# 7 Correction of Misconceptions

Inexperienced writers in their first professional position may find themselves tempted to emulate the traditional kinds of writing found in office filing cabinets, retrieval systems, or even media prose. However, writers must be careful to avoid copying inherently cumbersome and ineffective forms and styles. Too many reports and memorandums filed away from past years may not have been written effectively in the first place. Too often the writing comprises ready-made phrases and clichés strung together for the sake of convenience or done out of habit. Likewise, newspapers, textbooks, and other publications often contain errors, and readers need to understand that seeing the writing in a publication does not make it mechanically correct or stylistically sound.

Some basic misconceptions concern the writing process itself: that writers can achieve good results through some magic formula. Equally untrue is that some people can write well naturally while others can never learn. Writing is hard work even for the most talented writers, and writing well is a demanding and sophisticated task. Still, any writing assignment is controllable by using common sense and by editing logically and systematically. Seldom is writing an act of pure imagination. Mostly it requires the application of learnable skills, tried-and-true editing techniques, and a commitment by the writer to work effectively and efficiently. Good writers know there are no shortcuts to success. Instead, they trust in reliable techniques that consistently lead to proven results.

## Use Language Assertively

Figure 1 overviews some of the basic principles of practical editing and when applied help a writer develop a clean and straightforward prose style. For instance, such a sentence as "The *suggestion* of the *committee* was to *make a change* in policy" is more effective as "*The committee suggested* a change in policy." In this sentence, the verb, "suggest," lies hidden in a noun form, "suggestion," and by emphasizing a verb as opposed to a static noun the sentence becomes more forceful. "Nominalizations" are noun forms (such as recommendation, reaction, suggestion, discovery) containing a verb. Putting the action back into the verb or taking it out of the noun

# Figure 7.1

*Use Language Assertively*

    *Weak:*     Some confusion *is suggested* by the data with respect to consumer preferences.

    *Improved:*     The *data suggest* some confusion concerning consumer preferences.

    *Weak:*     *In the opinion of this writer, it seems* that the ITS data system can be feasibly used at the present time.

    *Improved:*     *I think* the ITS data system *is now ready* for use.

    *Weak:*     Bill's study revealed a *preference* of managers for dealing with a single company.

    *Improved:*     Bill's study showed that managers *prefer* to deal with a single company.

    *Weak:*     The researcher *made the discovery* of a new element.

    *Improved:*     The researcher *discovered* a new element.

*Be Concrete*

    *Weak:*     The *number of contracts* this year will be lower than previously anticipated.

    *Improved:*     Our company anticipated that the number of contracts would be *15 percent higher* than what now appears possible.

    *Weak:*     The experiment proved *various things*.

    *Improved:*     The experiment proved *that the containers are waterproof, durable, and portable.*

*Avoid Wordiness*

    *Weak:*     *There is a new feeling* among the engineering staff that the project will now succeed.

    *Improved:*     The engineering *staff feels* that the project will now succeed.

    *Weak:*     *The fact that* Mr. Denison is assuming the position of director of research pleased the department members.

    *Improved:*     Mr. Denison's becoming the director of research pleased the department members.

*Avoid 'Smoke' Talk*

    *Weak:*     Dr. Smith *affected a desire to withdraw* from *previous commitments* to the project.

    *Improved:*     Dr. Smith *no longer wished to participate* in the project.

*Weak:* The manager *disavowed his desire to terminate* personnel to be replaced with *certain mechanical contrivances.*

*Improved:* The manager *denied* that he had planned to replace employees *with robots.*

## Be Aware of False Elegance

*Weak:* As per your request to find an inexpensive solution to the paper waste problems, *I would like to offer the following solution* to the problem:

*Improved:* *I suggest* we solve the paper waste problem by . . .

*Weak:* *In regards to* your inspection of the *vehicular transportation* problem, I suggest that we *investigate and examine viable alternative means.*

*Improved:* I suggest that *we find alternate forms of transportation.*

## Recognize Tautology

*Weak:* The medical student examined the *dead cadaver.*

*Improved:* The medical student *examined the cadaver.*

*Weak:* The *burning fire* caused much damage to Building 22.

*Improved:* The *fire* caused much damage to Building 22.

## Avoid Meaningless Modifiers

*Weak:* The researchers investigated the pollution *problem.*

*Improved:* The researchers investigated the *pollution.*

*Weak:* A *famous* celebrity visited the college.

*Improved:* A celebrity visited the college.

## Watch Out for Euphemisms

*Weak:* The *sanitation engineer* picked up after the rally.

*Improved:* The *janitor* picked up after the rally.

*Weak:* The *maladjusted youth* received a light sentences.

*Improved:* The *juvenile delinquent* received a light sentence.

## Take Out Malapropisms

*Weak:* The patient *conspired* after a lengthy illness.

*Improved:* The patient *expired* after a lengthy illness.

*Weak:* The journalist sought a new *anglo* for the story.

*Improved:* The journalist sought a new *angle* for the story.

### Watch Out for Word Confusion

*Weak:*     The board *delegated* more funding for the project.
*Improved:*     The board *designated* more funding for the project.
*Weak:*     The *temperature* in the boiler was too *hot*.
*Improved:*     The *temperature* in the boiler was too *high*.

### Remove Trite Phrases and Mixed Metaphors

*Weak:*     *Each and every one* of the employees received a bonus.
*Improved:*     *Each* employee received a bonus.
*Weak:*     I can *see* what you are *saying*.
*Improved:*     I can *understand* what you are saying.

### Be Aware of Jargon

*Weak:*     Ms. Guggemos received the penicillin injection *subcutaneously*.
*Improved:*     Ms. Guggemos received a penicillin shot.
*Weak:*     The committees met *to interface with each other* about the new bill.
*Improved:*     The committees met *to discuss* the new bill.

### Watch Out for "Snow" Jobs

*Weak:*     In order to solve a problem, a person needs to understand what a problem is. A problem is a dilemma that needs to be resolved.
*Weak:*     The project needs more adequate funding. What is more adequate funding? It is funding that is substantial enough to meet the goals and aims of the project.

### Eliminate Sexist References

*Weak:*     A lawyer needs to understand *his* client's needs.
*Improved:*     Lawyers need to understand *their* clients' needs.
*Weak:*     The *mailmen* met to discuss their new routes.
*Improved:*     The *mail carriers* met to discuss their new routes.

achieves conciseness and better emphasis (recommend, react, suggest, discover). In general writers should use nominalizations sparingly and *only* for occasional emphasis. Too often, inexperienced writers overuse ineffectual verbs, such as *make, get, have, take, give, hold, do, went,* instead of using the more exact verb and end up relying on nominalizations. The following sentences exemplify such abuse:

*Make a measurement* of the room.
*Measure* the room.

We must *get some work done* on that project.
We must *work* on that project.

I *have to complete* the assignment by Friday.
I *must complete* the assignment by Friday.

*Take a look* at these findings.
*Look* at these findings.

They *gave encouragement* to the committee.
They *encouraged* the committee.

The group *held a rally* last weekend.
The group *rallied* last weekend.

We *need to do some research* on that situation.
We *need to research* that situation.

He further *went on to make a suggestion* that we hire more personnel.
He further *suggested* that we hire more personnel.

Thus, verb action keeps the writing accurate and forceful. This kind of editing logic is relatively simple and a matter of awareness and proofreading. Too often though, writers overlook such obvious problems, whose correction can tighten and clarify their meaning.

## Be Concrete

Another of the basic misconceptions about writing is that a long sentence generously sprinkled with polysyllabic words, stretches of specialized technical jargon, or verbiage reveals an enviable scientific or scholarly style and detachment. On the contrary, a good rule to follow is that the more concise and concrete the writing the better it will be. To do otherwise is to confuse the reader.

Sometimes inexperienced writers use words that contain little objective meaning, as in the use of words like "feel" or "thing," for example:

I *feel* that the committee should *do something* to improve working conditions.

This sentence contains little practical information. What is it that the writer wishes the committee to do? Perhaps such vague writing results from vague thinking. Still, even if the writer has no concrete recommendation for the committee, he or she will create a stronger impression by eliminating as much of the vagueness as possible and by making a declarative and meaningful statement:

> I *think* that the committee *should investigate* ways to improve working conditions.

Or better yet,

> The committee should investigate ways to improve working conditions.

This edited sentence calls for specific action, which is what the writer of the original sentence probably had in mind. Certainly, the revised sentence will create a stronger response in the reader.

## Avoid Wordiness

Words that have little practical meaning and which lead to overstatement, redundancy, and digression can obscure a message. The use of "it" in the following sentences is a good example:

> *It was found* in these studies that the equipment was inadequate.
>
> *It will be seen upon examination* of Table 5 that the tests are comparable.
>
> *It is obvious that* the committee will accept the proposal.
>
> *It is the intent of* this report to describe a newly-developed procedure for evaporation.

Deleting "it is" and other extraneous words corrects the unnecessary delay in reaching the point of the sentence and creates more forceful statements:

> *These studies show* that the equipment was inadequate.
>
> *Table 5 shows* that the test are comparable.
>
> *Obviously,* the committee will accept the proposal.
>
> *This report describes* a newly-developed procedure for evaporation.

"There is/are," "the fact that," and other empty phrases likewise contribute to vagueness in writing and muzzle the ideas the writer wishes to convey:

> *There are* many reasons why the project failed to meet its objectives.
> *The project failed* to meet its objectives for many reasons.
>
> *There is a feeling among* the secretarial staff that the rules are too stringent.
> *The secretarial staff feels* that the rules are too stringent.
>
> *There are many reasons why* projects fail to meet their objectives.
> *Projects fail* to meet their objectives for many reasons.

> *The fact that* the researchers received the award impressed their supervisor.
> *The researchers'* receiving the award impressed their supervisor.
>
> *The field of* medicine offers many rewards.
> *Medicine* offers many rewards.

Eliminating waste words in writing is often a matter of editing sensitivity and of objective proofreading—that is, training oneself to be aware of words often used habitually that do not relate directly to the meaning of the sentence.

The following example is typical of a writer who is not an active editor. Often such a writer will string together words without giving practical thought to the actual meaning. Writers uncertain of their message or insecure in their ability to convey the message often fall into this trap:

> At the time *of the first and initial* stage of the interviewing *process,* a *trained* psychoanalyst *possesses a plethora* of important responsibilities *to do;* focus*ing* the interviewing *procedure,* the creat*ion* of a productive *inter-personal* climate, and *to separate* the levels of patient response to *interviewing* questions.

This sample contains many basic flaws—in parallelism, redundancy, artificiality, deadwood, and lack of balance. Good editing would emphasize action, simplify the sentence structure, and remove meaningless, vague, or ambiguous words:

> During the *first interview,* a psychoanalyst should *focus* the conversation upon relevant topics, *create* an appropriate climate for discussion, and *separate* the relevant issues from relevant ones.

Good writers control their sentences and do not let their sentences control them. Conversely, bad writers merely go along with the flow of ideas without thinking through an appropriate strategy or anticipating the effect upon their reader. Effective revising requires the writer to keep in mind the relationship between form and content and to shape sentences and select words strategically for impact.

One of the basic strategies of all good writing is to achieve clarity without becoming unduly simplistic. Clarity, the goal of all communication, means writing at a level of understanding compatible with the sophistication of the audience. Good writers ask themselves two basic questions: Is the audience technically oriented and capable of understanding specialized terminology and concepts? Is the audience of a more general orientation, in need of specific definitions and further explanation of concepts?

Professional writers should also avoid falling into the style of pedantic writers whose writing sounds somehow knowledgeable but is difficult to decipher. These writers often give their materials artificial weightiness by using the largest and most obscure words and esoteric references. Examples of this kind of prose are readily—and unfortunately—apparent in publications for business, science, politics, and academe. Many college textbooks also exhibit such flaws. Although such writing could sound impressive, it usually is not very effective, as the following example from an economics text suggests:

> Extraneous habits and proclivities encroach upon the field of action occupied by this canon, and it presently comes about that the ecclesiastical and sacerdotal structures are partially converted to other uses, in some measure alien to the purpose of the scheme of devout life as it stood in the days of the most vigorous and characteristic development of the priesthood. (Veblen)

Translated into clear English, this passage means that "moneychangers can also be found in the temple." However, to understand this message the reader must become a detective looking for clues. This passage suggests that such writers are more interested in elaborating than in delivering an objective message. Inflated diction can alienate a reader; its egocentricity and pomposity leave a negative image of the authors in the reader's mind.

Gobbledegook, another form of wordiness, relies on cliché-ridden vocabulary and overly specialized hackneyed items. A high-school principal in Houston, Texas, fell into the gobbledegook pit a few years ago when he wrote the following letter announcing a special meeting on a proposed education program:

> Our school's *cross-graded, multi-ethnic, individualized learning program* is designed to enhance *the concept* of an *open-ended learning program* with emphasis on a *continuum of multi-ethnic, academically enriched learning* using the *identified intellectually gifted* child as the agent or director of his own learning.
> 
> Major emphasis is on *cross-graded, multi-ethnic learning* with the main objective being to learn respect for the uniqueness of a person.

After receiving this mishmash of words, a parent wrote the principal the following response:

> I have a college degree, speak two foreign languages and four Indian dialects, have been to a number of county fairs and three goat ropings, but I haven't the faintest idea as to what you are talking about. Do you? (Associated Press)

The principal transmitted more noise than message—and did not, no doubt, leave the impression with the reader which he had hoped to create. Usually such writing reveals much more about the insecurities and inabilities of the writer than anything else. It tends to distance an audience rather than gain its support. By choosing a simple, straightforward prose style, the principal could have avoided a needless conflict.

The following paragraph further exemplifies this type of problem:

> It is the *responsibility and duty* of *each and every* department *head or manager to correctly submit* the *budget and/or the appropriations request* necessary for *his or her* depart-

ment. *He or she* must *make this request* in such a *way or means* that all *elements, areas, and concerns* of *his or her* services will receive enough financial *substantiation* for the *six-month* or *half-year* production *requirements, wants, and needs*.

Concisely stated this message states, "Chairs should submit their comprehensive six-month budget immediately." The rest of the words merely fog the communication and force the audience to read unnecessary words. Having to wade through such wordiness not only tries the readers' patience but causes readers to question the writers' other abilities as well. The writer of the above passage could have achieved better results by being simple, by stating the issue directly, and by deleting redundancy. As Mark Twain once observed, "When in doubt, leave it out." A good rule to follow is that the best English is that which gives the sense in the fewest short words.

## Avoid "Smoke" Talk

"Smoke" talk is a kind of wordiness that some writers think adds scholarly sophistication to their writing; instead, it merely beats around the proverbial bush. Such words have little meaning and delay the message. This substitution of bureaucratic language for concise, concrete words only serves to irritate the audience. If a word does not add any real value to a sentence, then the writer should eliminate it as the following sentences indicate:

*According to Webster's,* a circle has no beginning and no end.
–A circle has no beginning and no end.

We *hope and trust* that we can *collaborate together* to eliminate any and all repetitious effort among departments that work in close proximity together.
–We hope to eliminate the duplication of departmental services.

This kind of language often occurs in specific professions, and writers should avoid such federalese, commercialese, medicalese, legalese or officialese as the following:

The politician urged his followers *to organize spontaneous cheering.*

The writer described the *energetic disassembly* and *rapid oxidation* that followed.

The psychologist encouraged his clients to overcome alienation by *increasing sensory awareness—interpersonal relations with cognitive feedback.*

The physician felt that he had gotten caught up in *therapeutic misadventures.*

The bureaucrat complained that he had *misspoke himself* and had engaged in an *inoperative statement.*

## Be Aware of False Elegance

False elegance is the pretentious use of words. English provides many words with similar meanings; as a general rule, words with Latin origins often have a formal connotation, whereas their Germanic or Celtic counterparts have an informal one:

| Formal | Informal |
|---|---|
| canine | dog |
| conflagration | fire |
| remuneration | pay |

Writers should adjust the level of word usage to the needs of their audience and strive for consistency.

*In the event that* a fire occurs, do not use the elevators.
*If* a fire occurs, do not use the elevators.

*In the not too distant future,* people may colonize the moon.
*People may soon* colonize the moon.

*It is incumbent on me* to make the decision.
*I must* decide.

We *need to proceed in our investigation of* the situation.
We *should study* the situation.

This experiment *will involve the necessity of* using clinical studies.
This experiment *will require* clinical studies.

The *aquatic biota had expired.*
The *fish had died.*

## Recognize Tautology

Tautology is the unnecessary repetition of an idea. It occurs when a writer fails to consider the literal meaning that the words already convey. It often results from unclear thinking.

The surface was ten by fifty inches *in size.*
The surface was ten by fifty inches.

They were European *in origin.*
They were European.

Sales increased *in the range* of eighty to ninety percent.
Sales increased eighty to ninety percent.

The apartment was adequate *enough* for our needs.
The apartment was adequate for our needs.

The automobile was red *in color.*
The automobile was red.

We will cooperate *together.*
We will cooperate.

The managers decided to base their *future* plans on their *past* experience.
The managers decided to base their plans on their experience.

## Avoid Meaningless Modifiers

Similar to tautology, meaningless modifiers are adjectives that add no objective meaning to the words they precede. They are either meaningless words or subjective calls too open to interpretation to be purposeful:

Inflation appears in *periodic* intervals.
Inflation appears in intervals.

The road was *in a wet condition.*
The road was wet.

The report was *of a confidential nature.*
The report was confidential.

We were in *close range* of our goal.
We were close to our goal.

The woman was *very* pregnant.
The woman was pregnant.

We received *sufficient* time for the test.
We received two hours for the test.

The parts manager said that he would give us a *fair price.*
The parts manager said that he would sell us the engine block for $500.

We felt that we had made an *excessive payment* for the supplies.
We felt that we had paid $200 too much for the supplies.

## Watch out for Euphemisms

Euphemisms are synonyms that change the impact of words by softening or changing their meaning. Euphemisms are often silly or pointless. They are rationalizations that make the reader think that the writer is trying to hide something.

He was an *undocumented worker.*
He was an *illegal alien.*

The student was an *underachiever.*
The student was *failing.*

The psychologist suggested that Smith had undergone *stimulus impoverishment.*
The psychologist suggested that Smith was lonely.

We need to make certain that each child receives an appropriate *learning experience.*
We need to make certain that each child receives an *education.*

The physician prescribed a *chemotherapeutic agent.*
The physician prescribed a drug.

He underwent *aversion therapy.*
He underwent shock treatment.

## Take Out Malapropisms

The word malaprop means out of place. The term comes from a character, Mrs. Malaprop, who became famous for misusing words in an 18th-century play by Richard Sheridan. Malapropisms occur when the writer just misses using the right words. Their use makes the writer appear ridiculous. Writers must take care to use the right word:

He was chastised for his *sedimentary* habits.
He was chastised for his *sedentary* habits.

For all *intensive* purposes, he was still alive.
For all *intents* and purposes, he was still alive.

The student had a *shrewd* awakening.
The student had a *rude* awakening.

She was as headstrong as an *allegory* in the River Nile.
She was as headstrong as an *alligator* in the River Nile.

They decided to create a new *contest* for the study.
They decided to create a new *context* for the study.

## Watch Out for Word Confusion

Good writers do not mistake the exact meaning of words—especially words particular to the writer's profession. Taking the time to look them up is one mark of a professional. Good writers do not trust their memories or the sound of words alone. Misusing a word common to one's own profession is a cardinal sin.

This idea is *universally* accepted.
This idea is *generally* accepted.

That condition is *hereditary.*
That condition is *congenital.*

The measurements were *precise.*
The measurements were *accurate.*

The investigation team worked *systemically.*
The investigation team worked *systematically.*

Smith *assumed* that the committee would meet on Friday.
Smith *presumed* that the committee would meet on Friday.

The supervisor's method was *judicious.*
The supervisor's method was *judicial.*

In the above examples, the words share similar meanings, but they are not interchangeable. Therefore, the writer needs to be certain of the exact definition of such terms before using them. Otherwise, the reader will misconstrue the meaning, or worse, question the ability of the writer.

## Remove Trite Phrases and Mixed Metaphors

Trite phrases and mixed metaphors indicate a lack of creativity or a no-care attitude on the part of the writer. Good writers do not rely on ready-made language because it lacks effect. Overused words seldom have an impact on a reader; instead, such words dissolve into pointless generalizations:

We need to send up *a trial balloon.*

In this *day and age* everyone needs an education.

The team decided to *take the bull by the horns.*

*At this point in time,* Smith can offer no solution to the problem.

*It goes without saying* that the project will continue.

*Slowly but surely,* investigators will resolve the issue.

The accountant suggested that the company strengthen its *bottom line.*

All of the *major players* in the contract dispute drew up a new *game plan.*

Sometimes using an analogy or metaphor is good if it could clarify the concept for the reader. However, an inappropriate, difficult to understand, or illogical image is out of place. Such was the case with the writer who suggested his colleagues take an idea and "run it up the flag pole to see if it can hold water." The following from a report co-authored by representatives of the computer industry illustrates a similar problem:

> *Rationale:* Given the rapid *expansion* of the use of computer technology on campus and the need for quality educational software tools, we are *witnessing* new *models of collaboration* between industry and the academy. . . . Some universities are *viewing* software commercialization as a new *revenue stream.* . . . *Software houses* are trying to determine how best to capitalize on this *evolving new frontier* and government agencies and associations are *studying the problem with an eye* on developing *support mechanism* for their *constituencies.* . . . It was clear that the *parties* representing the various . . . *sectors* needed to be brought together . . . . Each participant would provide *insight* into his/her sector and ultimately some *cross-fertilization* might occur.

This report is a hodge-podge of conflicting visual images and mixed metaphors. The writer is too removed from the needs of the audience; the result is a series of long, illogically developed images and ineffectual sentences. The same information becomes much more accessible by simplifying sentences and by strategically using *simple, plain, and concrete* words as the following rewrite shows:

> In response to the increased use of computers on university campuses, industry and academe should collaborate to determine needs and capabilities. Faculty are finding a growing market for new software which universities would like to market . . .

## Eliminate Jargon

Jargon is specialized or technical language related to a trade, profession, or fellowship. For people outside of the group, it seems to be a kind of "secret" language that only members of the in-group may understand. A major corporation in the Midwest sent out the following press release inviting business managers to a conference on management techniques:

> What would you do if several directors of personnel from various divisions told you their *first-line supervisors* needed some training? This is just one of the many items that will be covered as we review the *background needs* for an *interpersonal skills training* for first-line supervisors. Also, we will cover the various *interpersonal skills modules* [sic] that were used. . . . We will present the *evaluation methodology* involving several manufacturing locations over a nearly two-year period. We will share with you the supervisor's *behaviorally anchored rating scale questionnaires* that were both used to gather the data before and after the training.

This writing is so infested with jargon and abstract terms that it is very difficult to understand. This passage forces the audience not only to speculate about the meaning of the message but also about the intent or the competency of the writer trying to express it.

The following letter also suffers from an acute case of business jargon and clichés:

*My dear* Mr. Brown:

*Re* your communications of the *5th inst., contents duly noted.* In acknowledgement of same *we beg to reply* that the matter of filing system changes is now under our *strictest consideration and perusal.*

*As per your request,* we will *make every effort* to handle the matter to your best interests and all concerned.

Please *be advised and note therewith* that the latest report in our files *pertains to April last,* and we enclose a *copy herewith.*

*Thanking you kindly in advance* for your consideration, *we desire to remain*

*Very truly* yours,

The following edited version, revised in straightforward prose, improves the communication considerably:

Dear Mr. Brown:

In response to your letter of May 5, 1990, I will make every effort to handle the filing system changes quickly and efficiently.

I have also enclosed a copy of our latest report (April 20, 1990) concerning the need for this change.

Sincerely,

The second version of the letter is simple but not simplistic. It provides relevant details and relies on logical sentences to convey the information. Conversely, the original letter has too many prepackaged stock phrases and archaisms, such as "as per your request" and "be advised and note therewith." Such prefabricated English is imprecise and out of step with the communications realities of the time. A cliché-ridden approach reveals much about the writer's ego or insecurity but fails to convey specific ideas very well.

## Watch Out for "Snow" Jobs

The above examples, like most poorly written prose, indicate the writer's lack of knowledge or sensitivity concerning a subject or audience. The reader could interpret such writing as an attempt to overcome ignorance with a steady flow of words rather than succinct ideas. Other times the fault may lie with a writer's insensitivity to the reader's needs. The result could be a "snow job," such as the following paragraph written by a student trying to fake an assignment:

According to the definition of an event, both of these happenings would be classified as an event. One definition of an event is that it is a noteworthy happening. What makes something noteworthy? What is noteworthy? Noteworthy is a very broad and vague term. Noteworthy really doesn't have well-defined limits. It would depend on the situation and the people involved in the situation to decide if the situation is noteworthy.

The writer of this paragraph set out to define an event and somehow became lost in digression and repetition. The reader suspects the writer has nothing of value to say and, therefore, is using words as camouflage. The passage illustrates the student's disregard for the value of his own work. None of the definition has anything to do with the presentation of a valid message. The writer is merely filling up space to fulfill an assignment and would have been better off not wasting his or his reader's time.

The snow job is common in introductions when a writer is uncertain how to handle the material. Some writers habitually introduce their subject with a cliché or a quotation from a dictionary or some other reference source. More often than not, such allusions are only a waste of the reader's time.

## Eliminate Sexist References

Another basic error common in professional writing concerns sexism; that is, the unprofessional use of chauvinistic terms, which are often derogatory. The most common is the reliance upon "he," "him," and "himself" as universal pronouns when the person referred to is unknown, as in the following.

*Sexist:* Each chair*man* should direct *his* department to reduce spending by 5 percent.

This, of course, implies that all of the department chairs are men; besides being inaccurate, such generalizations alienate informed readers. To remove the sexism, the writer should use "he or she" consistently, or whenever possible use a plural reference. It would also be appropriate to shorten chairperson to chair, as in the following examples:

*Non-sexist:* Each chair*person* should direct *his or her* department to reduce spending by 5 percent.
*Non-sexist:* Chairs should direct their departments to reduce spending by 5 percent.
*Sexist:* The physician should first check for signs of shock in his patient.
*Non-sexist:* The physician should first check for signs of shock in his or her patient.
*Non-sexist:* The physician should first check for signs of shock in the patients.
*Non-sexist:* Physicians should check first for signs of shock in the patients.

Sexism causes many needless problems in professional writing. Letters addressed "Dear Sir" or "Gentlemen" sent indiscriminately often offend both women and men. The maxim "You think as you speak and you speak as you think" further indicates why such salutations are offensive. Automatically referring to a male reader shows prejudice and ignorance on the part of the writer and demeans the audience. Likewise, snide remarks, such as "snowperson" for snowman, belittle the writer and the reader and are not funny. Such insensitivity creates a poor image of the writer and indicates a lack of professionalism.

Many companies have eliminated using first names and titles altogether, choosing instead to rely on initials which give no clue to the employee's sex or marital status. Thus, letters for H. R. Brown cannot go to Mr. Harold R. Brown, for example. In the same spirit, many companies have found it convenient to substitute a "regarding" line for the salutation in letters:

May 7, 1990

H. R. Brown
Acme Equipment Company
1455 Industrial Parkway
Minneapolis, MN 45663

*RE:* Shipment of Replacement Parts, AX123-AZ488

The same holds true for in-house communications:

May 7, 1990

**TO:** H. R. Brown

**FROM:** H. Gross

**RE:** Shipment of Replacement Parts, AX123-AZ488

Similarly, the same form is appropriate when the writer has only the name of the company available. The "regarding" line replaces the salutation, and the body of the letter follows immediately. To write "Dear Sir or Gentlemen" or "Miss, Mrs., Ms" when the writer has only the company name is not appropriate. If a writer feels that the salutation is important, such information is available through corporate registers in most libraries or by a phone call to the company. If there is no salutation (Dear Mr. Brown), there is also no complimentary close (such as Sincerely):

May 7, 1990

Acme Equipment Company
1455 Industrial Parkway
Minneapolis, MN 45663

*RE:* Shipment of Replacement Parts, AX123-AZ488

Most writing problems result from ignorance—either misconceptions about writing or about the needs of the particular audience receiving the communication. Developing an awareness of the problems discussed in this chapter will promote clear, concise, and effective prose. The most effective writing occurs when a message is straightforward and neither patronizing, condescending, nor obscure. Writers should avoid being ostentatious or artificial. Most readers respond best to writing that gets to the point quickly, states ideas logically and concretely, and displays a good prose style.

# Questions

1. Discuss how language creates a persona in politics and business.

2. Analyze the strengths and weaknesses of prose taken from various professional journals or publications.

3. Overview the kinds of writing misconceptions you see around you: in business, the media, academe. What other form would be more appropriate?

4. Explain what it wrong with each phrase or word:

   a. it is extremely obvious that due to the fact that
      it is noted that
      it is reported that
      it is apparent that

   b. a certain degree of
      a high level of
      in a satisfactory manner
      along the lines of
      may or may not be
      with the possible exception of
      defined as
      due in large amount to
      for the purpose of
      of a dangerous character
      proceed to investigate

   c. subsequent to
      take appropriate measures
      terminate
      the question as to whether or not
      to be cognizant of
      to summarize the above
      within the realm of possibility
      with this in mind

modification
due to the fact that
for the reason that
implement
at this point in time
plan for the future
completely full
The reason is because

d. very unique
resultant effect
totally dead
single unit
final completion
true facts
first (or initial) beginnings
ultimate end
a funding level of $100,000
in magnitude
main essentials
in an upward direction
necessary requisite
melt down
in a postoperative type of situation
minimize as far as possible
modern methods of today
past history
fewer in number
close proximity
hydroxylation reaction
component parts
actual experience
absolutely necessary
two equal halves
completely eliminated
relative unimportance
aluminum metal
each and every

e. considerable attention
   negligible amount

f. community release
   inoperative statement
   credibility gap
   the disadvantaged
   the deprived
   maintenance engineer
   categorical inaccuracy

g. ligature/suture
   prevalence/incidence
   sensitivity/specificity
   causal/casual
   sample/specimen
   maximum/optimum
   usable/useful
   filtrate/filter
   replace/reinstall
   proportion/part
   waste/wastage

# 8 Grammatical Specifics

Grammatical specifics stresses the relationship of grammatical understandings to clear, concise, and effective communication. Essential knowledge for any writer or speaker is how the various elements of the sentence—parts of speech—collaborate to provide meaningful concepts. Meaning results from the patterned sequences of properly selected word forms and structures. Writing, as is speaking, is really a carefully engineered product.

Good writers or editors sense a weak or an incorrectly written structure. However, they must also have the know-how of what to do about it. Diagnosis and remedy require a good grasp of basic grammatical concepts. Thus, having a knowledge of certain features of the main elements of the sentence is necessary and appropriate.

## The Noun

Identifying the noun in the sentence or phrase (of all the parts of speech) is the least mystifying. Most people recall the early definition that "a noun is a name of a person, place, or thing." But, more specifically, there are three types of nouns and two types of transform structures that serve as nouns.

*Common* nouns name a general class of things, such as paper, pens, girl, democracy, crackers, books, table, etc.

*Proper* nouns name a particular person, place, or thing, such as Mary, Chicago, United States, Ireland, Rossetti Stone, etc. The first letter of these nouns requires capitalization.

*Collective* nouns name a group but a group interpreted as a single unit, such as family, jury, committee, class, etc.

### Transform Structures

Noun Phrases:
　　Gerund phrase—*Writing the letter* was a difficult and sad task.
　　Infinitive phrase—*To become* the best in his class was his chief goal in life.

Object of Preposition—The rejection of *middle class values* may result in some type of deviant behavior.

Noun Clause: *What he does tomorrow* will determine our future action.
He did not know *what the letter said.*

In English, the noun has only three inflectional forms—plural, singular possessive, and plural possessive. This is true regardless of whether the noun is serving as the subject, object, or object of a preposition. Most singular nouns form their possessive with *'s*. For a writer always to think singular possessive *'s* (not possessive singular) or plural possessive *s'* (not possessive plural) makes it easier to select the right form.

| Singular | Plural |
| --- | --- |
| The girl is here. | The girls are here. |
| I see the girl. | I see the girls. |
| The girl's hat is pretty. | The girls' hats are pretty. |
| I liked the girl's hat. | I liked the girls' hats. |

Some nouns, however, due to phonological need or historical logic may form their plural in seemingly irregular ways.[1]

Nouns ending in *ch, sh, s, or z* require an *es* ending instead of just an *s* for their plural.

| Singular | Plural |
| --- | --- |
| The church is very pretty. | The church*es* have beautiful chimes. |
| The bush has many flowers now. | The bush*es* are in full bloom. |
| The class started at noon. | The class*es* started at six P.M. |
| The buzz was very noticeable. | The buzz*es* were very annoying. |

Nouns ending in *f* or *fe* may change form completely for their plural: wife, wives; half, halves; shelf, shelves; calf, calves; life, lives.

Nouns ending in *o* may add an *s* or an *es:* solos, pianos, altos, mottos; potatoes, tomatoes, echoes, heroes.

Some nouns make internal changes rather than adding a suffix: foot, feet; tooth, teeth; man, men; woman, women; goose, geese; mouse, mice; child, children; ox, oxen.

Some foreign words retain their foreign endings even though they have become an important part of our vocabulary: datum, data; stimulus, stimuli; locus, loci; analysis, analyses; basis, bases; curriculum, curricula or curriculums; thesis, theses.

---

1. A writer unsure of the correct plural form should consult a dictionary.

Although these irregularities in forming the noun plural seem rather confusing, the English language is really considerably less complicated than most foreign languages. In Latin, for example, the noun has five cases—nominative, subject; the genitive, possessive; dative, indirect object; objective, object; and the ablative, manner, instrument, agent—each with different singular and plural inflectional endings. Moreover, English has natural gender; that is, a thing is an *it* and a person is either a *he* or *she*. In French, what would be an *it* in English (neuter) may be either masculine or feminine. For instance, a table in French is masculine and a pen and chair are feminine. This also means that French verbs and adjectives must adjust their endings accordingly.

## The Pronoun

### The Personal Pronouns

A pronoun takes the place of the noun in a sentence. The noun that it refers back to is its antecedent (it precedes). Every pronoun must have an antecedent and must agree with its noun in number, gender, and person.

> The *girl* is going to the game on Tuesday, and *she* will buy some tickets for the game on Wednesday.

> The *girls* are going to Montreal next week; *they* should have a very interesting excursion.

> *He* sent the book to me yesterday, but *it* was the wrong edition. I had to send *it* back to *him* this morning.

Figure 8.1 indicates the personal pronouns and their forms and uses in the various cases. As the chart shows, the *nominative* form (case) has four uses—as subjects, as complements, in comparisons, and as subjective appositives. The *who*, the relative pronoun, relates adjective clauses to the nouns *they* modify and serves as the subject or complement in these structures.

> Subject: The *boy who* lives down the street delivers our paper every morning.

> Complement: It is sometimes difficult to decide on *who* our outstanding student is for the year. (our outstanding student who)

Even as an interrogative pronoun, *who* serves in the subject position:

> *Who* will be the recipient of that award this year?

The *objective* form (case) has six uses—as the direct object, indirect object, object of a preposition, objective appositive, in implied verb comparisons, and as the subject of an infinitive.

# PRONOUNS

| Case: Nominative (Subjective) | Objective | Possessive + Noun | Possessive (Complement) |
|---|---|---|---|
| I | me | my + (book) | (It is) mine |
| you | you | your | yours |
| he | him | his | his |
| she | her | her | hers |
| it | it | its | its |
| we | us | our | ours |
| they | them | their | theirs |
| who | whom | whose | whose |

**Subject:**
We are going tomorrow.
She saw the painting then.
Mr. Hall and I will attend the meeting.

**Complement:**
The leaders will be Mary and I.
It was she who called.
This is he.

**In Comparisons:**
He understood the problem better than she.
Mary is better at mathematics than I.

**Appositive in Subject:**
Two students, James and she, did the packing.

**Who:**
He did not know who would take his place.
Give the samples to whoever asks for them.

**Direct Object:**
Mr. Behn saw him at the meeting.

**Indirect Object:**
The librarian gave them the book.

**Object of Preposition:**
The manager gave the check to them.
Mr. Parks went to the meeting with us.

**In Comparisons: Implied Verb**
Mary always gave Bill a larger share than (she gave) me.

**Appositive in Object:**
Mr. Bard appointed two people—Mark and me—to count the ballots.

**With Infinitive:**
He told Bill and her to ask the question.

**Whom:**
He did not know whom they would choose.

That is *my book* on the table.

*Whose books* were they?

It is *our opinion* that he is very talented.

**With Gerund:**
We objected to *his working* on that project.
*His writing* that letter did no good.

It is *mine*.

It was *theirs*.

It might be *his*.

The books were *hers*.

This check is *yours*.

That notice is *ours*.

**Figure 8.1**

| | |
|---:|:---|
| Object: | He saw *me* at the store yesterday. |
| Indirect object: | The clerk gave *me* the package for the club. |
| Object of Preposition: | The librarian gave the money for the Encyclopedia *to them*. |
| Objective appositive: | The committee appointed two people—Alden and *her*—to chair the finance committee. |
| Comparison—Implied Verb: | He always sent the club more money than *her* (he did send her). |
| Subject of Infinitive: | The manager wanted *Bill and him to decide* the question of increasing the personnel. |

*The whom*, the objective form (case) of the relative pronoun, can serve as the object of the clause or as an object of a preposition.

| | |
|---:|:---|
| Object: | Dr. Mills *whom I knew in college* is now President of that firm. |
| Object of Preposition: | I did not know to *whom* our supervisor was speaking. |

*Whom* also serves as an interrogative pronoun maintaining its same case.

*Whom* did the children believe about the party mixup?

Pronouns have two *possessive* cases: one preceding nouns and the other serving as the complement to a Be-Verb sentence.

| | |
|---:|:---|
| Preceding a Noun: | *My book* is on the table.<br>She saw *your book* at the library.<br>He put *his book* in *her car*.<br>It was *their turn* to drive to the University.<br>The bank confused *our accounts*. |
| As a complement: | The book is *mine*.<br>The phone call is *yours*.<br>The ticket was *his*.<br>The brown car was *hers*.<br>That house is *ours*.<br>That lawn is *theirs*. |

*Whose* is the possessive case form for who or whom. It also precedes a noun.

*Whose* book is that on the table?
That book is *whose*? (meaning whose book)

Although nouns add an *'s or an s'* to indicate possession, the pronouns do not require any apostrophes. Their change in form from Case to Case signals the proper meaning. Figure 8.1 shows no apostrophes for any of the pronouns.

The pronoun *its* causes the most confusion. Writers too often use the contraction *it's* meaning *it has* or *it is* when they really want to use *its*, the possessive pronoun.

> *It's* been a long year for everyone.
> *It has* been a long year for everyone.
>
> *It's* just as well that he did not come last.
> *It is* just as well that he did not come last night.
>
> The dog acted as though it was *its* house.
> The exterior of the house revealed *its* age.

Under the Case "Possessive + Noun," Figure 8.1 indicates that pronouns in this list also precede gerunds in sentences. A *gerund* is a *verb* + *ing* serving as a *noun*. Thus, the gerund really becomes a noun and as such also requires the possessive form of the pronoun and the possessive form of the noun to precede it.

> The manager was opposed to *his leaving* the office so soon.
> She was opposed to *his coming* home after what had happened.
>
> The company objected to *Mary's writing* that letter to the paper.
> *Bill's noting* the temperature discrepancy probably saved the building.

The manager is not opposed to *him* or the company to *Mary*. Rather the manager is opposed to *his leaving* and the company to *Mary's writing*. "Leaving, coming, writing, and noting" are gerunds serving as nouns and must receive the same privileges.

## The Demonstrative Pronouns

The demonstrative pronouns precede the noun—*this, that* (singular) and *these, those* (plural)—and point specifically to things or people.

> *This book* contains many interesting stories about Iceland.
> *That character* showed nothing of the honesty portrayed by the brothers.
> *These children* were orphaned by the street fighting.
> *Those men* have formed a committee to investigate the traffic problem.

In the above examples, each demonstrative pronoun agrees in number with the noun following it. Careless writers could overlook the following slips.

> wrong: *These* are the *type* of *problems* that can upset a good project.
> corrected: *These* are the *types* of problems that can upset a good project.
> or *This* is the *type* of *problem* that could upset a good project.

>   wrong:     *This* is the *kind* of *typewriters* that really thinks for the typist.
>   corrected: *This* is the kind of *typewriter* that really thinks for the typist.
>   or         *These* are the *kinds* of *typewriters* that really think for the typist.

As the corrected examples indicate, the demonstrative pronoun, noun, and object of *of* must all be either singular or plural.

## The Reflexive Pronouns

The reflexive pronouns—myself, yourself, himself, herself, ourselves, and themselves—turn the action to the doer or doers. To use one of these forms correctly, the writer must have the corresponding personal pronoun already in the sentence.

> *He* scratched *himself* on that file door.
> *She* studied *herself* in the mirror.
> *They* enjoyed *themselves* at the company picnic yesterday.

The reflexive pronoun is *not* a substitute for the objective case of the personal pronoun. Recently this mistake has become prevalent in speaking situations especially:

>   wrong:     She told her story to the lawyer and *myself*.
>   corrected: She told her story to the lawyer and *me*.
>
>   wrong:     He had nothing further to say to Bill and *myself*.
>   corrected: He had nothing further to say to Bill and *me*.

## Impersonal Pronoun One

The impersonal pronoun *one* not only provides for redundancy but also is often unnatural and clumsy in the sentence. Writers sometimes use *one* to avoid using an *I* or *we* as a subject believing it offers some objectivity to their writing.

> *One* should know that if *one* continues in this vein of thinking, the committee may decide to forget the project until next year.

Many journals now are encouraging authors to use the first person, active voice—*I tested, I noted, I know*—if they are responsible for the thinking or the action. This represents quite a change for many writers, particularly those in the scientific and technical fields. For decades they have avoided using the first person pronouns as indicating a too subjective approach. Often the result has been the development of a stilted and presumed academic style.

## Pronoun Agreement

Besides being in the right case, pronouns must also agree with their antecedents in person, number and gender. The antecedent is the noun the pronoun refers back to or replaces in the sentence. If the antecedent is singular, the pronoun must be singular. If plural, the pronoun must be plural.

Singular: *Mary* left for Cleveland where *she* is to meet her children.
*William* left *his* book in the car. *He* will pick *it* up tomorrow after class.

Plural: The *children* have just opened *their* gifts which *they* received yesterday.

Singular: *Each* of the students exhibited *his or her* painting at the party.
The *jury* did not complete *its* deliberations until late today.

Plural: A *few* of the *students* had sold *their* paintings before the exhibit opened yesterday.
*All* of the members of the committee accepted *their* assignments graciously if not eagerly.

## Indefinite Pronouns

The indefinite pronouns include such words as *any, anybody, anyone, each, either, neither, everybody, everyone, no one,* and *nobody*. Although some of these pronouns seem to sound plural, they all require a singular verb form and a singular pronoun to refer back to them. Most writers have no problem with the verb agreement but do have problems with the pronoun reference form.

*Everyone is* going to the lecture today.
*Everybody was* happy to welcome the students home from China.

Sometimes there is a temptation in informal writing to use the plural pronoun as reference. A writer disturbed by such a sentence as the following can easily rewrite it to exclude the problem structure.

Faulty: After *everyone* had finished the dessert, the chairperson instructed *them* to go to the lecture hall for the afternoon discussions.

Rewritten: After *everyone* had finished the dessert, the chairperson asked *the committee* to go to the lecture room for the afternoon discussion.

Careful writers treat the indefinite pronouns as well as the collective nouns (family, jury, group) or the generic nouns (person, kind, sort) as singular in all situations.

Faulty: *Everyone* needs one thing to excel in if *they* are to gain some self confidence.

Rewritten: *Everyone* needs one thing to excel in if *he* or *she* is to gain some self confidence.

Faulty: *Each* of the alternatives had *their* disadvantages, but the second approach seemed more viable.

Rewritten: *Each* of the alternatives had *its* disadvantages, but the second approach seemed more viable.

Faulty: *Every person* is unique; *their* likes or dislikes are quite different from those of any other person.

Rewritten: *Every person* is unique; *his or her* likes or dislikes are quite different from those of any other person.

Faulty: *Everyone* on the team must learn *their* signals if the team is to be coordinated and efficient.

Rewritten: Everyone on the team must learn *the* signals if the team is to be coordinated and efficient.

Rewritten: *All players* on the team must learn their signals if the team is to be coordinated and efficient.

Rewritten: *Everyone* on the team must learn *his or her* signals if the team is to be coordinated and efficient.

## The Verb

Verbs express action or states of being. Chapter V, "The Sentence," discusses the four types of verbs—Transitive, Intransitive, Be-Verb, and Linking verb. Chapter VI, "Sentence Structure and Style," notes the problems of too many verbs in the passive voice or too much shifting between the active and passive voice. Two other problems associated with the verb are subject-verb agreement and unnecessary or illogical shifts in tense. In English the number of the subject (singular or plural) controls the verb form just as the noun antecedent controls the number, gender, and person of its pronoun reference.

The *girls were* happy to hear that before the semester would begin *they* would receive all of the award money promised to *them*.

One of the problems of subject-verb agreement involves the third person singular of the present tense—he, she, it—and the past tense forms of the be-verb—was or were. The following paradigm indicates that the present tense changes form only once:

| Person | Singular | Person | Plural |
|---|---|---|---|
| 1 | I walk | 1 | We walk |
| 2 | You walk | 2 | You walk |
| 3 | *He, She, It walks* | 3 | They walk |

The be-verb is slightly irregular but the form changes are not difficult to remember and use.

| Singular | Present | Past | Plural | Present | Past |
|----------|---------|------|--------|---------|------|
| I | am | was | We | are | were |
| You | are | were | You | are | were |
| He, She, It | is | was | They | are | were |

The modals—can, may, will, shall, must (present tense) and could, might, would, should (past tense)—have the same form for all persons, genders, and numbers.

## Subject-Verb Agreement

The subject determines whether the verb will be singular or plural, but the decision has its complications. To be exact, *the verb agrees with the basic subject,* usually one word, as opposed to agreeing with the *complete subject* that may have a number of words. In the following sentence, *decisions* is the *basic* subject and "the decisions of the courts on such matters under the Pure and Food and Drug Act" the *complete* subject.

> The *decisions* of the courts on such matters under the Pure Food and Drug Act *have* deterred companies from engaging in such practices.

In the following example, *supply* is the basic subject and "the supply of trained, experienced maintenance workers" is the complete subject:

> The *supply* of trained, experienced maintenance workers *is* decreasing rapidly.

### *Compound Subjects*

Compound subjects joined by *and* require a plural verb form:

> Mary *and* William *were* the only two children close enough to come to the reunion last year.

> Jogging *and* walking *are* two of the best aerobic exercises.

However, if the two subjects refer to the same individual or if *and* joins two things considered as one unit, the verb remains singular.

> *My son and heir is* arriving by plane tonight.

> *His teacher and mentor*, Dr. Green, *has* been a true friend to that student.

In sentences with more than one subject-verb combination, each verb agrees with the subject that controls it.

> When *we were* in South America, our *group was* very interested in all of the Indian excavations, but our *guides were* not too well-informed about the history of many of them.

*Intervening Phrases*

Intervening phrases or clauses that come between the subject and the verb do not affect the number of the verb.

> The *rejection* of middle class values and rules *opens* the door to behavior problems.
>
> His white *hair*, as well as his friendly smile and ruddy face, *gives* him a patriarchal appearance.
>
> The maintenance *supervisor*, along with the rest of his shop crew, *was* accused of tampering with the sprinkling system.
>
> The *fact* that *people* in counseling *have* problems with convincing some of their clients of the right approaches to their living *is* not unusual.

*Subject Position Changes*

Changing the position of the subject either by a transform or by question inversion does not change the basic subject-verb agreement relationship.

> There *are three empty rooms* on this floor but by Tuesday *they will* all have occupants.
>
> Where *were the children* when the lights blinked?
>
> *Do the rooms* all have beds and chairs?
>
> In the library *are sand paintings and Japanese silk screens*.
>
> Near the two small lakes *is a view* of the high mountains with their snow-covered peaks.

*Alternative Subjects*

When *either or, neither nor, or, nor* join subjects in a sentence, the verb agrees with the nearer subject. Obviously, if both subjects are plural the verb is plural; if both subjects are singular, the verb is singular.

> Neither the Council nor its *attorneys were* prepared for the attack made by the prosecution.
>
> Either you or *Bill has* left the door to the laboratory open.
>
> *Neither* of us *plans* to go abroad this summer.
>
> Two single rooms *or one double room is* all that is available for tonight.

*Indefinite Pronouns*

Since indefinite pronouns are singular, they also require a singular verb. By thinking each *one*, either *one*, or neither *one*, the need for the singular verb is no longer as confusing.

> *Each man is* master of his own destiny.
>
> *Each* of the chapters *stresses* the culture of a different country.
>
> *Neither* of the proponents for the development of such a product *has* a large following at this time.
>
> *Everyone is* planning to attend the conference in Chicago.
>
> *Is everybody* ready for the trip down the rapids?

*Collective Nouns*

A collective noun is a noun that refers to a group, such as *committee, group, class, family, jury,* or *the number*. If the collective noun is regarded as a unit—the verb would be singular. If regarded as meaning individuals of the group, the verb would be plural.

> The French *group is* meeting in the library tonight.
> The French group *are divided* on their support of the textbooks.
>
> His *class was the* largest in the school at that time.
>
> Our *family is* holding *its* reunion in June this year.
> Our *family are* scattered throughout the country now.
>
> *The number* of people involved in the strike *was* very small.
> A *number of* people *were* involved in the strike.

*Words Ending in S*

Special rules of usage govern nouns that end in *ics* when they refer to a branch of academics or type of knowledge. Such words as *physics, economics,* and *mathematics* are thought of as singular and require a singular verb form.

> Mathe*matics is* a difficult subject for some students.
>
> Econo*mics is* sometimes called the dismal science.
>
> Linguis*tics is* the study of words and language.

Other words usually thought of as singular although they seem to have plural forms are *Mumps, Measles, news,* or *politics*.

*Measles is* a very serious disease for young children.

The *news has* not been very optimistic the last few days.

**Verb Tenses**

Native speakers of the English language select their verb tenses rather automatically. Most speakers or writers have few problems in selecting the simple past, present, or future tenses; however, some encounter problems when using and expressing the "perfect" forms of past, present or future, particularly if such forms must appear together in the same sentence or in the same paragraph. Understanding the make up of various tenses requires some knowledge of the principal parts of verbs; that is, the basic form for these tenses. Regular verbs have the following form for their five principal parts:

| | |
|---:|:---|
| Present tense: | walk |
| Third Person Present: | walks |
| Past Tense: | walked |
| Past Participle: | walked |
| Present Participle: | walking |

Irregular verbs also have five principal parts, but their past tense and past participle are not formed by the suffix -ed. An example of one type is as follows.

| | |
|---:|:---|
| Present tense: | speak |
| Third Person Present: | speaks |
| Past tense: | spoke |
| Past Participle: | spoken |
| Present Participle: | speaking |

Figure 8.2 provides a representative list of regular verbs and their principal parts; Figure 8.3 provides a list of the more familiar and often used irregular verbs.

| Infinitive Present | Third Person Present | Past | Past Participle | Present Participle |
|---|---|---|---|---|
| ask | asks | asked | asked | asking |
| burn | burns | burned | burned | burning |
| compel | compels | compelled | compelled | compelling |
| criticize | criticizes | criticized | criticized | criticizing |
| discuss | discusses | discussed | discussed | discussing |
| dream | dreams | dreamed | dreamed | dreaming |
| edit | edits | edited | edited | editing |
| fix | fixes | fixed | fixed | fixing |
| follow | follows | followed | followed | following |
| fund | funds | funded | funded | funding |
| grant | grants | granted | granted | granting |
| hate | hates | hated | hated | hating |
| jeer | jeers | jeered | jeered | jeering |
| knit | knits | knitted | knitted | knitting |
| lack | lacks | lacked | lacked | lacking |
| learn | learns | learned | learned | learning |
| lift | lifts | lifted | lifted | lifting |
| memorize | memorizes | memorized | memorized | memorizing |
| naturalize | naturalizes | naturalized | naturalized | naturalizing |
| open | opens | opened | opened | opening |
| permit | permits | permitted | permitted | permitting |
| point | points | pointed | pointed | pointing |
| plan | plans | planned | planned | planning |
| refer | refers | referred | referred | referring |
| reject | rejects | rejected | rejected | rejecting |
| rule | rules | ruled | ruled | ruling |
| stay | stays | stayed | stayed | staying |
| summarize | summarizes | summarized | summarized | summarizing |
| study | studies | studied | studied | studying |
| view | views | viewed | viewed | viewing |
| wait | waits | waited | waited | waiting |
| want | wants | wanted | wanted | wanting |

Figure 8.2  Regular Verbs

| Infinitive Present | Third Person Present | Past | Past Participle | Present Participle |
|---|---|---|---|---|
| begin | begins | began | begun | beginning |
| break | breaks | broke | broken | breaking |
| choose | chooses | chose | chosen | choosing |
| come | comes | came | come | coming |
| do | does | did | done | doing |
| drink | drinks | drank | drunk | drinking |
| drive | drives | drove | driven | driving |
| eat | eats | ate | eaten | eating |
| get | gets | got | gotten | getting |
| give | gives | gave | given | giving |
| forget | forgets | forgot | forgotten | forgetting |
| have | has | had | had | having |
| hide | hides | hid | hidden | hiding |
| hit | hits | hit | hit | hitting |
| know | knows | knew | known | knowing |
| lead | leads | led | led | leading |
| mean | means | meant | meant | meaning |
| pay | pays | paid | paid | paying |
| rise | rises | rose | risen | rising |
| ring | ring | rang | rung | ringing |
| say | says | said | said | saying |
| set | sets | set | set | setting |
| sing | sings | sang | sung | singing |
| sit | sits | sat | sat | sitting |
| shake | shakes | shook | shaken | shaking |
| speak | speaks | spoke | spoken | speaking |
| steal | steals | stole | stolen | stealing |
| take | takes | took | taken | taking |
| throw | throws | threw | thrown | throwing |
| tear | tears | tore | torn | tearing |
| win | wins | won | won | winning |
| write | writes | wrote | written | writing |

**Figure 8.3 Irregular Verbs**

Inconsistencies in the use of the verbal forms could disrupt the ideas and endanger proper interpretation. It is always best to select the tense carefully and stay with it.

The crew *noticed* the large crack in the pavement and *wondered* about its origin.

|  |  |  |
|---|---|---|
| Present Tense: | I walk | I am walking |
|  | I speak | I am speaking |
| Past Tense: | I walked | I was walking |
|  | I spoke | I was speaking |
| Present Perfect Tense: | I have walked | He has walked |
|  | I have spoken | He has spoken |
| Past Perfect Tense: | I had walked | He had walked |
|  | I had spoken | He had spoken |
| Future Tense: | I shall walk | He will walk |
|  | I shall speak | He will speak |
| Future Perfect Tense: | I shall have walked | He will have walked |
|  | I shall have spoken | He will have spoken |

**Figure 8.4. Verb Tenses**

Each tense has its own use for expressing what a writer wants his or her sentence to say. The **present** tense is correct for present action, habitual action, giving general truths, or describing literary events.

She *is walking* in the garden and *collecting* some cuttings for the table.

Every night, the storekeeper *locks* his door, *pulls down* the gratings, and then *steps* briskly to the curb just in time to catch his bus.

Columbus believed the earth is round.

The article I read last night *states* that travel will be up this year.

It is always necessary to use the tenses that show the correct relation of time between the main verb and the subordinate verb. The following sentences indicate that something had occurred previously to the time of the main verb.

Having learned the language in only one semester, I was ready to go to Germany at any time.

Having finished all my experiments, I felt free to take the weekend off.

In the sentence below, the action (had bought) had taken place before the action of the main verb. Since *mentioned* is in the past tense, *bought* must be in the **past perfect.**

My friend was very surprised when I *mentioned* that I *had bought* the tickets last week.

We *had been* home several days before I noticed that some of the pictures *were missing*.

We *wondered* what had happened to the animals that *had been* there earlier.

After we *had spoken* for several minutes, we *realized* the man did not understand English.

We *concluded* that everyone *had gone* home early.

However, a **present** not a **past** tense follows a statement introduced by the **present perfect.**

I *have known* for a long time that the case *is* a lost cause.

She *has always believed* that the shortest distance between two points *is* not always the best route.

The **future** tense does just what it says—it expresses something that is going to take place in the future.

She will leave for her trip next Monday.

The manager will hire as many security guards as the situation dictates.

The **future perfect** indicates a relationship between some future event and another future event which will happen before the first event has taken place.

Before the end of July, she *will have visited* fifteen countries in Europe.

Before the semester *is* over, the staff *will have tested* at least five hundred aspiring students.

## The Adjective

An adjective is a word that modifies, describes, or tells more about a noun.

The *clear, cold air* felt good after having been in the *hot, stuffy room* for so long.

Adjectives usually answer the questions of *what kind of* or *which kind of.* They make the noun more specific and concrete. In other words, in the sentence above it is not just air but *clear and cold* air. It is not just a room, but a *hot and stuffy* room.

Our *new* typewriter has a mind of its own which is sometimes very *inconvenient*.

The *blue* chair sitting beside the *oval* window is an antique.

Phrases and clauses can also serve as adjectives by providing more information about the noun they are attached to.

>The book *of poems* is on the table in the study.

*Of poems* is a prepositional phrase modifying and further explaining the type of book.

>The book *that my mentor loaned me* is lengthy but quite interesting.

>The dog *that our neighbors bought yesterday* howled all night.

In these two sentences, *that* introduces two restrictive adjective clauses—one provides essential identifying information about the book and the other about the dog.

As discussed in the "Sentence" chapter, the adjective also follows the verbs of the senses—*feel, taste, smell, sound.*

>The cake tastes *good.*
>He sounded *husky* this morning.
>I felt *unhappy* when I heard you were moving.

To say that something smells badly means that the something is capable of doing the smelling.

>The steam from the sulphur vent *smells bad.*

In this case, bad is describing the smell of the steam not saying that the steam is capable of doing the smelling on its own.

Three adjectives that cause some difficulty especially in speech are *good, real,* and *sure.* Speakers and some writers often use them incorrectly as adverbial intensifiers for adjectives.

>Incorrect: He is good and tired.
>Correct: He is very tired.

>Incorrect: That man is a real good writer.
>Correct: That man writes very well.

>Incorrect: He is sure unhappy.
>Correct: He is very unhappy.

## The Adverbs

An adverb is a word that modifies a verb, adjective, or another adverb. Adverbs usually answer the questions of how, why, where, when, for what reason.

>Verb modifier: Our guide *finally appeared* at the hotel.
>He *carefully constructed* his plots but did not *really develop* his characters *too well.*

|   |   |
|---|---|
| | He *hardly mentioned* his book in his speech. |
| | The floor *nearly collapsed* under the weight of the crowd. |
| Adjective Modifier: | He was *really* unhappy with the decision to close the plant. |
| | He was *usually* slow in answering our letter. |
| Adverb Modifier: | It was *so* very interesting to meet *so* many politicians at one time. |
| | The research indicated that people who did not watch the program were *generally* less aggressive in their actions. |

## The Comparison of Adjectives and Adverbs

Both adjectives and adverbs have three degrees of comparison:

|   |   |
|---|---|
| Positive Degree: | happy |
| Comparative Degree: | happier (comparison of two items or persons) |
| Superlative Degree: | happiest (comparison of more than two items or persons). |
| or | stately, more stately, or most stately. |
| | convenient, more convenient, or most convenient. |

The *more* and *most* are usually used for the comparative and superlative degrees respectively if the adjective or adverb has two or more syllables. Obviously conven*ienter* or conven*ienest* are very cumbersome, to say the least. No native speaker of the language would select such forms.

She was *much happier* than Mary about moving to Chicago.
He was the *happiest student on the bus* when he learned he had won the scholarship.

Their new home was *more conveniently located* than the previous one.
Their new home was the *most conveniently located* of any they had ever lived in anywhere.

Certain often-used words have irregular comparative forms. Most native speakers have few problems with them, however.

adjectives—good, better best
adverbs—well, better, best
with non-count nouns—much, more, most
with count nouns—many, more, most
adjectives—bad, worse, worst

concerning size—little, smaller, smallest
concerning amount or degree—little, less, least

There was too much liquid in the coffee pot.
There were too many people at the art exhibit yesterday.
Their house is smaller than any other house in the block.
They have the least amount of exposed area of any of the houses in the block.

The use of the double comparative or double superlative is unnecessary and incorrect.

He was *more unhappier* about having to miss the game than I had expected.
She seemed the *most saddest* loser of all the contestants.

# Questions

I. Revise the following sentences. Explain the problem in each sentence.

1. Everybody who submits a job application knows that they will have to work carefully and efficiently if they receive the appointment.

2. His secretary appeared much more capable and efficient in all ways than him.

3. I did not like the idea of him using my new bicycle when he had one just like it.

4. Him leaving the office so early developed into a serious problem for the company.

5. The new representatives to the senate will be Jones and whom?

6. Whom would you say was responsible for that problem?

7. No one in the office had given their permission for the purchase of that type of computer.

8. They were certain that all the employee needs to do is learn the facts and they will be satisfied.

9. They announced that the finalists for that position would be Bill and me.

10. James demonstrated clearly that he could write the reports better than me.

11. These are kind of pens that require only an occasional insert to keep them going.

12. The security officer told us—she and I—to report the theft to our insurance agent immediately.

13. Even though Mr. Alden was quite scientifically minded, he was unable to get it across to his classes.

14. The writer whom the editors believe is the most qualified will receive the study grant for Germany.

15. A child born into a deprived home does not have the resources to better their life.

16. The more the manager thought about the change to earlier hours, the more disturbing it's implication for customer relations became.

17. She promised to give the books to Mary and myself in the morning.

18. The security officer ordered both the driver and she to report to the station at once.

19. Everyone needs at least one thing to excel in if they are to gain a little self confidence.

20. There was not enough room in the laboratory for Tom and I to construct our model.

II. Revise the following sentences. Why might these sentences slip into a piece of writing? Explain your answer.

1. The problems of municipal government is his chief interest.

2. One of the major things that were troubling the employees were the matter of parking.

3. Physics is one of those subjects which attracts students who are better in mathematics than in verbal study areas.

4. This study—like the earlier studies—indicate the difficulty in trying to measure the effectiveness of such products.

5. Either Tom or you has left the blue light burning in the laboratory.

6. Neither of us are quite certain what the lawyer wants us to say at the trial.

7. There was enough rooms in the building to provide all the workers a with private office.

8. None of the headlines of the last few days have been concerned with the new drug discovery.

9. There is basically three reasons for adopting a retrieval system for this company.

10. The lack of good educational facilities give us a shortage of teachers, engineers, doctors, and many other type of professionals.

11. That big oak, as well as some of the less sturdy trees, were affected by the ice and high winds.

12. Just past the two small lakes were a view of green fields and patches of evergreens—a beautiful sight to behold.

13. Outside Building D-1 was a half starved and dirty poodle and a scrubby looking terrier.

14. There is rich rewards for the person finding a cure for that dreaded disease.

15. He nearly completed all of the tests yesterday but found, unfortunately, that he had omitted ten questions on the last page.

16. Our committed have not issued a statement yet about the findings in the bribery case.

17. He can't hardly believe that his friends could pull such a mean trick on anyone.

18. Our Laboratory supervisor needed someone to help her review her calculations badly.

19. Domain, range, and scope constitute the three main dimensions of political power, and determines the weight of that power.

III. Investigation and Research

Choose some article pertinent to your professional field that you have enjoyed reading. Investigate and analyze the writing:

What is it about the writing that attracts you?

What types of sentences, verbs, nouns, pronouns, adjectives, adverbs do the authors seem to have chosen the most?

Does the writer have a particular style? If so, how would you characterize it? Is he or she descriptive; that is, uses many adjectives? many adverbs? many clauses?

How would you characterize the intended audience?

# 9 Punctuation for Meaning

## Potential Ambiguity

Students often say and feel that if they could just give a speech, they would have no trouble communicating their ideas. Probably this is true, for most of them have some command of the spoken signals and patterns of language. They can rely upon the linguistic flow, pantomime, and vocal qualifiers to communicate meaning—and no one can pin them down. However, written English robs them of these convenient and important crutches, and they must be content with words and their arrangements and chunking to carry the load of meaning. To add to this dilemma, another inconvenience of writing—punctuation—also confronts them. Many see little connection between clear communication and the system of marks and scratches that they must learn with it.

Punctuation is not just a system of rules to be learned and applied; rather, it is a system of signals that indicate to the reader what to take together and what to separate. If writers come to understand this, they can begin to see that punctuation is a reading device marking the "joints" of thought—chunking the words into meaningful chunks—and serving the same purpose that pauses, voice inflections, and gestures do for speech.

Early grammars stated all punctuation rules in terms of grammar. Many students learned such rules blindly without understanding how they could help with sorting out the meaning of a sentence—often unaware that a comma or its absence would make a difference for the reader.

> Without oil transportation as we know it in this country would be impossible.
>
> Without oil, transportation as we know it in this country would be impossible.

This sentence needs something after the introductory prepositional phrase, "without oil." The insertion of a comma prevents the "without oil transportation" reading which would provide for no logical interpretation.

> Flexibility is the result of creativity and productivity is the result of both.
>
> Flexibility is the result of creat*ivity, and* productivity is the result of both.

The comma before the *and* in the second sentence signals to the reader that "flexibility" is not the result of "creativity and productivity." Rather, "productivity" is the subject of the second part of a compound sentence.

Good writers are aware that more than correct and complete punctuation and grammar are essential for good writing and good reading to result. The following compound sentence illustrates this very well:

The man has been in an automobile accide*nt, and he s*peaks broken English.

Placing a comma before the conjunction *and* joining the clauses of a compound sentence is correct according to the rule. However, these two sentences have no meaning relationship and logically should not have this type of close linking.

Writers need to construct their sentences to say what they want them to say and then punctuate them so the reader can interpret them that way. Thus, the meaning approach to punctuation should build good readers as well as good writers. Revision is more than checking for a display of grammatical dexterity; it is an opportunity for the writer or editor to become a reader and judge whether the sentences and marks are conveying his or her particular ideas.

The following illustrations further indicate the importance of punctuation in signalling the right meaning; both could be correct.

Don't take those shoes off, Melinda.

Don't take those shoes off Melinda.

One rule covering this situation states that a comma sets off a nominative of address (a name of someone being addressed) from the rest of the sentence. What does the writer mean to say here? Does he or she want to command Melinda not to do something or does he or she want to issue a command about Melinda to someone else? It is the comma or no comma that clinches the correct interpretation.

In the following examples, an essential comma is missing:

After the class finished reading the books were placed on the storage-return cart.

As the volume of blood increases the condition of the vessels improves.

The reader could easily chunk "finished reading the books" and "increases the condition" together, leaving incomplete phrases dangling at the end. However, a comma after "reading" and "increases" would set off the introductory dependent adverbial clauses from the main clauses of the sentences and restore order and meaning:

After the class finished reading, the books. . . .

As the volume of blood increases, the condition. . . .

The following words could also puzzle a reader. Do they make up an introductory dependent clause or a sentence?

If you want to ask John about his trip to Spain now   (, or . ?)

The subordinator "if" does signal a dependent clause, but the insertion of a strategically placed comma could provide another message as could the addition of another complete sentence.

If you *want to, ask John* about his trip to Spain now.
If you want to ask John about his trip to *Spain, we* suggest you do it now.

In either case, the comma stopped the train of thought sufficiently to provide the reader with a clear understanding of the intended meaning.

## Basic Chunking

True, all written sentences do not show such obvious evidence of potential ambiguity. However, punctuation or the proper chunking of the written material is essential in conveying the meaning and in the communication process. The following Figure 9.1, General Rules—Punctuation, indicates how different punctuation marks can change the emphasis and relationship of two sentences. A writer understanding these rules will also have a good grasp of basic chunking.

The *Example Sentences* in Figure 9.1 indicate that if the writer wants two sentences to stand alone and have only a nominal relationship, the period is the proper divider.

1. However, to show some relationship between the two sentences, the semicolon would be appropriate.
2. The use of one of the coordinating conjunctions—*and, but, for, or, nor*—preceded by a comma would bring the two ideas into an even closer meaning relationship.
3. The insertion of the semicolon plus one of the transition adverbs—*however, nevertheless, consequently,* etc.—would provide for another type of chunking and close tie-in of ideas. A comma before the transition adverb would not be strong enough to note this change of thought.

In the 1, 2, and 3 examples, both parts have retained their independent structure; that is remained complete sentences. But in 4 and 5, this changes.

4. Beginning with the use of subordinators, one of the sentences has become a dependent adverbial clause indicating a cause-effect relationship between the two ideas—something else happens or will happen *if, since, although,* etc. something is true. As in 4, when the subordinated structure appears at the end of the sentence, there is no punctuation (no comma) for this is the normal position of any adverbial in an English sentence pattern. The definition of the sentence at the bottom of Figure 9.1 summarizes this point. The adverbial construction can be a phrase, one word, or a dependent clause:

## GENERAL RULES—PUNCTUATION

Example Sentences:  The technicians stayed at the laboratory.         Complete Sentence (C.S.)
                   Their supervisors attended the ceremony.           C.S.

1. The technicians stayed at the laboratory; their supervisors attended the ceremony.
   Complete Sentence          ;          Complete Sentence          (C.S. ; C.S.)

2. The technicians stayed at the laboratory, *and* their supervisors attended the ceremony.
                                          , but
                                          , for                C.S.
   (Coordinators)         C.S.            , or
                                          , nor

3. The technicians stayed at the laboratory; *however*, their supervisors attended the ceremony.
                                           ; nevertheless,
                                           ; therefore,                C.S.
   (Transition words)      C.S.            ; consequently,
                                           ; thus,

4. The technicians stayed at the laboratory *while* their supervisors attended the ceremony.
                                             when
                           C.S.              since                      C.S.
                                             although
                                             even though
                           C.S.              as                   Subordinator + C.S.
                                             (if, before,
                                             after, etc.)

5. *While* their supervisors attended the ceremony, the technicians stayed at the laboratory.

   When
   Since        Subordinator  +   C.S.   ,   C. S.
   Although
   Even though
   As

                Complete Sentence   ⟶        Subject     +   Predicate   +   (Adverbs)
                                             (Adverbs),      Subject     +   Predicate

**Figure 9.1**

John went <u>to the store</u> <u>yesterday</u> <u>even though he had little money to spend.</u>
    phrase    one word         dependent clause

5. If the adverbial dependent clause appears at the beginning of the sentence as in 5, a comma is appropriate to set it off from the rest of the sentence. The subordinator is still signaling a cause-effect relationship, but this clause is out of its normal position; in speech a slight pause would indicate this—If, since, although, etc. something is <u>true,</u> <u>something</u> else happens or will happen.

Yesterd<u>ay, J</u>ohn went to the store even though he had little money to spend.

Even though he had little money to spen<u>d, J</u>ohn went to the store yesterday.

## Punctuation Specifics

### Semicolon

Figure 9.1 shows two uses of the semicolon: between two closely related sentences that have no coordinating word between them and between two closely related sentences joined by one of the transition adverbs.

Many effective ways of running this company are authoritarian; many are democratic.

I do not agree with your cost estimate for that computer conversion outlet at our plant; however, I am expressing only my opinion.

A third use of the semicolon not shown in Figure 9.1 involves a series when one or more of the items already contain commas.

Our company has mills in Maine, Michigan, and Wisconsi<u>n; </u>pulp suppliers in Canada, United States, and Europ<u>e; </u>and sales offices in five cities in this country, three in Canada, and five in Europe.

The counselor noted the things he needed to make his office really inviting: a new easy chair, not overstuffed to take up more of his needed space, but bright and attractiv<u>e; </u>a new rug for the floor, a thick, serviceable on<u>e; and</u> some pictures to fill up the dingy and gloomy walls.

Using only commas at the semicolon junctures in these sentences would cause some confusion for the readers. They would have difficulty sorting out the three main ideas of both sentences: the mills, the pulp suppliers, and the sales offices in the first sentence and the chair, new rug, and pictures in the second sentence.

The following **run-on sentences** indicate the need for some type of end punctuation. The term **run-on sentence** is self-explanatory. It refers to the collision of two sentences with the first one lacking the appropriate "breaking power" to avoid the crash—the semicolon or the period is necessary between them.

Some people take little interest in good drama productions their belief seems to be that such entertainment is not valuable.

The office space in our department should be more efficiently allocated there is one empty office on my floor.

The scheduling of business classes needs to be improved the reason is that business students have a difficult time getting their essential classes.

## Commas

Probably of all the marks of punctuation, the comma is the one most often overused and misused. The myth that writers insert a comma whenever they pause in a sentence is just that—a myth. Figure 9.1 indicates two necessary uses of the comma: to separate the two parts of a compound sentence joined by *and, but, for, or, nor* and to set off introductory adverbial clauses, phrases, and words. The comma, however, has several other functions:

**To separate items in a series:**

The writing was clear, concise, and effective.
Walking, running, and jogging are all popular exercise activities today.
What I do, where I go, or when I go is my personal responsibility.

Some examples of our products are corrugated containers, folding cartons, paper matches, and frozen food containers.

Two of these sentences also show that there is **no** comma after the last element when the series is serving as the subject or comes in the early part of the sentence.

**To separate words or phrases that could be joined incorrectly in reading:**

During the process of *bleaching the equipment* will need careful checking.
During the process of bleaching, the equipment will need careful checking.

After *eating the child*ren ran to the library to hear the story.
After eating, the children ran to the library to hear the story.

In *summarizing the 1990 outlook* for our industry indicates a moderate gain of 5% in sales.
In summarizing, the 1990 outlook for our industry indicates a moderate gain of 5% in sales.

*Below the earth* appeared parched, strangely quiet, and deserted.
Below, the earth appeared parched, strangely quiet, and deserted.

**To set off alternatives or appositives:**

The straight line, or zero interest, method is not always relevant.
William Acres, not Thomas Bradson, has volunteered to chair that committee.

Mr. Beardsly, the manager of the company, offered me a challenging and interesting opportunity at his plant.

Today, the once lowly placebo, an imitation medicine, is gaining considerable respect and serious attention even from medical scholars.

**To indicate nonrestrictive or nonessential relative clauses:**

Peak loads, *which seldom occur*, are the result of our extra generator.

Measured in terms of the Gross National Product, *which is a measure of the physical output of all goods and services in the country*, a gain of 3% a year on the average is possible for the 1990's.

Mr. Greason, *panting and puffing*, appeared in the doorway just behind them.

Nonrestrictive elements provide good additional information but are not crucial to the main import of the sentence and could even be omitted without any serious consequences to the meaning.

**However, restrictive or essential relative clauses require no commas to set them off:**

Students who have not paid their library fees by May will not be elegible for spring graduation.

Any ticket requests which indicate no return address will delay the processing.

**To enclose parenthetical elements or words that explain or qualify:**

This article, *I suppose*, suggests some worthwhile alternatives for our fund raising promotion.

A college, *or so I believe strongly*, must be able to meet the needs of all students both socially and academically.

Successful human relations training should result in the development of new habits and, *therefore*, should follow the rules for changing habits.

**To separate consecutive coordinate adjectives before the noun they modify:**

The quiet, deserted street at that hour of the day was mysterious but also interesting.

The slow, dangerous climb to the rim top was exciting but very exhausting.

The smooth, glistening, severe sides of the skyscraper reflected the chaotic life race below.

This comma is necessary only when the adjectives are coordinate—that is each adjective refers directly to the noun. If the word *and* could fit in between each adjective, the comma is the proper punctuation: the quiet *and* deserted street, the slow *and* dangerous climb, and the smooth *and* glistening *and* severe sides.

**To set off beginning participial phrases modifying the subject:**

>*Running* quickly up the stairs, t*he childre*n reached the classroom before the bell chimed.

>*Talking and laughing* loudly, the *visitors* climbed the rugged path leading to the haunted house.

**To note dialogue with quotation marks:**

>"Mary," said Bill, "is actually coming to the lecture."

>"For your next assignment," announced the professor, "please write a five hundred word paper about your most interesting job interview."

**To list geographical names, dates, and addresses:**

>The address you need is Mary Louise Acre, 367 Spruce Avenue, Chicago, Illinois 60521.

>Their school opened on March 2, 1909, in County Sussex, Boston, Massachusetts 82036.

## Comma Abuses

### The Comma Splice

>The equipment is in very poor condition, the belt is worn as well as the wall plug.

>The journal believes in truth, therefore, it will always try to print the truth.

>So you have decided to apply for another position, you're forsaking your major area of specialization forever.

The comma in these sentences is not a strong enough divider. The sentences require either a semicolon or a period.

### Compound Nouns and Compound Verbs Separated

The sentences below are examples of the **overuse** of the comma with coordinating conjunctions.

>I majored in both political science, and English, and received my degree in April.

>We will visit Scotland, and Iceland while on our trip this summer.

When he felt in his pocket, and found it empty, he began to worry in earnest.

It had snowed, and frozen the night before which made our trip to the farm quite risky.

Her work is very stimulating, but requires a great deal of concentration.

The coordinating conjunctions—<u>and</u>, <u>but</u>, <u>for</u>, <u>or</u>, <u>nor</u>—require a comma preceding them <u>only</u> to separate three or more words in a series or if followed by another sentence.

We will visit Scotland, Iceland, and Ireland while on our trip this year.

Her work is very stimulating, but it does require a great deal of administrative make-work.

### *Subject Noun Clauses Separated From Their Predicate*

Noun clauses serving as subjects in their sentences require *no* punctuation following them. This only separates them from their predicates.

|  | *Whoever plans to go to the concert, should leave now.* |
| --- | --- |
| corrected: | Whoever plans to go to the concert should leave now. |

|  | *Who done it, was the main theme of the book.* |
| --- | --- |
| corrected: | Who done it was the main theme of the book. |

|  | *Whatever he says, is always wrong.* |
| --- | --- |
| corrected: | Whatever he says is always wrong. |

# Colon

The colon introduces an item or a series formally. A general statement needing further clarification precedes the colon. The specifics of clarification follow the colon: examples, an itemized series, or a formal quotation.

General Statement = Specific Details

C. S. : list or another C. S.

This report will pose two very basic questions: Why has much classroom training in human relations been ineffective? What are some of the ways to make it more effective?

There are three essentials of good writing: thorough preparation, careful writing, and astute revision.

He noted two obvious ways to increase the wood supply: increase the land area and increase the yield of wood per acre.

Early in World War II, Winston Churchill sent the following appeal to the United States: "Give us the tools, and we will finish the job."

The general statement usually includes a reference to the number of specific items that will follow the colon. The material following a colon requires no capitalization unless normally capitalized, such as a proper noun, a quotation, or a sequence of sentences.

## Dash

The dash indicates an abrupt interruption or change of thought in a sentence. It is not a substitute for a semicolon or a period. The overuse of the dash reflects the work of an amateur writer. The dash sets off extraneous material, such as side comments or explanations. What occurs between the dashes may be one word, a sentence, a question, a phrase, or a clause.

> When water entered the cylinder during the priming—the technician had failed to shut off the water valve as called for—we found it difficult to start the motor.

> Size—the advantage of being part of a huge corporate structure—makes possible things impossible for a single industry.

> Bill Warren—a true mimic—caught the humor of the situation.

> Reid Anders—everyone knew Reid Anders—was the favorite candidate for that promotion.

In typing, the dash consists of two hyphens (--) typed flush against the words they separate. Using one hyphen ( - ) with a space on each side is incorrect representation. In current usage, no comma is necessary either before or after a dash.

## Parentheses

Parentheses ( ) like the dash enclose interrupting structures too strong for commas to hold but not abrupt enough for the dash. They often enclose supplementary material, references to previously cited concepts in other parts of a book or chapter, acronyms, numbers, or dates.

> Almost everyone "knows" (the quotation marks register some doubt) that $H_2O$ is the chemical formula for water.

> The various meanings conveyed by the verb are evident through its base form and its suffixes (inflectional endings).

> "Earth Day" (as was intended) demonstrated to the public that there was an environmental movement underway.

> The National Environmental Protection Act (NEPA) revolutionized the federal natural-resource business during the last year (1989).

## Brackets

Brackets [ ] have quite a different focus and use than the dash, parentheses, or comma. They are reserved chiefly for editorial use when a word or comment is inserted into the writing of another person. The insertion of [sic] into a quotation indicates that the quoter is aware of the error but not correcting it.

> "Last year [1988] the stock market experienced its greatest one-day drop of the last five years."

> The article stated quite emphatically, "Some of the Unions [sic] demands will be stoutly resisted by the company."

Brackets are also used as parentheses within parentheses.

> This common substance (water [$H_2O$]) is necessary for sustaining all life.

## Quotation Marks

Quotation marks indicate the actual words of a speaker as well as all words quoted from another author. They appear around all quotations even those set directly into the text.

> Aristotle said "know thyself"; Americans preach "know thy neighbor."

If the direct quotation is a question or an exclamation, the appropriate mark follows rather than a comma.

> "I will not take that test again!" the student yelled.

> "Do you wish to rescind any of your testimony at this time?" the committee asked.

If a quotation is interrupted in the middle by the speaker, a comma and quotation marks follow the first part and a comma and quotation marks precede the remaining ideas.

> "The reason for wanting Ann to go," noted Jim, "is that she has been closely in touch with the group since its beginning and is aware of its progress so far."

If the first part and the last part are both complete sentences, a comma and quotation mark precede the identified speaker who is followed by a period. The second sentence, of course, is enclosed in quotation marks.

> "Fortunately, John has retreated from his original stand against moving his office," the personnel director stated. "However, he has not accepted our suggestions totally yet."

Single quotation marks are for use only around a quotation within another quotation. They are not used to emphasize one or more words in a sentence. Double quotation marks are correct for such situations.

> Bill asked very quietly, "Didn't you say, 'I won't go to the conference this year' when I called you last week?"

She asked very loudly, "Can't images of the new, unknown, or uncharted characterize the sense of 'experience'?"

She told me last night that the word "quit" was not a part of her vocabulary.

## Quotations: Blocks of Prose or Poetry

Inset blocks of manuscripts require no quotation marks. Blocks of four lines or more of quoted material need to be separated from the rest of the paper, single spaced, and inset at least five spaces on both margins. The same rule applies for several lines of poetry quoted. With poetry, the verses would be indented and reproduced exactly as they appear in the original manuscript.

Block of Quoted Material:

Good writing means effective writing: it is a clear, concise, accurate, and appropriate expression of a well-focused and audience-oriented message. Bad writing means ineffective writing: it has lapses in spelling, grammatical usage, punctuation, and sentence-structure makeup. More unfortunately, it may also be the visible evidence of some inward confusion of thought. Clear and effective writing means clear thinking. It means making a piece of writing come "alive" and making it appealing and meaningful.

Lines of Poetry:

>     Whan that Aprille with his shoures soote
>     The droghte of March hath perced to the roote
>     And bathed every veyne in swich licour
>     Of which vertu engendred is the flour;
>     When Zephirus eek with his sweete breeth
>     Inspired hath in every holt and heeth
>     The tendre croppes, and the younge sonne
>     Hath in the Ram his halve cours yronne,
>     And slepen al the nyght with open ye
>     (So priketh hem nature in hir corages);
>     Thanne longen folk to goon on pilgrimages.
>                             —Chaucer, Prologue

## Quotation Marks: End Punctuation

*Periods* and *commas* are always inside the quotation marks even if only the last word or phrase is the enclosed part.

> I finally purchased a "time-sharing condominium."

> My friend found the book "challenging," but she noted that perhaps she had read it at a time when she had too many other things to do.

*Semicolons* and *colons* always come after the quotation marks.

> Bill said, "I want three things for you"; her response was not too optimistic.

> Bill said, "I want three things for you": health, wealth, and happiness.

*Question marks* and *exclamation points* come inside the quotation marks if the quotation is a question or an exclamation by the speaker.

> John asked, "Is there no hope?"
>
> Was it possible that the doctor said, "There is no hope"?
>
> Didn't Bremer state, "I want to assist you in every way I can with your yearly report"?
>
> John's reaction was immediate and happy: "I accept the nomination!"

## Other Uses

*Quotation marks* enclose the name of an article in a magazine or journal, a headline or article in a newspaper, and section or chapter titles of books. However, the name of a magazine, newspaper, or book appears in italicized print or is underlined in typed material. Respecting this convention of differentiation is important in alerting a reader wishing more information of where to begin the search.

> "It All Began with Conservation," an article in the April, 1990, issue of *Smithsonian*, is very informative concerning our need for environmental safety planning.
>
> Chapter V, "Getting Started" in *Pre-Professional Writing* provides some hints to help a writer organize and start a writing project.

## Uses in Technical and Scientific Writing

Technical and scientific writers do not use quotation marks too frequently. However, they must use quotation marks to note any quoted material and any titles of chapters.

## Hyphen

### Hyphenation of Compound Words

Today, many two words have progressed through a hyphenation stage into solid compounds. Familiar examples of these are "housekeeper, bookkeeper, everything, anybody, bankbook, bookcase, railroad, and roommate."

Other compound words have retained their entity and remain written as two words with no hyphenation but having only one meaning or reference: "stock market, all right, blood pressure, and school bell," to name a few.

Other very common compounds have remained hyphenated with no apparent need to progress further: "sister-in-law, clear-cut, post-mortem, French-fries, hot-foot, etc." Deciding on which of the various stages a compound may have reached is very confusing. In many cases, a trip to the dictionary will be the only solution. The use of the hyphen, however, does have some specific and solid rules:

1. Two or more words serving together as an adjective preceding a noun require the hyphen unless the adverb ending *ly* occurs on one of them:

    She is a *well-known person.*

    It was a *never-to-be-forgotten* evening.

    He has a very *up-to-date* record collection.

    The university-related research parks are *highly sophisticated, well-planned, quality-standard* controlled developments which attract much *sought-after* business and industries.

   However, these words remain unhyphenated if they follow the noun.

    That person is *well known.*

    He keeps his record collection *up to date.*

    The university park developments are *well planned* and much *sought after* by businesses.

2. Prefixes *post-, anti-, pro-, pre* when affixed to a proper noun or figure require a hyphen:

    un-American          pre-1990
    anti-American        post-1945
    post-World War II    pro-British

3. The prefixes *ex* (former) and *self* require a hyphen when added to a noun:

    ex-President       self-respect
    ex-professor       self-motivation
    ex-champion        self-taught
    ex-Ambassador      self-reliance

4. A hyphen can distinguish the meaning between two words spelled alike but having quite diverse meanings:

    recover      re-cover       reform      re-form
    recreation   re-creation    recount     re-count
    cooperate    co-operational recollect   re-collect

5. Fractions and numbers from twenty-one to ninety-nine require hyphens:

    one-third of a pound
    two-thirds of those present
    fifty-two
    four hundred sixty-two
    forty-two forty-fourths

6. The "suspended" hyphen, the hyphen for a series of hyphenated words, occurs after each modifier but the noun appears only at the end:

    twelve-, fifteen-, or twenty-year eras

    He prefers ten- to the eight-seat arrangement on a ship.

7. The hyphen is also essential in dividing words at the end of a line:
    a. One syllable words do not divide: through, names, many, signed, burned, trained, should, words, etc.
    b. The division of words of more than one syllable should be logical—between syllables:

        evi-dent          inter-action
        boy-ish           accom-modate
        treat-ment        com-pound
        divid-ing         some-times
        con-clusion       per-form-ing

8. The hyphen helps to differentiate the intended meaning of otherwise ambiguous phrases:

    three-hundred-gallon drums      a slow-moving truck
    three hundred-gallon drums      a slow moving truck

## Italics

When writers want to indicate that words or phrases should appear in italics, they merely underline them in the manuscript. The following types of material require italics:

1. Names of magazines, newspapers, books, or plays.

    We read that in *The Wall Street Journal* yesterday.

    *Alaska*, a novel by James Michener, provides the reader with a great deal of good historical background about the state.

    *Waiting for Godot*, a drama by Samuel Beckett, provides some glimpses of our style and times.

2. Names of works of art and music:

    *Beethoven's Fifth Symphony*

    *The Mona Lisa*

    *The Wild Duck*

3. Foreign words and expressions not yet assimilated (Americanized) enough to be a part of the vocabulary. A dictionary can be of help in deciding about such expressions.

    *fait Accompli*          *ideé fixé*          *quid pro quo*

4. Words or phrases that a writer wants to emphasize.

   Italicizing too many words for the sake of emphasis can be a devastating practice, however. But used with discrimination, this type of emphasizing can be effective.

   Who are *we* to judge his motives?

   Education is the *process* of learning, not the *accumulation* of dozens of tiny details.

## Apostrophe

The apostrophe has three uses, each one signalling a specific meaning to the reader. The omission or improper addition of an apostrophe not only can send the wrong message but also mark the sender as a careless if not illiterate writer.

1. *In Contractions:*
   *The apostroph*e indicates the point at which a letter (s) or part of a number is missing. The use of contractions is very common in dialects and in writing when trying to emulate specific speaking idiosyncracies of a region or people.

   | can't | cannot | mid- '80s |
   | don't | do not | class of '92 |
   | aren't | are not | it's   it is |
   | 'twas | it was | |
   | runnin' | running | |

   Writers of formal English (reports, proposals, articles, etc.) avoid using contradictions in their writing.

2. *In Possessives:*
   The apostrophe in the final syllable of an English noun signals possession. Most singular possessive nouns end in an 's and most plural possessives in s'.

   girl's hat—the hat of one girl

   girl's hats—the hats of one girl

   girls' books—the books of more than one girl

   girls' club—a club for girls.

   Nouns that do not add the *s* to form their plurals require the *'s* for their possessive:

   child's hat—hat of one child
   children's hats—hats of more than one child.

Compound hyphenated nouns add the 's possessive to the last word of the string. Such words form their plural by an *s* added to the first word of the string:

mother-in-law's coat
sister-in-law's cousin
somebody else's proposal

sisters-in-law's problem
brothers-in-law's business

3. *For Plural of Numbers, Letters, Symbols, and Words used as Words:*

Do not use so many "uh's" in your speaking.

Your "you know's" do not add anything to your speech.

He received all A's this semester.

You had better mind your p's and q's this year.

It was difficult to distinguish his 5's from his 6's.

## Punctuation with Abbreviations

When used within a sentence, either a comma, dash, or parenthesis appears in front of them; a comma separates them from the words that follow;

| etc. | (and so forth) | *et cetera* |
| et al. | (and others) | *et alii* or *et alia* |
| e.g. | (for example) | *exempli gratia* |
| i.e. | (namely, that is) | *id est* |
| viz. | (namely) | *videlicet* |

## Acronyms—Punctuation Conventions

Acronyms derive from the initial letter of each word of long titles and usually do not have periods after the individual letters. However, each one appears as a capital letter. Using an acronym without first providing all the words the letters represent can be confusing to an uninformed audience and the basis of a communication breakdown. To avoid any misunderstanding, the full phrase should appear the first time used with its acronym following immediately in parentheses:

The *U*nited *N*ations *E*ducation, *S*cientific, and *C*ultural *O*rganization (UNESCO) supports projects for better living and healthier living for peoples around the world.

The writer may use the acronym for any additional references in the article. In fact, the use of the full name several times—if a long title—would clutter the writing.

Some acronyms or abbreviations, such as YMCA, YWCA, ABC-TV, NBC-TV, are so general and well understood that they may no longer need prefacing with the full phrase. Others, such as *radar* and *laser,* have actually become words better known and understood than the words each letter represents. In scientific and technical writing, the acronym is easier to wield than repeatedly using the longer, wordier, and often Latin phrasing of the original version.

The increasing use of acronyms is evident in all areas, particularly for names of committees or commissions in business, government, or universities. Examples of some of these words would include the following:

| | |
|---|---|
| Home Ownership Savings Trust | (HOST) |
| Drug Asset Recovery Team | (DART) |
| Tuition Incentive Program | (TIP) |
| Student Assistance Program | (SAP) |
| Michigan Opportunity and Skills Training | (MOST) |

A recent Associated Press (AP) article provided the following hardcharging handles for narcotic enforcement and programs that have descriptive names for what they are talking about:

| | |
|---|---|
| Bay Area Narcotic Enforcement Team | (BAYONET) |
| Fugitive Investigative Strike Team | (FIST) |
| Down River Area Narcotic Organization | (DRANO) |

## Questions

Part I  Various Types of Punctuation Uses

1. In your reading—articles or textbooks—find three examples for each of the following punctuation marks. Explain why the author(s) selected them.

   | | |
   |---|---|
   | comma | quotation marks |
   | semicolon | parentheses |
   | colon | hyphen |
   | dash | apostrophe |

2. Write out one sentence of your own or select one from something you have written illustrating the use of each of the punctuation marks listed above.

3. Which of the marks do you use most often in your writing? Does your area of specialization have any influence on your use?

4. What abbreviations does the style manual of your professional society approve?

5. Make a list of common and frequently used words in your area of specialty that require a hyphen.

Part II  Sentences for Correction

Correct the punctuation in the following sentences. Explain the reason for any of your changes.

1. The equipment is in very poor condition, the belt is worn as well as the wall plug.

2. You have decided to apply for another position, you're forsaking your home town forever.

3. It had snowed and frozen the night before, therefore, our trip to the cottage at the lake was risky at best.

4. The group waited patiently at the station, the bus never arrived.

5. The Department of Health and Education has sponsored many safety programs, three-fourths of them, however, have had little effect on the accident rate.

6. The rejection of middle class values, and rules opens the door for acceptance of deviant life styles as a means to gain status, and material objects.

7. To choose what is briefly gratifying regardless of the consequences, is to choose the aesthetic life.

8. His biggest mistake however, was deciding to sell his oil stock, and buy municipal bonds.

9. The business office notified us that any students, who had not paid all of their bills by Tuesday, would not be able to graduate at the June ceremony.

10. You should guard against overstatement in your reports some people might question your motives.

11. His greatest error in judgment, was his decision to sell his house and cabin.

12. What he said to the judge, was kept in strictest confidence until after the trial.

13. Ticket voucher requests, which are not accompanied by the signature of the supervisor, will not be issued.

14. Mr. Richards, red-faced and puffing appeared in the window, just behind his son.

15. When the quantity is an unknown science adopts the symbol X or Y to indicate it.

16. Becoming known, means getting involved in community affairs.

17. He always has some useful historical information available, since he keeps his files up-to-date.

18. The multi-level home situated in a quiet affluent, neighborhood was the perfect backdrop for that commercial.

19. On this particular day, I not only won the street fight, but also made peace as well.

20. When that nature and wild flower trail was closed; it was only a small segment of the trail system in the state.


Part III Questions—Colon, Dash, Quotations, Apostrophe
1. The main topics to be covered in this report are: the increase in adult crime and the influence of the television hero on the viewers.

2. Many times success is measured by the big events; a substantial raise, an important promotion, and significant publicity.

3. Boards of Education are influenced in making decisions by: students, teachers, and administrators.

4. Some of the employees demands, such as: those for a guaranteed annual wave and for a two-week vacation pay, will be ruled out by that company.

5. Bill Andrews, everyone knew Bill andrews—was the most well qualified candidate for that position.

6. Guiding and directing students in areas they may plan to make into a lifes work is interesting and challenging.

7. The need for security by todays youth is the result of two major forces; unsettled world conditions and changing family relationships.

8. Was it possible that the doctor said, "There is no hope?"

9. Didn't Adams say, "I want to assist you in every day I can with your new business?"

10. Since I was the oldest I was the 'trail blazer' in everything, sports, games, and of course, school work.

11. At that time, the inspector would not determine whether the discharge was completely "safe".

12. "Up to this time", he said, "we cannot provide a dollar figure for the cost of the river clean-up".

# 10 Editing Challenges: Word Usage—Diction

Usage in English refers to understanding the exact definition and application of words similar in sound or meaning. Occasionally, the writer has some leeway with such words; however, often misusing a word has a detrimental impact on the reader, but writers who use words carefully show a high degree of professionalism. An awareness of differences in usage and diction raises the writer's consciousness and can affect a close reading of the text. Thus, understanding differences in usage and diction is very important. Following is a list of commonly misused words and phrases, along with examples of their accepted usage. Students often ask who determines nuances of meaning and correctness. A good reference source is *The American Heritage Dictionary* or any other dictionary that employs a "Usage Panel" of writers to determine how contemporary writers use such words. Such dictionaries provide explicit definitions for words of ambiguous usage. Dictionaries are worth consulting whenever a writer doubts the exact meaning of a word.

## Words that Sound Alike

**Accept/Except**

Both words function as verbs.

*Accept* means to receive, admit, or include:

We will *accept* your offer.

*Except* means to exclude or to exempt:

I will *except* you from doing the assignment because you have been sick.

*Except* also works as a preposition:

No one *except* Fred passed the examination.

**Adopt/Adapt**

*Adopt* means to accept

We will *adopt* the new procedures.

*Adapt* means to change according to circumstances:

Animals learn to *adapt* to their environment.

**Advice/Advise**

For some pairs of words, the noun form contains a **c** and the verb form contains an **s**:

*Advice* is a noun; *advise* is a verb:

I received good financial *advice*.

The counselor *advises* students about graduation requirements.

*Device* is a noun; *devise* is a verb;

The *device* did not work as well as he had hoped.

He *devised* a plan of action.

*Prophecy* is a noun; *prophesy* is a verb:

The Old Testament *prophecy* came true.

The broker *prophesied* that the Dow average would continue to climb.

*Revise* is a verb:

He needed to *revise* his manuscript.

**Affect/Effect**

As a general rule, *affect* as a verb means to influence or impress:

The drug *affected* his sense.

She *affected* a knowledge of Latin.

A verb form of *effect* also exists. It means to bring about change:

The government *effected* a change in trading policies.

*Effect* as a noun means result:

The *effect* of the drug wore off after two hours.

**Allusion/Illusion**

*Allusion* is a reference to something:

His *allusion* to Shakespeare's *Hamlet* impressed the professor.

*Illusion* is a fantasy:

I saw an optical *illusion* in the desert.

## Breath/Breathe

*Breath* is a noun.

She struggled to catch her *breath*.

*Breathe* is a verb.

She will *breathe* a sigh of relief when she graduates.

## Capitol/Capital

*Capitol* refers to a building:

We visited the *capitol* rotunda.

Capital refers to a geographical or political center, to material wealth, or to the chief or main thing:

The *capital* of Michigan is Lansing.

We needed more *capital* to secure the loan.

That was a capital idea.

## Censor/Censure

*Censor* as a verb means to cut out, examine, or remove objectionable ideas. *Censor as a noun* refers to the person responsible for the deleting of materials:

Hollywood producers would like the authority to *censor* their own movies.

The *censor* decided to cut the scene from the show.

*Censure* is a verb that means to criticize or to disapprove of something:

The union *censured* the company for unfair labor practices.

## Choose/Chose/Chosen

*Choose* is the present tense of the verb. *Chose* is the past tense.
Chosen is the past participle:

We need to *choose* a new chairperson.

They *chose* a new delegate to the assembly.

We *have chosen* a new representative.

### Cite/Site/Sight

*Cite* means to identify:

He *cited* five sources in his study.

*Site* refers to a place:

They had to choose a new building *site*.

*Sight* is visual:

He had very good eye*sight*.

### Clothe/Cloth

*Clothe* is a verb:

They need to *clothe* themselves.

*Clothes* refers to garments.

We purchased new *clothes* for the kids.

*Cloth* refers to items of fabric:

I need to find a polishing *cloth*.

### Complacent/Complaisant

*Complacent* is an adjective that means smug.

Her *complacent* attitude gets her into trouble.

*Complaisant* is an adjective that means agreeable:

Her *complaisant* attitude makes her a joy to be around.

### Complement/Compliment

*Complement* (a verb or a noun) means go with or complete.

Right angles *complement* each other.

Ms. DeRossett, the designer, says that blue is a *complement* of orange.

*Compliment* (a verb or a noun) means praise:

I *complimented* Loren on her taste in clothes.

Give my *compliments* to the chef.

### Contemptible/Contemptuous

*Contemptible* is an adjective that refers to *deserving* contempt:

Your attitude is *contemptible*.

*Contemptuous* is an adjective that refers to *feeling* contempt:

Your *contemptuous* opinions upset everyone.

## Continually/Continuously

*Continually* is an adverb that means intermittent:

Cats *continually* clean themselves.

*Continuously* is an adverb that means constant:

The sun shines *continuously* somewhere on Earth.

## Council/Counsel

*Council* is a noun or adjective that refers to a group of people:

We attended the meeting of the *council*.

We attended the *council* meeting.

*Counsel* is a noun or a verb that refers to giving advice:

I tried to give her good *counsel*.

I *counseled* her to quit smoking.

Consequently, a *councilor* is someone who serves on a council, whereas a *counselor* is someone who gives advice:

I met with my city *councilor* to discuss the tax rate.

They met with a marriage *counselor*.

## Divers/Diverse

*Divers* is an adjective that means several or many:

This investment offers *divers* opportunities.

*Diverse* is an adjective that means disperate:

It was a *diverse* group of students.

## Elicit/Illicit

*Elicit* is a verb that means to provoke a response:

We will *elicit* help from the committee.

*Illicit* is an adjective that means illegal:

He was arrested for carrying an *illicit* substance.

**Eminent/Imminent/Immanent**

*Eminent* is an adjective that means famous.

The Pope is an *eminent* person.

*Imminent* is an adjective that means just about to happen:

He thought that his promotion was *imminent*.

*Immanent* is an adjective that means inherent or objective

Diamonds have *immanent* value.

**Insure/Ensure/Assure**

*Insure* and *ensure* are verbs that mean guarantee or passify:

I need to *insure* my new car.

We need to *ensure* them that we can complete the project on time.

*Assure* is a verb that refers to a state of mind:

I can *assure* you that your daughter will be safe.

Note: *Insure* once referred only to insurance matters, but is now an acceptable synonym for *ensure*.

**Lay/Lie**

*Lay* (lay, laid, have/has laid, laying) is a transitive verb meaning to place or put:

I *lay* the book on the table

I *laid* the book on the table.

I *have laid* the book on the table.

*Lie* (lies, lay, lain, lying) is an intransitive verb meaning to rest or recline:

I want to *lie* down.

I *lay* down last night, but I could not sleep.

I *have lain* around all morning.

**Led/Lead**

*Led* is the past tense of the verb to *lead*:

If you will *lead*, I will follow.

The committee members *led* me to the meeting.

*Lead* as a noun is an element:

The X-ray room has *lead* walls.

**Loose/Lose**

*Loose* is an adjective that means unbridled and is the opposite of tight:

He wore a *loose* shirt.

The dog was running *loose*.

*Lose* is a verb that means to have misplaced something as well as being the opposite of win:

Did you *lose* your books?

They will *lose* the Series if they don't get better pitching.

**Morale/Moral**

*Morale* is a noun that refers to a positive mental attitude:

The team retained its good *morale* despite having lost the championship.

*Moral* is an adjective that refers to personal values:

Mark Twain wrote an essay on the "*moral* sense."

**Past/Passed**

*Past* is an adjective or noun that refers to time:

We can all learn from *past* mistakes.

We thought that she was living too much in the *past*.

*Passed* is a verb referring to move or put in motion:

We *passed* by the store but decided not to go inside.

**Personal/Personnel**

*Personal* is an adjective that means intimate or private:

Her decision to marry was a *personal* matter.

*Personnel* is a noun that refers to employees:

We need to hire more *personnel*.

**Precede/Proceed**

*Precede* is a verb that means to come before:

The speech will *precede* the banquet.

*Proceed* is a verb that means to move forward:

Before we *proceed* any further, we need to consider all facets of the problem.

**Prescribe/Proscribe**

*Prescribe* is a verb that means to order or advise:

The physician *prescribed* rest and antibiotics.

*Proscribe* means to forbid or to set forth:

A federal law *proscribes* smoking in airplanes.

**Principal/Principle**

*Principal* is a noun that refers to a person or to capital. As an adjective it means the main thing.

The *principal* of the school dismissed the student.

I went to the bank to discuss the *principal* and interest in my account.

To increase his income is the *principal* reason he works so much.

*Principle* is a noun that means rule or idea:

His new book is about the basic *principles* of democracy.

**Stationary/Stationery**

*Stationary* is an adjective that means to remain in one place:

Despite the earthquake, the buildings remained *stationary*.

*Stationery* is a noun that refers to paper:

I need to buy some new *stationery* for my business.

**There/Their/They're**

*There* is an adverb that refers to place:

*There* we had a nice view of the city.

*Their* is a plural possessive pronoun:

*Their* income increased dramatically once they started their own business.

*They're* is a contraction (they are):

*They're* trying to find an equitable solution.

**Too/To/Two**

*Too* is an intensifier and is a synonym for also:

She was *too* late to enter the contest.

She wanted to attend the conference, *too*.

*To* is a preposition and also an indicator for an infinitive:

We went *to* Chicago last summer.

They wanted *to* surprise me.

*Two* is a number:

The *two* of us have been friends for many years.

### Your/You're

*Your* is a possessive pronoun:

*Your* car is in the way.

*You're* is a contraction (you are):

*You're* going to have a great time.

## The Problem of Dropped D's

Certain expressions lend themselves to a dropped D if the writer is not careful:

We *used* to be friends.
(Not: We *use* to be friends.)

We were *supposed* to meet at noon.
(Not: We were *suppose* to meet at noon.)

He was a *prejudiced* person.
(Not: He was a *prejudice* person.)

She was a *biased* person.
(Not: She was a *bias* person.)

## Common Mix-ups

**Agree with** is correct—not agree at:

We *agreed with* her proposal.

**Aggravate** means to make something worse:

Complaining will only *aggravate* the situation.

(It does not mean to irritate. Not: His constant talking during the lecture aggravated me.)

**Also,** an adverb, often does not make a good beginning to a sentence. *Furthermore* is a good substitute:

*Furthermore*, I would like to propose a change in plans.
(Not: Also, I would like to propose a change in plans.)

You are **angry with** a person and **angry at** a thing.

I was *angry with* her.
I was *angry at* the car.

Likewise, you are **annoyed with** a person and **annoyed at** a thing:

I was *annoyed with* her behavior.
I was *annoyed at* circumstances.

**Apt/Liable/Likely** have distinct meanings.

*Apt* means appropriate:

The project was *aptly* done.

*Liable* means accountable:

They are *liable* if an accident should occur.

*Likely* means probably:

He will *likely* retire next year.

**As** is a conjunction or an adverb. **Like**, however, is a preposition.

Is the situation as bad *as it seems*?

My sister is *like me*.

**Bi** means two; therefore, biannual means every two years, bi-weekly means every two weeks, and bi-monthly means every two months:

The next meetings of that *biannual* conference will be in 1992 and 1994.

**Semi** means half; therefore semi-annually means every six months:

The store has two *semi-annual* sales: one during the summer and another sometime around Christmas.

**The Bible** is not put in quotation marks nor italicized:

I am taking a course in the Bible as literature.

Lowercase letters are standard when not referring to the scriptures:

His book is the bible of economics.

You **bring** things to someone or something. You **take** them away:

*Bring* your papers to my office.

I will *take* the grades to the records office.

**But, and, for, or, so,** and **nor** are not always appropriate words to begin a sentence:

*But* I think we need a new strategy.

*However,* I think we need a new strategy.

**Convince** means to change a point of view. **Persuade** means to cause something to happen:

He *convinced* me that his decision was the correct one.

We *persuaded* Dr. Madison to accept the new position.

**Disinterested** means unbiased; **uninterested** means not caring, lacking in interest:

I was a *disinterested* bystander.

The students were *uninterested* in the lecture.

**Dose** is a verb. It is also a noun used as an abbreviation of dosage and a word pertaining to the individual application of a drug. **Dosage** pertains to the amount of the drug administered:

He *dosed* the cat with the usual medication.

He received a *dose* of penicillin.

We will need to increase the *dosage*.

**Erratic** is an adjective that describes behavior. **Sporadic** is an adjective that describes iregular occurrances:

The boy's behavior was *erratic*.

The sound occurred in *sporadic* bursts.

**Etc.** is an abbreviation of *et cetera,* meaning so forth (best used sparingly):

His presentation involved slides, charts, *etc*.
(Not: His presentation involved slides, charts, *ect.*)

**Expect** means to anticipate; it is not a synonym for suspect:

I will *expect* you to be there at noon.
(Not: I *expect* that she has had an accident.)

**Feel** is an emotional state or a physical sensation. It is not a synonym for *think*:

*I think* the proposal is illogical (Not: *I feel* that the proposal is illogical.)

I *felt* sad about his accident.

**Hanged** refers to execution; **hung** refers to suspension:

The spy was *hanged* by the Iraqi government.

The tools *hung* in the shed.

**Have** is a verb of ownership and an auxiliary verb. **Of,** a preposition, is not a substitute for have:

I *have* several books on the subject.

I should *have gone* to the reception.
(Not: I should *of gone* to the reception.)

**Hopefully** is an adverb meaning with hope, a cliche too often used instead of *I hope:*

*I hope* that the plane will not crash.
(Not: *Hopefully*, the plane will not crash.)

I went *hopefully* to the bank to apply for a loan.

**Hypothesis** is a noun which refers to an untried assertion. **Theory** is a noun that refers to a systemized explanation of generally accepted principles.

I have a *hypothesis* about who stole my computer.

Einstein has given us many *theories* about the universe.

**Imply** means someone suggests something. **Infer** means someone concludes something from someone else or something else.

He *implied* that *he* was going to resign.

We *inferred* from *his anger* that he was going to resign.

**In** refers to placement. **Into** involves action:

He is *in* the English Center.

I went *into* the room.

**Irregardless,** a double negative, is not an acceptable substitute for **regardless:**

*Regardless* of your position in the company, you still need to assert yourself.

**Its** is a possessive form. **It's** is a contraction of *it is:*

The dog hurt *its* foot.
(Not: The dog hurt *it's* foot.)

*It's* going to be a great day.

**Lend** is a verb; **loan** is a noun but may be used informally as a verb:

Please *lend* me some money.

I went to the bank to apply for a *loan*.

Please *loan* me some money (informal usage).

**Mad** is an adjective that means insane or irrational; in informal usage it may be used in place of *angry*.

The situation was driving me *mad*.

I was *angry* with him.

I was *mad* at him. (informal usage)

**Momentarily** refers to the near future or at any time. **Temporarily** refers to being limited by time:

She will return *momentarily*.

It is *temporarily* out of commission.

**Most** is an indefinite pronoun and not a synonym for **almost**:

*Most* of them have arrived safely.
(Not: *Most* everyone has seen a picture of the Grand Canyon. Instead: Almost everyone has seen a picture of the Grand Canyon.)

**Myself** is a reflexive pronoun, not used in place of **me** or **I**:

I thought about *myself* as a teacher in a foreign country.

I told a story about *myself*.

They presented the award to Jones and *me*.
(Not: They presented the award to Jones and myself.)

Jane and *I* were welcomed at the conference in Chicago.
(Not: Jane and myself were welcomed at the conference in Chicago.)

**Nauseate** is a verb. Nauseous is an adjective:

The chemical fumes *nauseated* me.

It was a *nauseous* experience.

**Notorious** has a negative connotation and is not a synonym for famous:

He was a *notorious* gangster.

**Over with** is redundant:

> The game was *over*.
> (Not: The game was over with.)

**Presently** is an adverb that means soon. It does not mean at present.

> We will *presently* arrive.

> I am *at present* working in the Midwest.
> (Not: I am *presently* working in the Midwest.)

**Proved** is now the acceptable past participle of prove. **Proven** is an adjective:

> This procedure *has proved* safe.

> This is a *proven* commodity.

**Quote,** a verb, is unacceptable as an abbreviation for **quotation,** a noun:

> The newspaper *quoted* her in a story.

> The *quotation* came from Shakespeare's *Hamlet*.

**Raise** is a transitive verb or noun that means to lift or increase. **Rise** is an intransitive verb that refers to upward movement:

> The soldiers will *raise* the flag.

> I asked my supervisor for a *raise* in salary.

> The price of housing will *rise* with inflation.

**Rational** is an adjective that means logical. **Rationale** is a noun that means reason. **Rationalize** means to provide an excuse:

> Let us try to be more *rational* in our decision-making.

> What is the *rationale* behind your proposal?

> He will probably *rationalize* that the goods would not have sold anyway.

**Real** is an adjective that means genuine—not very, which is an intensifier:

> Is this *real* wood?

> I was *very* disappointed.
> (Not: I was *real* disappointed.)

**Respectfully** is an adverb that means with respect. **Respectively** is an adverb that means one after the other:

> We listened to the lecturer *respectfully*.

> We have lived in Chicago, Detroit, and Santa Fe, *respectively*.

**Sit** is an intransitive verb that means to take a position. **Set** is a transitive verb that means to place or put:

>The boxes *sit* in the corner.

>He *set* the boxes in the corner.

**That**, a relative pronoun, introduces an essential clause or phrase. The relative pronoun **which** introduces a non-essential one:

>Dogs *that* have rabies need quarantining.

>Dogs, *which* make nice pets, are often silly creatures.

**Themselfs** is an incorrect reflexive form for themselves:

>They need to learn to do something for *themselves*.
>(Not: They need to learn to do something for themselfs.)

**This** and **That** are demonstrative pronouns that refer to one. **These** and **Those** are demonstrative pronouns that refer to more than one:

>*That kind* of project interests me.

>*This kind* of project interests me.

>*Those kinds* of things never work right.
>(Not: *These kind* of things never work right.)

>*Those kinds* of cars have poor gas mileage.

**Thusly** is archaic, as are **firstly, secondly, thirdly,** and so forth:

>*Thus,* this proved correct.
>(Not: Thusly, this proved correct.)

>*Second,* he noted the problem of absenteeism.
>(Not: Secondly, he noted the problem of absenteeism.)

**Whether** expresses an alternative in which "or not" is implied. **If** expresses a situation in which there are no alternatives.

>We cannot decide *whether* to go.
>(Not: We cannot decide if we should go.)

>What would she do *if* he were to leave the company.

**Whose** is a possessive pronoun. **Who's** is a contraction for *who is:*

>*Whose* car is this?

>*Who's* going with you to Detroit?

**-wise** and **-ize** are trite suffixes that offend some people:

He did *well in business* last year.
(Not: He did well businesswise last year.)

We need to *complete* this study.
(Not: We need to *finalize* this study.)

## One Word or Two

**A lot** are always two words:

*A lot* of us were unhappy with the situation.
(Not: Alot of us were unhappy with the situation.)

**Already**, an adverb, is a time reference. **All ready** describes a group:

Is he here *already*?

We were *all ready* to begin the project.

**All right** are always two words:

His decision was *all right* with me.
(Not: His decision was alright with me.)

**Altogether** means entirely. **All together** describes a group:

We were *altogether* pleased with his efforts.

We were *all together* for the first time.

**Anyone** is an indefinite pronoun. **Any one** describes a group:

Is *anyone* there?

*Any one* of these will work.

The indefinite pronouns **anything, anywhere, anybody,** and **anyhow** are one word. **Any more** is a phrase:

If *anything* can go wrong, it will.
I cannot take *any more* of this medicine.

**Awhile** is an adverb. **A while** uses while as a noun:

She arrived *awhile* ago.

*A while* passed before we left.

**Maybe** means perhaps. **May be** is part of a predicate:

*Maybe* we will come; I'm not certain.

She *may be* stranded at the station.

# Words That Go Together

**Anyone** or **everyone** used in a comparison requires **else**:

He is smarter than *anyone else*.

*Everyone else* passed the test.

We **compare something with** something else, and we **contrast something to** something else:

They *compared* our program *with* theirs.

They *contrasted* our program *to* theirs.

Note: A comparison focuses on similarities while a contrast focuses on differences.

**Different from** is correct:

Your experiences are *different from* mine.
(Not: Your experiences are different than mine.)

**Not only** requires **but also** to reinforce parallel structure:

He is *not only* a good teacher *but also* an effective leader.
He enjoys *not only to see* plays *but also* to hear a symphony.

**Other** requires the use of **any** in a comparison:

He is faster than *any other* runner in the race.
(Other is necessary because he, too, is a runner in the race.)

**So** requires a **that**:

He was *so* happy that he went out to celebrate.
(Not: He was so happy.)

**Split infinitives,** while not always avoidable, are usually awkward:

He decided *to drive* slowly around the corner.
(Not: He decided to slowly drive around the corner.)

# Referring to Two or More

### Between/Among

*Between* refers to two people or things. *Among* refers to more than two:

*Between* the two of them, John was the better student.

*Among* the three of them, I prefer John.

This same principle applies to **comparatives** and **superlatives**. The comparative (-er, -ier, more) refers to two, whereas the superlative (-est, -iest, most) refers to more than two:

She is the *older of the two sisters.*

He is the *tallest person in the room.*

He is the *more intelligent of the two* brothers.

She is the *most intelligent student in the class.*

## Quantitative Differences

### Farther/Further

*Farther* refers to distance. *Further* refers to degree; it may also mean "additional":

How many miles *farther*?

The *further* my imagination goes, the more confused I become.

Can you provide *further* information?

### Fewer/Less

*Fewer* precedes nouns that are countable; *less* precedes nouns that are not countable:

*Fewer people* are here today.

I have *less time* now for this project.

### Number/Amount

*Number* refers to nouns that are countable. *Amount* refers to nouns that are not countable.

The *number of people* at the concert impressed us.

The *amount of knowledge* he possessed was impressive.

*The number* takes a singular verb. *A number* requires a plural verb:

*The number* of students in the class *is* decreasing.

*A number* of people *have* died.

## Singular or Plural

Determining the plural form of words borrowed from foreign languages is sometimes difficult:

His *analysis is* correct.
Their *analyses are* correct.

What *basis exists* for that remark?
On what *bases are* you projecting your results?

I prefer to deal with *one crisis* at a time.
At present, we are coping with at least *three crises*.

My *thesis* sentence *is* a good one.
The graduate students completed *their theses*.

I have only *one criterion*.
What *are* the *criteria* for this recommendation?

The full moon is *a natural phenomenon*.
Earthquakes *are* natural *phenomena*.

We have only *one agendum* item.
(Note: This is an archaic usage.)
How many *items* are on our *agenda*?

I went to the *curriculum* committee meeting.
We need to improve *curricula* in the various colleges.
(Note: *Curricula* is accepted in formal writing; however, *curriculums* is more prevalent.)

Please refer to the *datum line*.
(Note: This is an obscure usage.)
*These data are* incorrect.

The *medium is* the message.
The news *media are* not always fair or accurate.

I wrote *a memorandum* for the file.
We need to distribute *these memoranda*.
(Note: *Memorandums* is also an acceptable plural form.)

*He* is an *alumnus* of the college.
*She* is an *alumna* of the college.
*We* are *alumni* of the college.
*Those women* are *alumnae* of the college.
(Note: This refers to graduates from an all-female college.)

*He* is a professor *emeritus*.
*They* are professors *emeriti*.

What is the *stimulus* for his behavior?
What *are* the *stimuli* for his behavior?

# Awkward Words and Phrases

**Anyways** is not a word.

> I decided to go *anyway*.
> (Not: I decided to go anyways.)

**As to** is better off written as **about**:

> She was confused *about* my intentions.
> (Not: She was confused as to my intentions.)

**At** with **where** is redundant:

> Does he know *where it is*?
> (Not: Does he know where it's at?)

**Being that** or **being as** are better off replaced with *because* or *since*:

> Since he was late, we refused to meet with him.
> (Not: Being that he was late, we refused to meet with him.)

**Beside** means next to. **Besides** means in addition to:

> I sat *beside* her.

> *Besides* taking English, I am also taking French.

**Can't but** is unnecessary:

> *I can't help thinking* that she is crazy.
> (Not: I *can't but help thinking* that she is crazy.)

> I think that she is crazy.

**Can** means a person is able to do something. **May** refers to asking permission to do something.

> *Can* you run five miles?

> *May* I have a drink of water?

You **center in** or **on** something—not *around* it. The same is true of focus:

> The discussion *centered on* politics.
> (Not: The discussion centered around politics.)

> The discussion *focused on* politics.
> (Not: The discussion focused around politics.)

**Contractions** are out of place in formal writing.

I *cannot* write a new proposal until next summer.
(Not: I *can't* write a new proposal until next summer.)

**Equally as** is redundant. Use one or the other:

Harvard is as prestigious as Yale.
(Not: Harvard is equally as prestigious as Yale.)

Harvard and Yale are equally prestigious.

**Is When/Is Because** constructions create cumbersome sentences:

This *is the time when* I think the meeting will occur.
(Not: This is when I think it will occur.)

This *occurred because* the temperature was too high.
(Not: This is because the temperature is too high.)

**Like for instance** is redundant and cumbersome:

Some events interest me, such as the World Series.
(Not: Some events interest me, *like for instance* the World Series.)

**Reverend** is an adjective, not a noun, and thus requires "the" in a title:

*The Reverend* John Adams was in town.
(Not: *Reverend* John Adams was in town.)

# Questions

Correct the usage and diction errors in the following sentences:

1. The student was pleased to have been excepted by such a highly ranked university.

2. The architect noted that the structure would be adopted to its building cite.

3. Thompson's negative response to the proposal aggravated his staff.

4. After sitting through such a long meeting in a stuffy room, Smith felt nauseously.

5. Jones noted that he was presently at work on a master's degree in public administration.

6. The affects of the drug wore off after one hour.

7. The employees were altogether for their first staff meeting.

8. The amount of emigrants coming into the country worried some of the local politicians.

9. Mr. Norman says that he is liable to attend the seminar.

10. The California system of higher education is comprised of many colleges and universities.

11. Ms. Derose explained that her principle reason for attending the conference was to meet perspective clients.

12. The councilor suggested that the student should receive additional therapy.

13. The review committee felt that Ms. Becker's data was inaccurate.

14. The coach noted that Ellman had been running good all week during practice.

15. The manager decided to draft a new personal policy for her unit.

16. After work, we were suppose to meet for dinner.

17. After the rally, Ms. Canavan preceeded to become more involved in politics.

18. His letter inferred that he was going to change his proposal.

19. The phenomena of bird migration is an interesting topic for study.

20. The three companies worked out an agreement between them.

Look up the different meanings of the following pairs of words and write a sentence using each correctly:

discreet/discrete

demur/demure

precision/accuracy

exalt/exult

flaunt/flout
healthy/healthful

former/latter

amend/emend

Keep a list of the words commonly misused by professionals in your field. Make sure that you understand the accepted meaning and usage of each word.

Part 3  *Application: Reporting the Message*

# 11 Professional Documents

Following are examples of different kinds of documents and assignments commonly used in professional writing. Although the formats for specific documents may vary from one profession or office to another, the following examples are good models for study and emulation.

## Paraphrasing

Paraphrasing a piece of writing is exactly the opposite of reacting to a piece of writing. Paraphrasing is an objective summary. Reacting is a subjective evaluation of the ideas and contents. Both are essential types of communication but have quite different purposes.

With the profusion of communication on all subjects, it is often difficult for everyone to be able to read all of the current pertinent literature. In some companies or departments, some members may be asked to provide quick summaries of various reports to the staff. This provides a large number of the staff access to new information when their own commitments encroach too heavily on their reading time. A paraphrased summary of some report or investigation by a staff member is one solution to the problem of trying to keep up with the latest in a particular specialization.

As stated before, paraphrasing is objective reporting. Thus, the writer doing the paraphrasing has a unique obligation.

**Steps in Paraphrasing:**
1. Read the article (report) thoroughly.
2. Put the meaning of the text in new words but keep the original meaning.
3. Substitute synonyms.
4. Rearrange sentence structure
5. Provide no reactive statements—no arguments for or against the text.
6. Avoid qualifying words, such as *rarely, generally, hardly* or such phrases as *I concurred, I believe,* or *I thought.*

Compare the following exact quotation with its paraphrase that follows. What are the differences?

### Exact Quotation

Foretelling what may happen to the world if it should warm by even one or two degrees is the toughest problem facing climatologists today. Even though there have been times in the dim geologic past when temperatures were warmer—with no ice at all on the polar regions—there are vast differences today. No one knows whether the "wild card" of human activity will disrupt or make more extreme the cycles ordained by nature.*

### Paraphrasing

The most difficult problem facing climatologists today is trying to determine what might occur should the world warm by one or two degrees. In our geologic past, there have been periods when the polar areas had no ice at all and the earth temperature was warmer. No one today can predict whether the "unknown quantity"—human activity and its ramifications—will or can prove more disruptive or even bring about dire extremes in the cycles of nature.

### Paraphrasing Assignment

Choose a paragraph or two from some newspaper, magazine, or journal concerned with an issue relevant to your field. Write a good paraphrase for your selection. Provide a full bibliographical citation for the source.

## Reaction Paper

A reaction paper is an evaluation paper. The evaluation may be favorable, unfavorable, or both. However, it is the reviewer's point of view about the context not necessarily the same as the original writer intended. There is nothing wrong about the reviewer or reactor disagreeing or maybe even misinterpreting the material. What is wrong is the readers accepting as fact the reviewer's viewpoint without question. In doing so, they are no longer independent thinkers and indicate it is very easy to lead them.

The following paragraph is a reaction to the exact quotation above and differs considerably from the paraphrase.

## Reaction

Today, our climatologists are attempting to determine what catastrophes await civilization if the world should warm by a few degrees. They are well aware that at one time in the far geologic past, earth temperatures were warmer and the polar areas devoid of ice. We all are aware that such knowledge should be of little comfort to today's populations. Obviously, the vast and unpredictable stepped-up human activity in all parts of the world can not help but provide for only an extremely disruptive effect on nature's ordained cycles.

---

*Samuel W. Matthews, "Is Our World Warming?," *National Geographic* (October, 1990), p. 77.

**Reaction Paper Assignment**

React to a newspaper or magazine article concerned with some important and current issue. Take a stand on the issue; that is either support or refute the position taken by the journalist or writer. Be sure to include a full bibliographical citation for the source article (Author's name, "Title," *Magazine or Newspaper,* Date, Page).

As you write, be aware of the *three basic elements* of a good paragraph. Each paragraph has one central idea as expressed in its topic sentence, usually the opening sentence.

Good paragraphs also contain a generous supply of *details* to clarify the idea expressed in the topic sentence. These details include such things as facts, statistics, observations, listings, examples, definitions or personal experiences. Each detail is one piece of the larger picture and adds to the interest and the information. Inadequate support—insufficient detail—will provide only a vague or even muddled impression for the reader.

Good paragraphs also have good "linking" devices. These are types of *transitions* that make the sentences within the paragraphs flow smoothly so the reader can follow the progression of thought easily from sentence to sentence. They act as signposts to the reader.

# Definition Paper

Defining is a narrowing or limiting process, distinguishing a particular word or concept from all others. A short phrase or one sentence may provide an adequate definition for such a simple term as "plagiarism"; that is, "the copying of another's work." However, providing a definition of a technical or social term, such as "consumerism," "corporate responsibility," or "bureaucrat" will require a much more extended discussion.

Writing a definition involves three basic steps: choosing the subject, establishing a formal definition, and expanding this definition.

Once you have chosen your topic, the next step is composing a one-sentence formal definition which will serve as the thesis sentence. In this way you put the term in a broad category and also note how it differs from others in the same category:

> Examples: "A pediatrician is a physician who limits his/her medical practice to the treatment of diseases in children."
>
> "Plastics are man-made materials, in contrast to nature's materials like wood and metal."

You can expand your definition by comparing your topic with another familiar item or concept, by analyzing or breaking the topic into separate categories, by providing illustrations or examples (especially good when defining abstract terms, such as happiness, respect, esteem), by saying what it isn't (negation), or by using a combination of these approaches.

> Example: "The Mysterious Placebo" (Opening paragraphs of an extended definition)
>
> The word *placebo* comes from the Latin verb meaning 'to please.' A placebo in the classical sense, then, is an imitation medicine—generally an innocuous milk-sugar tablet dressed up like an authentic pill—given more for the purpose of placating a patient than for meeting a clearly diagnosed organic need. The placebo's most frequent use in recent years, however, has been in the testing of new drugs.
>
> For a long time, placebos were in general disrepute with a large part of the medical profession. The term had connotations of quack remedies or "pseudomedicaments." Some considered them shortcuts for too busy doctors. Today, however, the once lowly placebo is receiving serious attention from even medical scholars. They are finding substantial evidence that the placebo not only can be made to look like a powerful medication but can actually act like a medication. Doctors may prescribe a placebo in cases where reassurance for the patient is far more useful than a famous-name pill three times a day.*

## Definition Paper Assignment

Write an extended definition of some term you are familiar with or are interested in clarifying for some audience. Some topic suggestions are "salesmanship," "preventive medicine," "isometric exercises," or some term from your field of study or occupation. When in your work might you have to resort to writing a definition?

# Process Paper

Explaining a process is one of the most widely used types of communication. The process explanation provides step-by-step directions about how to carry out a procedure or how to do something. Regardless of what field you may be working in or planning to work in (medicine, police work, social work, computer programming, engineering, science, teaching), you will find it essential at some time or other to explain a process.

Writing a process paper involves five basic steps:

1. **Develop the thesis statement.**
   After choosing your subject, develop the thesis statement which provides the focus and thus controls the direction of the explanation.

---

*Norman Cousins, "The Mysterious Placebo." *Saturday Review,* October 1, 1977, p. 9

Examples: Training my dog proved to be a very arduous and challenging task.

Film developing is a procedure not only demanding considerable knowledge but also requiring some very specific equipment.

2. **Compose the introduction.**
List any items needed and any special conditions or skills essential to a successful completion of the process.

3. **Order the steps.**
Include a list of the steps in the order in which your reader must complete them.

4. **Develop the steps.**
Provide the proper amount of detail to make the steps understandable to your audience. Besides discussing each one, indicate its value and purpose as well as how to perform it.

5. **Write the conclusion.**
Avoid an abrupt ending. Include a summary, an evaluation of the results, and an added comment about the importance of the process.

## Process Paper Assignment

Write a paper in which you explain how to do something or how something was done. Use the steps explained above as a guide.

# Analysis

Analysis is a useful way to explain a large or hard-to-grasp topic. An analysis paper breaks a broad topic into separate categories and then discusses these categories one at a time. The explanation is thus simplified, for a writer deals with the topic in small, manageable parts. This technique of organization is used frequently, for it is a natural way for the mind to deal with many subjects. It allows the reader to understand two things clearly: the separate categories and the way these categories relate to each other.

|  |  |  |
|---|---|---|
|  | (Title) | The Eternal <u>Triangle</u> in Personnel Affairs |
|  | Paragraph I: | Introduces the topic |
|  |  | "There are <u>three general philosophies</u> of personnel management. The first is based on <u>organizational theory</u>, the second on <u>industrial engineering</u>, and the third on <u>behavioral science</u>. |
|  | Paragraph II: | The organizational theorists believe that . . . |
| (beginning of topic sentences | Paragraph III: | The industrial engineer holds that man . . . |
|  | Paragraph IV: | The behavioral scientist focuses on group sentiment . . . |
|  | Paragraph V: | Summarizes: There is always a lively debate as to the overall effectiveness of <u>the approaches</u> in personnel management. . . . Actually the <u>three philosophies</u> can be depicted as a <u>triangle</u> with each one claiming the apex angle. |

You will notice that the topic sentences in the above paragraphs clearly indicate what the remaining subject matter of the paragraph will cover. The topic sentence, the first sentence of the paragraph, announces to the reader what the main idea of that paragraph is to be.

The following introductory sentences provide a good preview analysis of what their authors plan to say.

> Case analyses involve three basic steps: defining the problem, formulating and analyzing the alternatives in terms of strengths and weaknesses, and selecting the best alternative to recommend.

> Three fundamental feelings about labor and its organizations exist in our nation: those who feel there is absolutely no need for a union advocate the open shop; others who feel there is no need for a closed shop approach support the quasi-union attitude; and those who are totally committed to the union concept support the closed shop approach.

In reading that you do, how many articles or paragraphs show an analysis or division organization? How many paragraphs begin with a topic sentence?

## Writing Assignment: An Analysis (or Division) Paper

Choose some topic that interests you and develop your discussion by using analysis for your organizing pattern. Your paper should have five paragraphs—each headed by a topic sentence as shown in the example above.

# A Proposal

Realistically proposals can vary in length from the five-sentence memorandum to one of almost book length depending on the significance of the subject matter.

The format of a proposal should include some or all of the following parts:

- *Heading.* — State the subject.
- *Introduction.* — State exactly what you are proposing and why.
- *Statement of the Problem.* — Convince the reader that the problem or need exists and requires some immediate solution. Use evidence, such as statistics, personal experience, and opinions (outside experts or those of other colleagues or fellow workers).
- *Recommendations.* — Offer specific suggestions. Show the feasibility of the solution or plan. Mention the advantages of the change; perhaps even cite other companies or departments that have benefited from such an adoption.
- *Discussion of means of implementation.* — Discuss each step of implementation and mention any key personnel or facility changes possibly required.
- *Conclusion.* — Try to prove the feasibility of your proposal. Restate any benefits. Mention the consequences of nonadoption or the *status quo.* Stress the ease of implementation. Suggest meeting with the reader to discuss the proposal and perhaps to clarify some of the information.
- *Attachments.* — Add any display material or extra support material that if included in the body of the proposal would clutter and be an interruption in the presentation. This could include charts, testimonials, test results, etc.

Much planning and research should precede any proposal. The amount, of course, depends upon the subject of the proposal. Many good ideas may never gain favor simply because the writer fails to do adequate "homework." A proposal for new equipment or an addition of a new facility may have many readings—from the immediate supervisor or department head on up the ladder to the directors, or Chief Operating Officer. A good writer takes all of this into consideration in planning and writing his or her proposal.

## Proposal Assignment

Write a short proposal (3–5 pages) using the above guidelines.

# Memorandums

For the most part, memorandums are short letters used within organizations to provide data, announce or suggest policy changes, request action, give recommendations, explain procedures, etc. They are also the primary means by which members of an organization keep one another informed. Both your co-workers and your superiors may judge your professional ability somewhat by the memos you write. Thus, it is essential to your career that you learn how to make your memos clear, concise, and effective. Such messages need to be brief and readable.

Memos provide a flow of ideas among persons and departments of similar rank as well as those occupying different positions in the chain of command. Besides conveying information horizontally and vertically, memos provide a permanent record of actions and decisions.

Large companies very often have especially printed memo forms. However, if your company does not have such forms, the following pattern is the one usually used for the heading.

Date:
To:
From:
Subject:

It is important that the subject line reflects accurately whatever you are writing about. Otherwise, the message could go unread or be discarded entirely if the receiver felt the memo lacked relevance for the department.

## Memorandum Assignment 1: Prescription Outline for Writing

a. State in one sentence the nature of some problem in your area; then in two sentences, why you think the problem exists; then in two sentences, your suggestions to correct it.

b. Recommend some improvement of a specific facility, operation, or procedure in your department. In two sentences state the reason(s) for your recommendation; then in two sentences how you think the change could be implemented.

## Memorandum Assignment 2: Samples for Revision

1. Concerning: Electrical Problem

   All of the electrical outlets in our laboratory will be converted. In this way standard extensions can be utilized. Each time an outlet is used, an adapter must be located. We never use the three prong system, therefore they are not necessary. Implementation of this proposal could easily be conducted. An electrician will alleviate this problem.

2. Concerning: Office Rumors

    The nature of rumors in the field of public relations causes problems. It may be caused by the lack of authentic data or information. Rumors may also be caused by employees of an organization who may feel they are no longer in control of their own fate. Therefore, the state of rumors may be very satisfying when a rumor is stated, the correct information should immediately be provided. A healthy communication system should be maintained in order to prevent rumors.

3. Subject:

    Excessive noise in the office has become a problem because the only blockage of sound between desks is a small partition. Moreover, another reason heavier traffic in and out of the office has started. One way to alleviate the problem would be to put in larger office-like partitions to enclose the desks. A second way would be to provide a reception area for visitors rather than letting them disrupt employees.

# Trip Report

Reporting on trips as a part of an employment assignment is an important professional responsibility. Such trips can range from an afternoon visit to another business to a week- or two-week study seminar in another part of the country or world or to a regional or national conference concerned with some aspect of the work.

Anytime an employee is on company business away from the regular routine, he or she will be expected to file a report on these activities. Trip or travel reports serve three functions: inform colleagues of activities outside the plant, clinic, or office; document whatever seen or learned; and provide information for use in later reports or research projects. Such trips may be field trips, site inspections, study seminars, or just daily investigations of some project.

Trip reports need to be written promptly before important items are forgotten. Also they should include only relevant details not everything seen or done, such as where you stayed or what you had to eat.

## Trip Report Assignment

Write a trip report about some field trip or work-related activity that you have taken or participated in during the last few weeks. Indicate why you took the trip, any individuals you met, what you learned, and how that information is relevant or important to you or your work. Your report should be approximately 400–500 words long.

# Letter of Inquiry (for Information) or Application

A letter of inquiry is a request to an outside source (a person, a governmental unit, or a company) for needed information. You might want further information about some piece of equipment, some subject you had read about in a magazine or newspaper, a clarification of some statistics or rating programs, or just additional material about a subject that interests you. The answers that you request should not be ones that are easily available to you in reference books, journals, or other such sources.

Besides the usual *Heading,* a letter of inquiry has three rather distinct sections:

- Section I. Identify yourself. Indicate the general subject of your request for information. State why you need it.
Some organizations or individuals might be reluctant to provide information for unknown reasons to unknown writers; thus, out of courtesy, explain your interest and how you plan to use any of the material furnished you. Also mention why you have addressed your request to this particular person or organizations.
- Section II. Mention the points that you would like to have answered or further explained. Frame your questions in such a way that your source could answer them in a few short sentences.
- Section III. Make the final section a brief one. Express your appreciation. If appropriate, offer to send a copy of your finished report showing how you used the requested materials. Avoid writing "Thank you in advance for your help." This presumes too much on your source.

## Letter of Inquiry Assignment: For Information

Write a letter of inquiry using the above guidelines.

# Letter of Inquiry
# (for position)

(to company to determine openings in your field)

Date

To:

From:

Concerning:

    Purpose of letter—to inquire whether the company (school) has any positions open in your field.

    Provide significant experience in your field which could make you a desirable employee for that company (or school). Also mention specific courses taken or outside interests that might recommend you as a likely prospect in case there is an opening.

    Refer to your attached résumé and list of references. Mention the availability of other credentials (where they are on file and how to obtain them).

    Restate your interest in the company (school). State your availability for interviews and that you will look forward to hearing from them.

Enclosure

## Letter of Inquiry Assignment: For Position

Write a letter of inquiry for a position using the above suggestions.

# Letter of Application

(to officials of schools or company in which you know openings exist in your field)

> Return Address
> City, State Zip Code
> Date

Inside Address to Company

Title

City, State Zip Code

Subject: Application for . . .

Purpose of letter—identify position for which you are applying. Mention briefly source of information concerning opening.

Explain concisely why you are interested in working for this particular institution or company and your interest in this type of endeavor. If you have had related experience, point out briefly your achievements in the field.

Refer to the attached résumé and the availability of references (if not included).

Indicate where any other credentials are on file.

Restate your interest by indicating your availability for an interview.

Full Name Signed

Full Name Typed

Enclosures

## Letter of Application Assignment

Write a letter of application using the above format.

# Personal Data Sheet (Résumé)

The résumé (data sheet or vita) is a factual and concise summary of a person's qualifications for some position. It is a persuasion instrument, actually the initial personal "representative." It is a one or two page outline that would accompany a letter of application. Its main purpose is to present any qualifications accurately and quickly so that a busy department head or personnel manager may read it and be impressed enough to want an interview. Obviously, the résumé should not include any mention of salary or fringe benefits expected, travel restrictions, or work schedule preferences.

## Personal Data Sheet (résumé) Assignment

Prepare a résumé that you would be proud to send to any possible employer. It should be neat, easy to read, and well organized. The accompanying sample indicates the major information to include on a data sheet. It is necessary to select and emphasize the skills and employment opportunities most relevant to a position. Any professional person should always have an up-to-date résumé on file. Writing a good résumé takes time, time a person may not have if some opportunity for a change of positions should come along quickly. Use the following example as a guideline.

# Sample Resumé

William E. Smith  
2853 South Oak Drive  
Cleveland, Ohio 34900  
Phone: (256) 387-2624

| | |
|---|---|
| <u>Professional Objective</u> | Marketing Analyst or Retail Sales Manager |
| <u>Education</u> | MBA Western Michigan University, April 1989<br>BBA Western Michigan University, April 1987<br>Major: Marketing<br>Minors: Accounting, Business Law<br>Considerable work in data processing<br>Internship in Sales, Fall Semester, 1988, at the Role Company Outlet in Muskegon. |
| <u>Experience</u> | |
| 1989–Present | Majors, Inc., Cleveland, Ohio<br>Coordinator for all storewide modernization and merchandising reorganizations. |
| 1987–1989 | Industrials, Inc., Kalamazoo, Michigan<br>Assistant to the manager in charge of all advertising and copy layout for this large retail outlet. Worked closely with buyers in sales campaigns. |
| 1985–1987 | Woodsons, Inc., Kalamazoo, Michigan<br>Started as assistant to display manager. Promoted to sales promotions at the end of three months. |
| Summers 1981–1985 | Assistant to the Manager of the Hillside Club Pro Shop. Also in charge of the caddy corps and served as starter for tournaments and busy weekend play. |
| <u>Military Service</u> | |
| 1979–1981 | United States Navy, Communications Specialist<br>Most of tour of duty in the Far East (Japan and Korea) as a Communications and Personnel Relations Coordinator. |
| <u>Background</u> | Born in Marquette, Michigan, but moved with my family to Detroit when I was five years old. Always interested in community affairs. Served on several teen-adult community study committees. |
| <u>Interests</u> | Enjoy symphony and chamber music concerts. Play tennis and golf and am a football and basketball armchair sportsman. |
| <u>References</u> | List three references with all information: title, company, address, phone. |

# 12 Formal Report

## The Structure of the Formal Report

Following are the basic components of a formal report, an essential communications tool for most businesses and professions.

The purpose of the formal report is to convey accurate and thorough information in as succinct a format as possible. The writer should use multiple headings and supporting charts, graphs, figures, and appendices whenever possible.

- **The cover**—title, writer, department authorizing the study, the date.
- **Letter of Transmittal**—(optional)
  Serves merely as a record of the submission of a report. Includes material otherwise contained in an introduction or preface.
- **Title page**—title of the report, name and title of writer, date.
- **Table of contents.**
- **List of illustrations.**
- **Abstract**
- **Executive Summary**—particularly for long reports.
- **Preface**—(optional)
  The reason for the report.
  Statement concerning the organization.
  Relevant material concerning qualifications point of view of author. (authors).
- **Text**—Introduction, the body (the developing paragraphs or parts), conclusions and recommendations.
- **Reference material**—appendix, charts, tables, graphs, statistical data, bibliography
- **Credits** to those who assisted with or contributed to the report.

The structure of a formal report always relates to the informational needs of the reader:

- The purpose of the study.
- The most significant results.
- The interpretations of the results.
- Any recommendations for specific action.
- The methods of investigation.

Every aspect of a report should relate to the following:

- Its function or intended use
- The audience
- The person or group communicating
- The material to be communicated

The following variations in format are common:

## Reports Concerned with Providing Information:

- **Introduction**—background, purpose, divisions
- **Summary**—main facts and interpretations, conclusions and recommendations.
- **The body**—details of methods and procedures, full explanations of the facts.
- **Reference materials.**

## Reports Concerned with Reporting Investigations:

- **Introduction**—background, definition of the problem, methods or procedures of investigation, organizational division of the report.
- **Conclusions**—*relevant* observations and recommendations.
- **Body**—the development section
  The technical sections:
  Details of apparatus, methods, procedures.
  Details of the experiments and investigations.
- **All material to support or justify conclusion or recommendation.**
- **Material presented according to divisions outlined in the introduction.**

Other important communication considerations for articles: relevance, need, timeliness, interest, accuracy, demand.

Basic format criteria—*appearance, readability,* and *objectivity.*

## Formal Report Assignment

Draft a formal report describing a research topic of interest to you and relevant to your professional interest. The report need not be long; however, it should be thorough. Support the writing with relevant figures and a bibliography.

# Letter of Transmittal

The letter of Transmittal accompanies the formal report and provides any information and instructions needed for use of the document.

## Sample Letter of Transmittal

**BRADSHAW SMITH LIVERMORE, INC.**
1 Sawyer      Columbus, MO. 57231
Phone: (577) 667-4358

December 20, 1990

Robert Jones
2121 Green Valley Drive
Grand Rapids, MI 49001

Dear Mr. Jones:

Enclosed are the galley proofs and a xerox of the typescript of your entry for the <u>Encyclopedia of Literature</u>. I have edited the entry for clarity, conciseness, and style. You may find that some of your authorial "voice" has been lost in this process, but please keep in mind that the <u>EL</u> is a reference work which must maintain a certain uniformity and tone from entry to entry.

Please note the following when making your revision:

- Please check the proofs for typographical errors; also please check to make sure that my editing has not distorted your meaning.
- You may find tags attached to the typescript containing requests for clarification or for more information. Please respond to these queries.
- Please make all corrections and revisions on the proofs, in the right-hand margin; or, if the revisions are too lengthy, please make them on separate sheets and indicate where they are to be inserted.
- Please return the corrected galley proofs to me within <u>two weeks</u> of your receipt of this letter, or as soon after that as possible. There is no need to return the copy of the typescript.

Incidentally, in correcting the proofs, please disregard the absence of a crossbar on the lower-case "f." That is a peculiarity of the printer we use for the proofs, and the crossbar will automatically be restored when we print the final version.

Thank you for your help with this volume.

Sincerely yours,

Charles Wesley
Editor, <u>EL</u>

## Letter of Transmittal Assignment

Write a ltter of transmittal appropriate for your formal report.

# The Abstract

An abstract is a short summary of the contents of a report, article, proposal, dissertation, or some paper to be presented at a professional meeting. It may be the only part of a report that everyone will read. In some fields, the major products of research are reports and publications. Proper abstracting assures that reports and articles will attract readers. An abstract must be objective, clear, accurate, and concise, and contain no criticism or evaluative statements. It should not exceed more than *one paragraph*.

There are two types of abstracts: the *descriptive* and the *informative*. The *descriptive* type is a short description of the report. It indicates only the topics covered in the report and is similar to a table of contents in prose form.

## Example: Descriptive Abstract "Crisis Centers"

> This study defines crisis centers as local voluntary associations in which counseling and sometimes other services are provided to members and clients free of charge. It investigates and describes six crisis centers in relation to why some of them underwent dissolution and why some of them survived. It concludes with a discussion concerning the differences in the capacity and services of the surviving centers.

The *informative abstract* is a short report of the report. It objectively discusses the investigation or problem presented. It summarizes principal findings, stresses the objectives of the work, emphasizes what is new, and gives the chief results, conclusions, and recommendations. It omits supporting details and provides only the essential message.

## Example: Informative Abstract "Community Change"

> This study identifies and examines specific processes of community change through the use of case examples and through a test of four qualitative hypotheses. It also takes into account community decision-making and power structures, but only in relation to identifiable processes of community change. The methodology is primarily a participant-observer approach. The findings of this community-change study indicate four basic community patterns: 1) small communities are similar to large urban areas in population characteristics and change processes; 2) Particular people in small communities develop and maintain linkages to the larger society which places them in powerful positions to bring about change in their communities; 3) Community change policy occurs through private settings; 4) Small communities are changing and a good deal of the change is traceable to new residents. These four patterns suggest that any assessment to coordinate population growth and change strategies must acknowledge the process and character of change now under way. Local, as well as state governments, must recognize population shifts and the new value systems of the recent community settlers.

## Example: Informative Abstract "Danish Bronze Age Wool"

Measurements of twelve new samples of Danish Bronze Age wool showed them to be hairy medium fleeces. The supporting evidence indicated that a high proportion of fine fibers in yarn results from the plucking of wool during the moult before the hairy fibers have been released from the skin. The fine fibers were closer in diameter to the underwool of the wild ancestor than to those of the soay sheep indicating a more primitive fleece. The samples described include the first Bronze Age wool. Those with natural pigmentation in every fiber could be black or brown, while those with pigmented and white fibers are thought to be a mixture of brown and white (by analogy with the Soay) rather than grey which in unknown in the Soay. (M. L. Ryder, *Journal of Archaeological Science,* June 1983, p. 327)

### *Steps in Writing an Abstract*

In writing the final abstract a writer needs to review the material carefully. Many days or months could have elapsed between the first and final drafts of a long report or dissertation. Many changes and revisions could have been a part of the long process.

The following five steps will be helpful in writing the abstract, either type.

- Read the report thoroughly again and objectively.
- List in order the points covered by the report.
- Be sure the draft follows the organization of the original report.
- Check all basic information to be sure the reporting is correct.
- Be sure of the accuracy as the abstract may be the only part read by the reader.

### *Types of Beginnings for Abstracts*

1. Brief Statement of Main Ideas:
   The problem arising from the increasing use of heavy fuel oil under industrial boilers is the basis for this study on corrosion involving the mechanism and the involved parameters.

2. Scope: A statement of the limitations of the subject.
   Two major classifications of computer applications, their value, cost and manpower talent requirements are the bases of this paper: financial management and distribution management.

3. Point of View—The author states his or her position on a topic:
   My aim here is to show the achievements of this department in the use of computers in the last six months.

4. Specific Detail:
   Our new purchases of paper stock are at the lowest volume in many years, and the prices for some grades are at discouragingly low levels.

5. Background—background to the need of the report:
   Assembly line modernization is an old problem, but trying to modernize every machine, increase production and quality, and change products 15 times a day without dropping the ball . . . that is a real challenge.

6. Asking a Question:
   How long can the current inflated real estate and stock prices last?

7. Defining—Classifying:
   A confluent education is that sort of learning situation in which the cognitive and affective aspects of learning are joined into one.

8. Purpose:
   The primary objective of this research is to review the economics involved in this production changeover.

9. Beginning with a quotation.
   "The American, from the beginning, has been the most ardent of recorded rhetoricians—his politics bristles with pungent epithets; his whole history has been bedizened with tall talk; his fundamental institutions rest far more upon brilliant phrases than upon logical ideas." H. L. Menchen, *The American Language*

10. Scientific Focus
    1. This investigation concerns the antitumor action of some xylitol compounds possessing alkylating potency at 1 and 5 positions of the sugar skeleton

    2. This study indicates that the capacity factors determined by reversed-phase micro-HPLC can be used as 1 of the descriptors in Qsar studies.

    3. This investigation concentrates on the carbohydrates accumulation profiles of 70 strains of cyanbacteria in 3 organic osmotics (glucoslyglcerol, sucrose, and tribalose) using both freshwater and marine isolates under conditions of osmotic stress.

    4. This study explored the effects of assertion role-play variations on physiological arousal as a function of scene length (single vs multiple responses), scene type (live prompts, tape prompts and taped prompts with imaginal responses), and subject type.

    5. This current assessment is of a previously described aspects of host defense responsiveness as well as aspects that several laboratories now have under investigation.

6. This study of physician distribution in the United States demonstrates that there will be some overcrowding at all community levels and in all nine of the specialty fields of surgery by the year 2000.

7. This review concerns the technique of in vivo neutron activation analysis and broadly examines its utility in pre-operative care.

## Assignment 1: Writing an Abstract

a. Write a descriptive and an informative abstract for some journal article you have read, for a chapter in a textbook, or for some lecture you have heard recently. Be sure you provide an accurate bibliographic reference for your source (author, *title*, "title of chapter," place of publication, publisher's name, date of publication, page numbers of chapter).

b. Write a descriptive and an informative abstract for your report.

## Assignment 2: Evaluate the following abstract:

- Is the writer objective in the treatment of the material?
- Are the ideas stated clearly and concisely?
- Does the abstract make you want to read the whole report?
- Is "What the Public Thinks of Industry" an appropriate title for the article?

## Sample abstract:

The present trends of public opinion concerning technology are upward in favorability. The uncommitted percentage of the public is enough, however, to actually exert unfavorable pressure on the trends of public opinion. Although there is less public demand for government intervention, the public concern for high prices and poor quality products coupled the lack of knowledge concerning conservation, reforestation, and recreation steps undertaken by the pulp-wood industry should be of prime concern. The author has tried to sample public opinion by supposedly accepted statistical techniques. I disagree that the present percentage of favorable answers to uncommitted answers is correct as he examined them. His concern over high prices and poor quality and over pollution and other such problems is commendable. Government and regulation of industry was mentioned to some extent. Public opinion and knowledge concerning conservation and reforestation policies is not accurate. Justification of public relations and expenses was stressed.

## Questions

- What is the function of the abstract?
- What are some of its characteristics?
- Where would you find the abstracts published in your area of specialization?
- When might abstract writing be important to you?
- How does a summary differ from an abstract?

# Executive Summary

An executive summary reports key concepts and important data contained in the formal report. The purpose of the executive summary is to allow a reader to grasp ideas and conclusions quickly. It can provide a nontechnically oriented audience with essential facts but without too much spcialized detail.

## Sample Executive Summary: Evaluation of a Training Program

This week-long basic immunocytochemistry techniques course at the Marine Biology Laboratory in Massachusetts provided intensive laboratory experience using the principles and current technologies of immunocytochemistry. The lectures and discussions presented a wide variety of sectioned and whole mount material to examine at the light microscope level with the aid of immunocytochemical methods of antigen localization. Specifically, the course covered tissue preparation—including vibrotome and cryostat sectioning, immunofluorescence, and immunoperoxidase and avidin/biotin systems. Each participant designed his/her own experiments. The instructors were always available to help solve experimental problems, such as background, cross-reactivity, and nonspecific binding of antibodies. The last day included formal presentations of experimental designs, problems and solutions, and results. This excellent course instructed by experts offered intensive laboratory experience combined with expert instruction in a stimulating, science-oriented environment.

## Assignments:

a. Write an executive summary of your formal report.
b. Write an executive summary of a journal article relevant to your field.

# Sample: Student's Sample Formal Report

Letter of Transmittal

JULIE ZAGON
2830 Tattersall Road
Dearborn Heights, MI 48127

April 17, 1990

Dr. Brad Hayden
921 Sprau
Western Michigan University
Kalamazoo, MI 49008

Dear Dr. Hayden:

Here is my report, "The Tumbling Tokyo Stock Market," which you asked for on March 13.

The report concerns the recent downfall of the Tokyo Stock Market. I provided some background information to the strong Japanese economy before discussing its current status. I also listed the major causes of the decline and the effects it has had on the United States' economy.

I hope this report will help you see how a decline in one international market influences the markets in the rest of the world. I will answer any questions this report may arise.

Sincerely,

Julie M. Zagon

# Abstract

Japan's postwar economic history began on August 16, 1945, with the end of World War II. Japan sustained crushing damages to the economy during the war and found itself completely deprived of the former empire. Amazingly, the Japanese rebounded with a miraculous economic expansion. The accelerated growth brought on some notable structural changes, including active participation in the stock market.

Actively participating in the stock market brought on a fierce competitor for the United States stockholders. After the stock market crash in 1987, the United States lost its title of having the world's biggest and most profitable stock market to the aggressive Japanese. Recently, however, the stock market's performance has surprised the Japanese investors.

After hitting on all-time high in December 1989, the Tokyo Stock Market declined rapidly. Soaring interest rates, high price-earnings ratios, increasing inflation, the weakening of the yen, and the apprehension about the political strength of the Japanese government resulted in the battered Japanese shares. The United States recaptured its title of having the world's biggest and most profitable stock market.

The Japanese investor switched into the U.S. market to take advantage of the low price-earnings ratio. Whole this keeps the United States' economy strong, it may just be advantageous in the short run. The long-term effects could be detrimental. When the Japanese find their market more attractive, they will quickly leave the U.S. market. This, in turn, will cause the United States market to fail.

# Background

Japan's postwar economic history began on August 15, 1945, with the announcement of the end of World War II. With the end of the war, the opportunity arose for launching a new, modern economy without a war. However, at the time of a brutal defeat, the country had been almost totally devastated. The country's vast colonial empire was lost, its economic infrastructure was in a state of ruin, and its population was barely able to survive from day to day. The war left its cruel marks on every aspect of life.

Japan sustained crushing damages to its economy during the war and found itself completely deprived of its former empire. The loss of Manchuria, China, and Southeast Asia reduced the territory of the Japanese empire by 56%. The end of many businesses and the halt of military production put 13.1 million people out of work (Uchino 1983). This, along with a sudden increase in population, resulted in a demand for essential raw materials and basic daily necessities. Mass hysteria characterized the economy. The feelings of confusion and disillusionment left the prole with no clear vision of what the post war would bring.

Amazingly, this confusion and disillusionment lessened with a miraculous economic expansion. Japan's resurgence as one of the great industrial and trading nations of the world is one of the most surprising developments of the post war period. No one anticipated this extraordinary achievement. Yet, Japan produced a rapid recovery with determination. In only a decade, the Japanese rebuilt the national economy. Close cooperation between organized business and the government accompanied this astonishing growth.

The accelerated growth brought on some notable structural changes, including some Westernized tactics. Participation in the stock market and foreign investment became popular. The Nikkei 225 characterizes the Tokyo Stock Market. The Nikkei 225 is comparable to the Dow Jones Industrial Average of the United States market. The Dow Jones Industrial Average has 30 stocks that accurately represent the entire United States Market. The Nikkei, on the other hand, has 225 stocks that represent the Tokyo Stock Market. In other words, the direction of these particular 225 stocks is the direction of the entire market.

Actively participating in the stock market brought on a fierce competitor for the United States stockholders. After the stock market crash in October 1987, the United States lost its title of having the world's biggest and most profitable stock market to the aggressive Japanese.

## Summary

The title of being the world's biggest and most profitable stock market was an accurate assumption following the United States stock market crash in 1987. The Tokyo Stock Exchange experienced a huge expansion. Recently, however, the strong exchange incurred a rapid decline.

On December 29, 1989 the Tokyo Stock Exchange hit an all-time high with 38,916 points (*Business Week* 2-12-90). The pleasant feeling of security and safety was replaced with feelings of uncertainty and speculation. Just as in the economies of other advanced nations, interest rates recently changed in Japan. After a fairly long period of continuous growth, disruptions in the Tokyo Stock Market caused it to lose stability quickly. Graph 1 shows that the past few months have proved to be disastrous to Japan's market.

Soaring interest rates, high price-earnings ratios, increasing inflation, the weakening of the yen, and the apprehension about the political strength of the Japanese government resulted in the battered Japanese shares. The United States recaptured its title of having the world's biggest and most profitable stock market.

In hopes of retaining and stabilizing their market, the Japanese switched to foreign markets. This switch appears to be quite profitable to the United States in the short run.

Graph 1: Decline of the Tokyo Stock Exchange

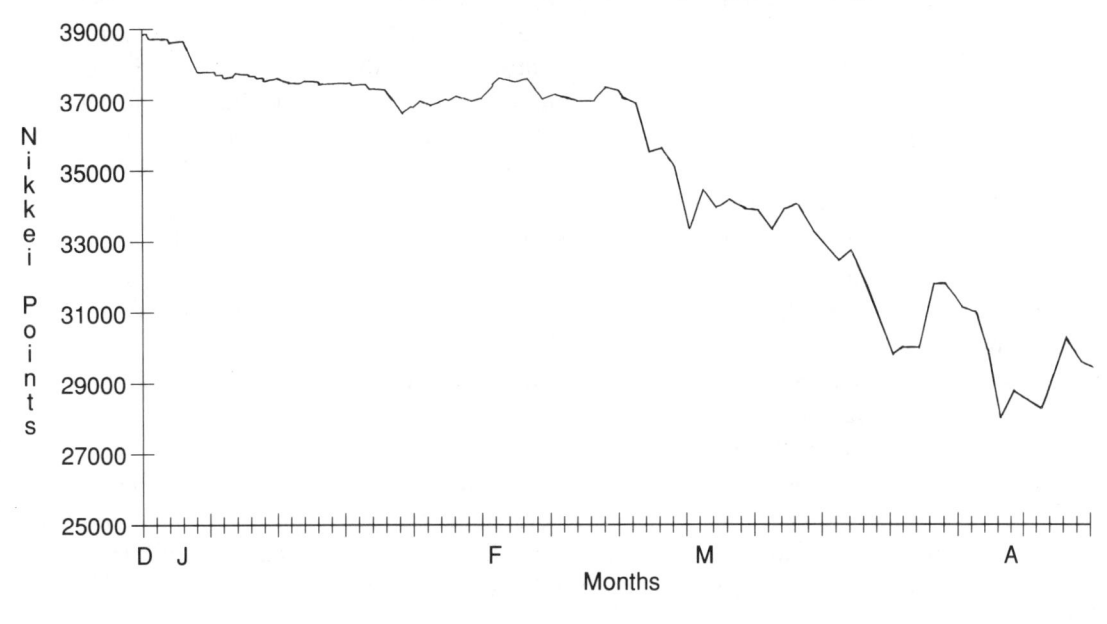

**Graph 1.**

However, when the Japanese switch back to their market and out of the U.S. market, the United States will experience some detrimental long-term effects.

The Tokyo Stock Exchange is now down to 29,000 points (*Wall Street Journal* 4-11-90). This figure leaves many Japanese, as well as foreign, investors wondering when and if the downfall will pivot upward back to the typical strong Japanese average.

## Discussion

Many individuals find international stock markets intimidating. In this section, I attempt to alleviate the unsure feeling. I divided up the causes of the Tokyo Stock Market decline and discuss each cause individually. I also emphasize the effect on the United States.

### High Price Earnings Ratios

When the Tokyo Stock Exchange hit an all-time high on December 12, 1989, the price-earnings ratio average 60 on the Nikkei 225—compared to 11 on the Dow Jones Industrial Average (*Business Week* 2-12-90). Simply stated, this means that an investor in the Japanese market invests $60 in the market for every dollar earned—an extremely high comparison. Obviously, the Japanese investor found the U.S. market more attractive. The Japanese bailed out of their market and poured into the U.S. market.

Although this move seems appealing to the United States at present, I think the long-term effects could be disastrous. Investing in the U.S. market allows the Japanese to take advantage of the low price-earnings ratio. When the Japanese ratio decreases, they will leave the U.S. Market. This switch will cause a sharp decline in the United States' stock prices, creating a serious dilemma for U.S. investors. Another stock market crash may result if the decline is too sharp for the typical investor. This scenario preceded the crash in October 1987.

It is difficult to predict exactly when the Japanese will make the shift back to their market. In my opinion, the Japanese are extremely shrewd. The Japanese companies do not report quarterly results. This secret does not give the investor any insight into the hottest profits. This presents a problem of U.S. money managers. Trying to predict the direction of the Japanese stock prices, the managers are devising many strategies to value Japanese companies.

I think that not disclosing quarterly profits is an advantage for the Japanese investor. The Japanese, perhaps, may have some ulterior motives. By not sharing company reports, the Japanese could wait until their companies appear to be most profitable and leave the U.S. market. Thus, the U.S. market will fall, and the Japanese will recapture the status of having the world's most profitable stock market.

## The Weakening Yen

In order to recapture this comforting title, investors are focusing on the yen. As the yen weakens, it loses power against major currencies.

The Japanese left their own market due to uncertainties and trouble. The money flow is going from Japan to overseas markets. Sales are yen-denominated investments and purchases are dollar-dominated securities. I expect the stock market to remain unstable due to the unbalance of the currency exchange. In an effort to make the yen strong against the dollar, the Bank of Japan has bought billions of U.S. dollars. With the large flow of money from foreign investors, the U.S. dollar should continue to rise.

## Soaring Interest Rates and Rising Inflation

Lingering uncertainty over Japan's election has made stabilizing the economy difficult. Apprehension due to the possibility of a new political government prevented investors from buying enthusiastically. The Liberal Democratic Party survived the election, and the Bank of Japan had the opportunity to raise the official discount rate. (The discount rate controls the money supply.)

On March 20, 1990 the discount rate increased a full percentage point to 5.25% (*Chicago Tribune* 3-20-90). This increase was inevitable to slow the rate of inflation in Japan's economy. Of all the causes of inflation, high energy prices dominate. The weak yen boosted oil prices. Japan is dependent on imported oil which is priced in U.S. dollars. Oil becomes more expensive as the yen weakens.

Raising the discount rate was the only alternative the Bank of Japan had. This increase will have a strong impact on other interest rates making it more expensive for companies to borrow. Rising interest rates makes outside investments more appealing.

Risk-free investment with sufficient returns at present interest the Japanese. U.S. Treasury Securities are extremely attractive to satisfy these needs. Savings accounts in Japan yield a mere 0.75%; investors can obtain an 8.5% return on U.S. Treasury Securities (*Business Week* 2-12-90).

I think the switch to U.S. securities is extremely beneficial for financing the U.S. deficit in the short run. The long run, however, is not as beneficial. With the Japanese obtaining a large volume of U.S. securities, the United States is no longer the master of its own destiny. If Japanese savings account rates jolted upward, the Japanese would linger away from U.S. securities to invest in their own. The U.S. deficit would suffer considerably. I feel this move might inevitably lead to an increase in United States prices and a decrease in output, which would ultimately lead to an economic recession.

## Concluding Remarks

The Tokyo Stock Exchange is now down to 29,000 points. The market will probably continue to tumble approximately another 5000 points before it begins to stabilize. Amazingly, this sharp decline will not have a major effect on other markets. I think foreign investors have not felt the stock price plunge because foreign investors' portfolios are underweighted in Japanese stocks compared with their holdings in other markets. This finding is a result of the Japanese market being overvalued. The overvalued stocks were prevalent when the price-earnings ratio was an outrageous 60 times earnings in December. The ratio is now down to only 45 times earnings. It is apparent that the Japanese have a long way to go before their market stops declining.

## Sources

### I. Bibliography

Tsoukalis, Loukas. *Japan and Western Europe.* New York: St. Martin's Press, 1982.

Uchino, Tatsuro. *Japan's Postwar Economy.* Tokyo: Kodansha International Ltd., 1983.

Woronoff, Jon. *World Trade War.* New York: Praeger Publisher, 1984.

### II. Data

*Business Week:* March 12, 1990

*Chicago Tribune:* March 20, 1990

*Wall Street Journal:* December 29, 1989—April 11, 1990

# Information Sources

The ability to locate quickly and accurately what has been published or is being published about some given subject is an essential skill for the professional writer and researcher. The following bibliography contains some of the more widely used sources to published information. Readings in these sources can serve as actual models for good writing style for all areas of expertise.

## Guide to On-line Reference Databases

**ABI/INFORM:** Contains citations and abstracts to English language and selected foreign journal literature on administration, banking, human resources, information science, law, management, marketing, and other areas of interest to business decision makers. Subject term and keyword Boolean searching* is available. Covers the five years. Updated monthly.

**APPLIED SCIENCE AND TECHNOLOGY INDEX:** Provides access to journal citations in areas such as aeronautics, atmospheric sciences, computer science, electronics, energy resources, engineering, food industry, geology, textile industry, and transportation. Indexes over 300 English language journals. Subject term and keyword Boolean searching* is available. Three levels of searching (from basic to advanced) can be used. Updated quarterly.

**BIOLOGICAL AND AGRICULTURAL SCIENCE INDEX:** Provides journal citations in areas such as agriculture, biochemistry, biology, botany, ecology, entomology, environmental science, food science, genetics, nutrition, physiology, and zoology. Indexes over 300 English language journals. Subject term and keyword Boolean searching* is available. Three levels of searching (from basic to advanced) can be used. Updated quarterly.

**BUSINESS PERIODICALS INDEX:** Provides access to journal citations in areas such as accounting, computers, finance, international business, management and marketing. Indexes approximately 345 English language journals. Subject term and keyword Boolean searching* is available. Three levels of searching (from basic to advanced) can be used. Updated quarterly.

**BUSINESS PERIODICALS ONDISC:** Contains the ABI/Inform database (see description above) and the full text of actual articles for approximately one third of the journals indexed. Updated monthly.

**ERIC:** Indexes and abstracts over 780 journals and ERIC (Educational Resources Information Center) documents. Covers education and related fields such as counseling, psychology, and the social sciences. The ERIC documents are available on microfiche in the Education Library. Subject term and keyword Boolean searching* is available. Consult the print copy of the *Thesaurus of ERIC Descriptors* for subject terms. An online tutorial is available for help in searching the database. Covers 1966 to the present. Updated monthly.

**INFOTRAC:** Indexes 900 general interest, business, and academic magazines and journals covering approximately the last 9 years. Uses Library of Congress Subject Headings. Updated monthly.

**MATHSCI DISC:** Indexes articles from approximately 2,000 journals, books, and conference proceedings in the areas of biology, computer science, engineering, mathematics, operations research, physics, and other fields that contain mathematical or statistical applications. Includes coverage of the printed indexes: *Mathematical Reviews* and *Current Mathematical Publications*. Subject term and keyword Boolean* searching is available. Updated on a semiannual basis.

**MLA INTERNATIONAL BIBLIOGRAPHY:** Indexes periodicals and series, monographs, book collections, dissertation abstracts, festschriften, and other sources. Areas covered include modern languages and literature, folklore, linguistics, literary themes, genres, and related topics, across national literatures or other classified boundaries. Subject term and keyword Boolean searching* is available. Three levels of searching (from basic to advanced) can be used. Updated annually.

**NEWSBANK:** Indexes newspaper articles on a variety of topics from selected papers across the country, not just large city papers. Includes files on: **Business; Names in the news; Film and Television; Fine arts and Architecture; Literature.** Subheadings are available to help narrow a topic.

**OARS (Online Automated Reference Service):** A large number of commercially available databases covering a wide range of subjects can be accessed through OARS. This fee-based information retrieval service is a supplement to the computerized reference databases available as well as the standard printed bibliographic indexes.

**SPORTSDISC:** Indexes over 1,000 international sport periodicals along with many medical and related journals. Books, conference proceedings, dissertations, reports, and other monographs on sports are also included. Covers 1975 to the present. Subject term and keyword Boolean searching* is available. Updated on a seminannual basis.

**SUPERMAP:** Provides access to statistical data combined with digital mapping capabilities. The system provides over 2,400 demographic, economic, social, and financial statistics for more than 3,700 counties in the United States. Retrieved data can be viewed as tables which can be manipulated, ranked, and mapped. Tables or maps that have been constructed can be printed in black and white or color. Data can be downloaded or uploaded from spreadsheets like Lotus tutorial in order to create simple applications.

***(Boolean Searching) Allows a searcher to cross one subject with another, using subject headings or keywords. (Example: computers and training)***

## Indexes to Interdisciplinary Scholarly Journals

*Humanities Index.* 1974–present

A subject index to over 200 journals in literature, languages, archaeology, history, folklore, philosophy, religion, and other humanities areas. Before 1974 this source was known as the *Social Sciences and Humanities Index,* AI 3 .R49 (Ref). From 1907 to March 1965 this index, in turn, was called the *International Index,* AI 3 .R49 (Ref).

*Social Sciences Index.* 1974–present

A subject index to over 300 journals in anthropology, economics, geography, history, law, political science, psychology, sociology, and related social science areas of study. (See the note above on the *Humanities Index* for previous names of this index.)

*Social Sciences Citation Index.* 1970–present

Covers about 2000 journals in the social sciences. Use the *Permuterm* Subject Index for a keywords in title approach, the *Source Index* if you're looking for publications by a specific author, and the *Citation Index* if you want references by other scholars to specific publications you already know.

*Arts and Humanities Citation Index.* 1977–present.

Covers about 1300 journals in the arts and humanities. This has the same format as the three divisions of the *Social Sciences Citation Index.* (See note above.)

# Subject Encyclopedias

**Archaeology**
*Larousse Encyclopedia of Archaeology.*

**Afro-Americans**
*Afro-American Encyclopedia.*

**American Economic History**
*Encyclopedia of American Economic History.*

**American Ethnic Groups**
*Harvard Encyclopedia of American Ethnic Groups.*

**American Foreign Policy**
*Encyclopedia of American Foreign Policy.*

**American Literature**
*The Oxford Companion to American Literature.*

**Architecture**
*Encyclopedia of Architecture, Design, Engineering and Construction.*

**Art**
*Encyclopedia of World Art.*

**Australia**
*The Australian Encyclopedia.*

**Bible**
*The International Standard Bible Encyclopedia.*

**Canada**
*The Canadian Encyclopedia.*

**Communications**
*International Encyclopedia of Communications.*

**Criminology**
*Encyclopedia of Crime and Justice.*

**Drama**
*McGraw-Hill Encyclopedia of World Drama.*

**Economics**
*The New Palgrave Dictionary of Economics.*

**English Literature**
*Oxford Companion to English Literature.*

**Feminism**
*Encyclopedia of Feminism.*

**Film**
*New York Times Encyclopedia of Film.*

**Japan**
*Kodansha Encyclopedia of Japan.*

**Law**
*Encyclopedia of the American Judicial System.*
*The Guide to American Law.*

**Library Science**
*Encyclopedia of Library and Information Science.*

**The Middle Ages**
*Dictionary of the Middle Ages.*

**Music**
*The New Grove Dictionary of Music and Musicians.*

**Native Americans**
*Encyclopedia of Indians of the Americas.*

**Peoples of the World**
*The Illustrated Encyclopedia of Mankind.*

**Philosophy**
*Encyclopedia of Philosophy.*

**Psychology**
*Encyclopedia of Psychology.*

**Religion**
*The Encyclopedia of Religion.*
*Encyclopedia of the American Religious Experience.*
*The Encyclopedia of American Religions.*
*New Catholic Encyclopedia.*
*Encyclopedia of Islam.*
*Encyclopedia Judaica.*

**The Social Sciences**
*International Encyclopedia of the Social Sciences.*

**Social Work**
*Encyclopedia Of Social Work.*

**South Africa**
*Standard Encyclopedia of Southern Africa.*

# Subject Dictionaries

**American History**
*The Encyclopedia of American Facts and Dates.*

**Anthropology**
*Dictionary of Anthropology.*

**Archaeology**
*Facts on File Dictionary of Archaeology.*

**Architecture**
*Dictionary of Architecture and Construction.*

**Art**
*A Dictionary of Art Terms and Techniques.*

**The Bible**
*The Interpreter's Dictionary of the Bible.*

**Communications**
*Longman Dictionary of Mass Media and Communication.*

**Economics**
*Economics Dictionary.*

**Folklore**
*Standard Dictionary of Folklore.*

**History**
*Dictionary of Dates.*
*Macmillan Concise Dictionary of World History.*

**Law**
*Black's Law Dictionary.*

**Librarianship**
*Dictionary of Library Science, Information and Documentation.*

**Linguistics**
*Longman Dictionary of Applied Linguistics.*

**Literary Terms**
*A Handbook to Literature.*

**Names**
*Dictionary of First Names.*

**Philosophy**
*Dictionary of Philosophy.*

**Political Science**
*Dictionary of Political Science.*
*A Dictionary of Modern Politics.*

**Psychology**
*Comprehensive Dictionary of Psychological and Psychoanalytical Terms.*
*Dictionary of Behavioral Science.*

**Religion**
*The New Dictionary of Theology.*

**Social Sciences**
*Dictionary of the Social Sciences.*

# Scholarly Book Review Sources

*An Index to Book Reviews in the Humanities.* 1960–present.

Lists by author citations to reviews in approximately 225 English journals in art, architecture, drama, dance, language, literature, music and philosophy.

*Social Sciences and Humanities Index.* 1907–present.

(Since April, 1974 this has become two separate indexes, *Social Sciences Index* and *Humanities Index.* From 1907 until 1965 this source was called *International Index.*) List reviews by author of the book reviewed in a separate index following the main index.

*New Technical Books.* 1958–present.

(Recent volumes in Science Reference, earlier volumes in book stacks.) A selective, annotated list of reviews by subject of English language books in pure and applied science, mathematics, engineering, industrial technology, and related subjects. There are separate author and title indexes.

*Social Sciences Citation Index.* 1970–present

This is a very broad inter-disciplinary index, covering hundreds of journals in the social sciences as well as applied areas of the social sciences, including anthropology, area studies, business, economics, education, geography, history, political science, psychology, sociology, and many more disciplines. This source has three separate indexes: the **Source** index, the **Citation** index, and the **Permuterm Subject** index. If you are searching for reviews of a book by title, look up key words of the title in the **Permuterm Subject** index. If you are looking for reviews by the author of the book, look up his/her name in the **Citation** index. If you are looking for reviews by a specific reviewer, look up his/her name in the **Source index.**

*Arts and Humanities Citation Index.* 1977–present.

This interdisciplinary index covers hundreds of journals (and some books) in art, dance, film, history, language, literature, linguistics, theater, theology, philosophy, and numerous other humanities subjects. This is organized in the same way as the *Social Sciences Citation Index* described above.

*Science Citation Index.* 1961–present.

This interdisciplinary tool covers hundreds of journals in the pure and applied sciences, such as chemistry, biology, mathematics, physics, engineering, etc. This is organized in the same way as the *Social Sciences Citation Index* described above.

## Social Sciences Indexes

### Anthropology
*Abstracts in Anthropology.*
*International Bibliography of Social and Cultural Anthropology.* 1955–present.

### Black Americana Studies
*Index to Periodical Articles by and About Blacks.* 1950–present.

### Communications
*Communications Abstracts.*

### Criminology
*Crime and Delinquency Literature.* 1968–present.
*Criminology and Penology.* 1965–present.
*Police Science Abstracts.*

### Economics
*World Agricultural Economics and Rural Sociology Abstracts.* 1967–present.
*Economic Abstracts.* 1953–present.
*Journal of Economic Literature.* 1963–present.
*Index of Economic Articles.* 1886–present.
*International Bibliography of the Social Sciences—Economics.* 1952–present.

### Education
*Current Index to Journals in Education.* 1966–present.
*Education Index.* 1957–present.
*Resources in Education.* 1966–present.

### Geography
*Geographic Abstracts: Part C. Economic Geography.*
*Geographic Abstracts: Part D. Social and Historic Geography.*
*Geographic Abstracts: Part F. Regional and Community Planning.*

### History
*Historical Abstracts.* 1955–present.
*America: History and Life.* 1964–present.

**Law**
*Index to Legal Periodicals.* 1970–present.

**Library Science**
*Library Literature.* 1933–present.
*Library and Information Science Abstracts.* 1950–present.

**Political Science**
*International Political Science Abstracts.* 1951–present.
*International Bibliography of the Social Sciences—Political Science.* 1952–present.
*United States Political Science Documents.* 1979–present.

**Psychology**
*Psychological Abstracts.* 1927–present.
*Index Medicus.* 1960–present.

**Social Work**
*Social Work Research and Abstracts.* 1978–present.

**Sociology**
*Sociological Abstracts.* 1953–present.
*International Bibliography of the Social Sciences—Sociology.* 1956–present.

**Women's Studies**
*Women's Studies Abstracts.* 1972–present.

## Specific Subject Sources

*Anthropology Sources*

**Guides to the Literature**
*The Student Anthropologist's Handbook.*

**Dictionaries and Encyclopedias**
*Dictionary of Terms and Techniques in Archaeology.*
*Dictionary of Anthropology.*
*Encyclopedia of Anthropology.*

**Handbooks**
*Handbook of Method in Cultural Anthropology.*

**Annual Reviews**
*Annual Review of Anthropology.*

**Periodical Indexes and Abstracts**
*Abstracts in Anthropology.* 1970–present.
*International Bibliography of the Social Sciences—Anthropology.* 1955–present.

*Architecture Sources*

**Encyclopedias**
*Encyclopedia of Architecture, Design, Engineering and Construction.*
*Encyclopedia of World Architecture.*
*The Architecture of the United States.*

**Dictionaries**
*Dictionary of Architectural Science.*
*Dictionary of Architecture and Construction.*
*Historic Architecture Sourcebook.*

**Histories**
*A History of Architecture.*
*A Visual History of Twentieth-Century Architecture.*

**Biographical Sources**
*Macmillan Encyclopedia of Architects.*
*Contemporary Architects.*

*Economics Sources*

**Guide to the Literature**
*The Use of Economic Literature.*

**Dictionaries**
*Dictionary of Modern Economics.*
*The Encyclopedic Dictionary of Economics.*

**Encyclopedias**
*Encyclopedia of Economics.*
*The New Palgrave Dictionary of Economics.*

**Handbooks**
*Economic Handbook of the World.*
*Commodity Year Book.*

**Periodical Indexes**
*Journal of Economic Literature.* 1963–present.
*Index of Economic Articles.* 1886–present.
*International Bibliography of the Social Sciences—Economics.* 1952–present.

*English Language Dictionaries*

**Unabridged**

*Webster's New International Dictionary.*
About 600,000 words, earliest meanings given first, many usage labels.

*Webster's Third New International Dictionary.*
About 450,000 words, earliest meanings first, fewer usage labels, new words in Addenda at front of volume.

*Random House Dictionary of the English Language.*
About 260,000 words, most recent meanings first, often less detailed definitions than *Webster's*.

**Abridged**

*Webster's Ninth New Collegiate Dictionary.*
About 160,000 words, based on *Webster's Third*, frequently reprinted.

*American Heritage Dictionary of the English Language.*
About 200,000 words, most recent meaning first, considerable guidance on usage, some in the form of usage notes, many graphic illustrations.

**Historical**

*The Oxford English Dictionary.* (2nd ed.)
Most complete English language dictionary, defines more than a half-million words, 2.4 million quotations used to illustrate meanings, quotations arranged chronologically, includes all varieties of English from all over the world. (20 vols.)

*A Dictionary of American English.*
Defines and gives chronologically arranged quotations for words of American origin, or which have special meanings in the United States. Covers from Colonial period through the 19th century.

**Synonyms**

*Roget's International Thesaurus.*
Look up synonyms in index at back of volume, then find corresponding numbered entries for lists of similar words. No definitions given.

*Webster's New Dictionary of Synonyms.*
One of a number of dictionaries which **define** as well as list synonyms, but doesn't have as many entries as *Roget's*.

**Foreign Language (Bilingual)**

To find these in the catalog look up the language name, followed by the sub-heading, Dictionaries, e.g.: French language—Dictionaries—English.

*The New Cassell's French Dictionary.*
*Muret-Sanders Dictionary: German-English.*
*Larousse Gran Diccionario Moderno: English-Spanish.*

**Abbreviations**
*Acronyms and Initialisms Dictionary.*

**Usage**
*Fowler's Dictionary of Modern English Usage.*
   One of a number of sources giving detailed advice about when to use (or avoid using) certain words and expressions.

**Slang**
*New Dictionary of American Slang.*
   Includes informal, mostly spoken, rather than written language of the United States.
*A Dictionary of Slang and Unconventional English.*
   Focuses mainly on British, not American slang.

**Regionalism**
*Dictionary of American Regional English.*
   Multi-volume set, published over many years, defining words associated with specific geographic regions in the United States.

**Etymology (Word origins)**
*The Barnhart Dictionary of Etymology.*

**Pronunciation**
*Dictionary of Pronunciation.*

**Rhyming**
*New Rhyming Dictionary and Poet's Handbook.*

**Phrases**
*Idioms and Phrases Index.*

**New Words**
   No dictionary can keep up with all the new words and new meaning for old words constantly entering English. Recent editions of classic sources, such as the unabridged third edition of *Random House,* the *Oxford English Dictionary,* and the Addenda section at the front of *Webster's Third New International Dictionary,* include many new words. The following sources are other places to look:
*The Barnhart Dictionary of New English Since 1963.*
*The Second Barnhart Dictionary of New English.*
*The Barnhart Dictionary Companion.*
   This quarterly service updates the two previous dictionaries. All three provide extensive definitions and quotations using the new words and phrases.

*Fine Arts Sources*

**Guides to Research**

*Guide to the Literature of Art History.*
*Fine Arts: A Bibliographic Guide to Basic Reference Works, Histories, and Handbooks.*

**Encyclopedias**

*Encyclopedia of World Art.*
*McGraw-Hill Dictionary of Art.*

**Dictionaries**

*North Light Dictionary of Art Terms.*
*A Dictionary of Art Terms and Techniques.*
*The Oxford Companion to Art.*

**Directories of Institutions**

*The Official Museum Directory.*
*American Art Directory.*
*International Directory of Arts.*

**Biographical Sources**

*A Biographical Dictionary of Artists.*
*Dictionnaire Des Peintres, Sculpteurs, Dessinatateurs, Et Graveurs.*
*Kunstler-Lexikon.*
*Kunstler-Lexikon Dex Zwanzigsten Jahrhunderts.*
*Contemporary Artists.*
*A Dictionary of Contemporary American Artists.*

**Index to Reproductions**

*World Painting Index.*

**Indexes to Periodicals**

*Art Index.* 1929–present.
*Arts and Humanities Citation Index.* 1977–present.
*Repertoire D'Art Et D'Archeologie.* 1910–1980.
*Repertoire International De La Litterature De L'Art.* 1975–present.

*Geography Sources*

**Guides to the Literature**

*Bibliography of Geography: Part I. Introduction to General Aids.*
*Bibliography of Geography: Part II. Vol. 1, The United States.*

## Dictionaries

*Longman Dictionary of Geography.*
*Dictionary of Human Geography.*
*Dictionary of Concepts in Geography.*

## Handbooks

*Countries of the World and Their Leaders.*

## Periodical Indexes

*Geography Abstracts: Part C, Economic Geography.*
*Geography Abstracts: Part D, Social and Historical Geography.*
*Geography Abstracts: Part F, Regional and Communal Planning.*
*Geography Abstracts: Annual Index.*

*History Sources*

## Guides to the Literature

*The Modern Researcher.*
*Library Research Guide to History.*
*The Historian's Handbook.*

## Dictionaries and Encyclopedias

*Macmillan Concise Dictionary of World History.*
*Dictionary of American History.*

## Biographical Sources

*Dictionary of National Biography.*
*Dictionary of American Biography.*

## Documents Collections

*The Annals of America.*
*Documents of American History.*

## Handbooks

*Chronology of the Modern World, 1763–1968.*

## Annual Reviews

*Annual Register of World Events.*

## Periodical Indexes and Abstracts

*Historical Abstracts.* 1955–present.
*America: History and Life.* 1964–present.

## Statistics

*Historical Statistics of the United States.*

*Law Sources*

## Guides to Legal Research

*Legal Research in a Nutshell.*
*How to Find the Law.*
*Fundamentals of Legal Research.*

## Statutes

*United States Code.* (U.S.C.)
*United States Code Annotated.* (U.S.C.A.)
*United States Statutes at Large.* (Stat. or Stat. at L.)
*Public and Local Acts of the Legislature of the State of Michigan.*
*Michigan Compiled Laws Annotated.*

## Administrative Law

*Federal Register.* (FR)
*Code of Federal Regulations.*
*Michigan Administrative Code.*

## Case Law

U.S. Supreme Court

*United States Reports.* (U.S.)
*U.S. Supreme Court Reports, Lawyer's Edition.* (L.Ed., and L.Ed., 2d)
*U.S. Supreme Court Reports Desk Book.*
*U.S. Supreme Court Decisions.*

Other Federal Courts

*Federal Reporter* (F. and F. 2nd)
*Federal Supplement.* (F. Supp.)
*American Law Reports—Federal: Cases and Annotations.* (ALR-Fed)
*U.S. Court of Claims Reports.* (Ct. Cl.)

State Appellate Court Decisions

*American Law Reports: Cases and Annotations.* (A.L.R., A.L.R. 2d, A.L.R. 3d)
*Northeastern Reporter.* (N.E. and N.E. 2d)
*Northwestern Reporter.* (N.W. and N.W. 2d)
*Pacific Reporter.* (P. and P. 2d)

Citators

*How to Use Shepard's Citations.*
*Shepard's U.S. Citations: Statutes.*
*Shepard's U.S. Citations.*

*Shepard's Northeastern Reporter Citations.*
*Shepard's Northwestern Reporter Citations.*
*Shepard's Pacific Reporter Citations.*

**Secondary Materials**

Law Dictionaries
*Black's Law Dictionary.*

Law Encyclopedias
*American Jurisprudence.* (Am Jur 2d)
*Corpus Juris Secundum.* (C.J.S.)
*Callaghan's Michigan Civil Jurisprudence.*
*Michigan Law and Practice Encyclopedia.*

Legal Periodicals Indexes
*Index to Legal Periodicals.*
*Index to Periodical Articles Related to Law.*

*Philosophy Sources*

**Guides to Research**

*Research Guide to Philosophy.*
*Philosophy: A Guide to the Reference Literature.*
*The Philosopher's Guide to Sources. Research Tools, Professional Life, and Related Fields.*

**Encyclopedia**

*The Encyclopedia of Philosophy.*

**Summaries of Major Works**

*World Philosophy: Essay-Reviews of 225 Major Works.*

**Dictionaries**

*A Dictionary of Philosophy.*

**Biographical Directory**

*Directory of American Philosophers.*

**Indexes**

*Humanities Index.* 1974–present.
*Arts and Humanities Citation Index.* 1977–present.
*Bulletin Signaletique 519: Philosophie.* 1972–present.
*The Philosopher's Index.* 1967–present.

*Political Science Sources*

## Guides to the Literature
*Information Sources in Political Science.*

## Dictionaries and Encyclopedias
*The Blackwell Encyclopedia of Political Thought.*
*Public Administration Dictionary.*
*American Political Dictionary.*

Clio Dictionaries in Political Science

*Soviet and East European Political Dictionary.*
*Latin American Political Dictionary.*
*Dictionary of Political Analysis.*
*Presidential Congressional Political Dictionary.*
*International Relations Dictionary.*

## Handbooks
*International Handbook of Political Science.*
*Handbook of Political Psychology.*
*Political Handbook of the World.* 1975–present.

## Annual Reviews and Yearbooks
*International Year Book and Statesman's Who's Who.* 1957–present.
*Almanac of American Politics.*
*Political Science Reviewer.*

## Periodical Indexes and Abstracts
*International Political Science Abstracts.* 1952–present.
*United States Political Science Documents.* 1979–present.

## Government Sources
*Monthly Catalog of U.S. Government Publications.*
*Congressional Information Service (CIS) Annual.* 1970–present.
*Congressional Index.* 1951/52–present.
*U.S. Government Manual.*
*U.S. Code.*
*Federal Register.*
*Code of Federal Regulations.*
*Michigan Compiled Laws.*
*Michigan Documents.*
*Michigan Manual.*

*Psychology Sources*

## Guides to the Literature
*Library Use: A Handbook for Psychology.*
*Research Guide for Psychology.*

## Dictionaries and Encyclopedias
*Dictionary of Key Words in Psychology.*
*Encyclopedia of Psychology.*
*Longman Dictionary of Psychology and Psychiatry.*
*Dictionary of Behavioral Science.*
(Ref) *International Encyclopedia of Psychiatry, Psychology, Psychoanalysis, and Neurology.*

## Handbooks
*Steven's Handbook of Experimental Psychology.*
*Handbook of Operant Behavior.*
*Handbook of Developmental Psychology.*
*International Handbook of Behavior Modification and Therapy.*

## Annual Reviews
*Annual Review of Psychology.*
*Annual Review of Behavior Therapy.*

## Periodical Indexes and Abstracts
*Psychological Abstracts.* 1927–present.
*Index Medicus.*, 1960–present.

*Religion Sources*

## Guides to Research
*Research Guide to Religious Studies.*
*Tools for Theological Research.*

## Encyclopedias
*The Encyclopedia of Religion.*
*The Encyclopedia of American Religions.*
*New Catholic Encyclopedia.*
*Encyclopedia of Islam.*
*Encyclopedia Judaica.*

## Handbooks and Directories
*Yearbook of American and Canadian Churches.*
*Handbook of Denominations.*

### Dictionaries

*The New Dictionary of Theology.*
*The Oxford Dictionary of the Christian Church.*

### Indexes

*Humanities Index.* 1974–present.
*Arts and Humanities Citation Index.* 1977–present.
*Bulletin Signaletique 527: Histoire et Sciences Des Religions.* 1972–present.
*Religion Index Two: Multi-Author Works.* 1970–present.
*Religion Index One: Periodicals.* 1949–present.
*Index Islamicus.* 1906–present.

*Sociology Sources*

### Guides to the Literature

*Library Research Guide to Sociology.*
*The Student Sociologist's Handbook.*
*Criminal Justice Research Sources.*

### Dictionaries and Encyclopedias

*Encyclopedia of Sociology.*
*A Modern Dictionary of Sociology.*
*The Criminal Justice Dictionary.*
*Encyclopedia of Crime and Justice.*
*Dictionary of Criminal Justice Data Terminology.*
*An Encyclopedia of Marxism, Socialism and Communism.*

### Handbooks

*Handbook of Small Group Research.*
*Handbook of Social Psychology.*
*Handbook of Aging and the Social Sciences.*
*Sourcebook of Death and Dying.*
*Handbook of Criminology.*

### Annual Review

*Annual Review of Sociology.* 1975–present.

### Periodical Indexes and Abstracts

*Sociological Abstracts.* 1953–present.
*Criminology and Penology Abstracts.* 1978–present.
*Criminal Justice Periodical Index.* 1975–present.
*Current Literature on Aging.* 1969–present.

# General Book Review Sources

*Infotrac.* 1980–present.

This computerized index includes **references** to book reviews from about 900 general and business magazines. Locate these reviews under the author's name or the title of the book.

*Book Review Digest.* 1905–present.

References to book reviews are listed under authors' names, but there are separate title and subject indexes. Often, **selections** from the reviews are included. Notice that this source goes back to 1905.

*Book Review Index.* 1965–present.

Includes more book reviewing sources than *Book Review Digest*, but does not include the selections from the reviews. However, you'll often find more reviews of a book you're looking for here than in *Book Review Digest*.

## Indexes to General Interest Periodicals

*Readers' Guide to Periodical Literature.* 1900–present.

Indexes about 200 general interest magazines by subject and author. While *Infotrac* is often the first choice for **recent** magazine articles, notice that *Readers' Guide* back to 1900.

*Public Affairs Information Service Bulletin.* 1915–present.

A subject index to current literature relating to social and economic issues. Includes some books and government publications as well as periodical articles.

## Newspaper Indexes

**Newsbank**

**Indexes newspapers from over 450 U.S. cities.** Coverage from 1982 to the present (print indexes go back to 1970). Search by subject in a variety of sections within the database. For example, the Newsbank section covers social, economic, and political news, Names in the News covers biographical articles, etc.

**Print Indexes**

*Christian Science Monitor Index.* 1960–present.

A subject, with separate personal name index.

*Detroit News Index.* 1977–present.

A subject, with separate personal name index.

*The New York Times Index.* 1851–present.

A subject index, often with brief summaries of the articles. A separate personal name index is shelved next to this index.

*The Times (of London).* 1785–present.

A subject index with brief summaries of some articles.

*Washington Post Index.* 1972–present.

A subject index (with personal names listed under subject).

## Quotation Sources

*Bartlett's Familiar Quotations.*

This is the best known general collection of quotations, arranged chronologically, with separate author and key word indexes. Earlier editions, contain some quotations not included in later editions.

*The Home Book of Quotations.*

A very large collection of quotations, arranged by subject, with separate key word and author indexes. Some overlap with *Bartlett's,* but each book contains quotations not found in the other.

If your quotation is the first line of a poem, try:

*Granger's Index to Poetry.*

If you don't find your quotation in one of these sources, try one or more of the following, or browse other quotation books:

*The Oxford Dictionary of Quotations.*
*The Home Book of American Quotations.*
*The Home Book of Humorous Quotations.*

## Film Reviews and Film Review Indexes

*New York Times Film Reviews.* 1913–present.

Reporting reviews, in chronological order, from the *New York Times* newspaper. Consult the index volume under the film's title to locate reviews of films between 1913 and 1968. After 1968 each two-year volume has its own index.

*The Motion Picture Guide.* 1927–present.

Arranges film reviews alphabetically by title. Reviews are usually briefer than in the *New York Times.*

*Magill's Survey of Cinema.*

Has rather long plot summaries, with some interpretation, of major films only. Arranged alphabetically by title.

## Style Guides

Professional associations rely on style guides to ensure consistency for bibliographical citations. Often the style guides provide guidelines for other writing considerations as well—such as the use of numerals, spelling, and so forth. At times, companies and offices develop their own in-house skill. Writers should use a relevant style book consistently in order to achieve professional results. Following is a list of common styles:

APA style (American Psychological Association)

CBE style (Council of Biology Editors)

MLA style (Modern Language Association)

University of Chicago style (University of Chicago Press)

## Questions

1. Information Source Assignment:
   Research a topic of interest to you using four of the services listed above. Include at least one on-line database.

2. Style Guides Assignment:
   Compare the differences in the citation formats for the above-mentioned styles. The guides are usually available in the reference section of most libraries. If submitting an article for publication, consult the "Author's Guide Lines" used by professional journals in your field.

# Index

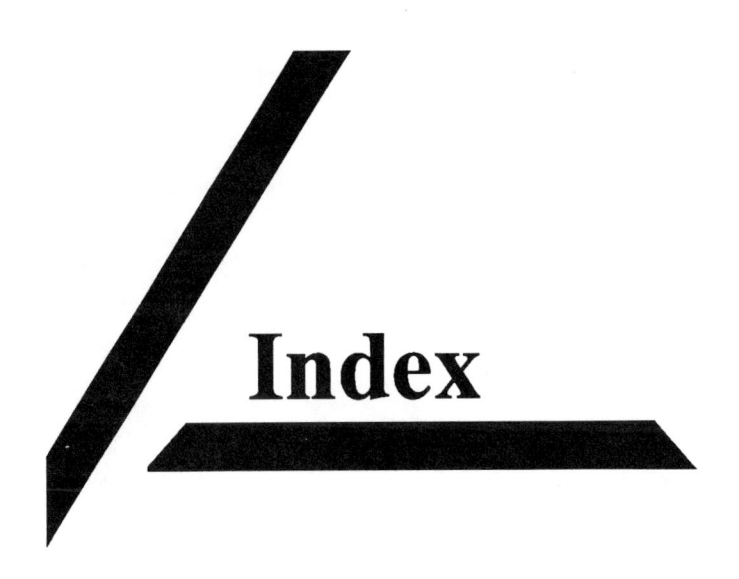

*A lot*, 184
*A while* versus *awhile*, 184
Abbreviations, punctuation with, 161
Abstract
   assignments, 213
   beginnings for, 211–212
   defined, 210
   examples of, 210–211, 215
*Accept* versus *except*, 169
Acronyms, punctuation conventions for, 161–162
Active–passive voice, 69–73
*Adapt* versus *adopt*, 170
Adjective clause, *who* as subject of, 62–63, 121
Adjective complement of linking verb, 56–57
Adjective phrase used with verb "to be," 56
Adjectives, 135–136
   adverbs compared with, 137–138
   coordinate, 151–152
   following verbs of the senses, 57, 136
   nouns used as, 91
   parallelism with, 78
   prepositional phrase used as, 136
*Adopt* versus *adapt*, 170
Adverbial clause at beginning of sentence followed by comma, 149
Adverbial phrase
   of place, 56
   used with intransitive verb, 55

Adverbs, 136–138
   adjectives compared with, 137–138
   parallelism with, 79–80
   problem, 91–93
   transition, 89, 147
*Advice* versus *advise*, 170
*Affect* versus *effect*, 170
*Aggravate* versus *irritate*, 177
*Agree with*, 177
*All ready* versus *already*, 184
*All right*, 184
*All together* versus *altogether*, 184
*Allusion* versus *illusion*, 170–171
*Almost* versus *most*, 181
*Already* versus *all ready*, 184
*Also* at beginning of sentence, 178
*Altogether* versus *all together*, 184
Ambiguity
   caused by missing punctuation, 145–147
   of compared elements, 88
   of meaning caused by squinting modifier, 85–86
*Among* versus *between*, 185
*Amount* versus *number*, 186
Analogy
   to clarify concept, 111
   comparison topic sentence, 33
Analysis
   assignment, 197–198
   and division topic sentence, 33
*Angry with* versus *angry at*, 178
*Annoyed with* versus *annoyed at*, 178
Anthropology sources, 229
*Any more*, 184

*Anyone*
   in a comparison with *else*, 185
   versus *any one*, 184
*Anything, anywhere, anybody,* and *anyhow* as single words, 184
*Anyways* as awkward, 188
Apostrophe
   in contractions, 160
   in possessives, 124, 160–161
   in some plurals, 161
Application assignments, 201–203
Appositives, commas to set off, 150–151
*Apt, liable,* and *likely*, 178
Archaisms, 113
Architecture sources, 230
Art, italics for names of, 159
*As to* as awkward, 188
*As* versus *like*, 178
*Assure, ensure,* and *insure*, 174
*At* awkward with *where*, 188
Audiences
   adjustment of emphasis and quantity scale according to, 10
   defining, 21–22
   distortion probability to, 11
   messages geared to different, 9–10, 15, 31
   professional communication for different, 9
   reaction to communication of, 12
   word usage adjusted to level of, 108
*Awhile* versus *a while*, 184
Awkward words and phrases list, 188–189

Bacon, Francis, 3
Balanced sentence, 65
*Being as* or *being that* as awkward, 188
*Beside* versus *besides*, 188
*Between* versus *among*, 185
*Bi* versus *semi*, 178
Bible, nonitalicization of, 178
Bibliography, sample, 219
Body of a written communication, 31–32, 49
Book
   approach of this, viii
   audience for this, vii
   philosophical concerns of this, vii–viii
Book review sources
   general, 240
   scholarly, 227–228
Brackets
   for editorial use, 154–155
   as parentheses within parentheses, 155
*Breath* versus *breathe*, 171
*Bring* versus *take*, 178–179
Business
   communication needs of, viii, 2
   decentralization of, 2

*Can* versus *may*, 188
*Can't but* as awkward, 188
*Capital* versus *capitol*, 171
Capitalization of acronyms, 161–162
*Capitol* versus *capital*, 171
Carroll, Lewis, 54
Cause and effect
   complex sentence to show, 60
   sentence connectives, 40
   shown by subordinating words, 43
*Censor* versus *censure*, 171
*Center around* as awkward, 188
*Choose, chose,* and *chosen,* 171
Chronological arrangement topic sentence, 33–34
Chunking, 147–149
Churchill, Winston, 13
Circulation of completed communication, 21, 26–28
*Cite, site,* and *sight,* 172
Clarity defined, 105
Clauses, parallelism with, 79
Clichés
   eliminating, 112–113
   introducing subject with, 114
   level of usage problem from using, 76
   used for convenience, 99
*Clothe* versus *cloth,* 172

Coherence
   defined, 40
   parallelism to provide, 42
   pronoun references to aid, clear, 42–43
   repetition of key word or idea to provide, 41
   subordination of sentence part to provide, 43–51
   transition devices to provide, 40–41
Colon
   to introduce series, 153–154
   placed outside quotation marks, 156
Comma, 150–153
   abuses, 152–153
   after adverbial dependent clause at beginning of sentence, 149
   after subordinator, 146–147
   before *and* to join clauses, 146
   impact on meaning of, 145–146
   misused to separate compound nouns or compound verbs, 152
   placed inside quotation marks, 156
   to separate words or phrases that could be joined incorrectly, 150
   to set off beginning participial phrases, 152
   splice, 152
Commas
   to enclose parenthetical elements, 151
   to indicate nonrestrictive clause, 151
   to list geographical names, dates, and addresses, 152
   to note dialogue with quotation marks, 152
   to separate consecutive coordinate adjectives before noun, 151–152
   to separate items in a series, 150
   to set off alternatives or appositives, 150–151
   to set off nonessential clauses from rest of sentence, 62
Communication
   audience's reactions to, 12
   breakdown, 11, 17
   function of professional, 9
   horizontal, 16
   purpose of, vii, 1
   schema, 13–15
   in upper management levels, 4–5

Comparative degree
   double, 138
   irregular, 137–138
   *more, –er,* or *–ier* used with, 137–138, 186
*Compare* versus *contrast,* 185
Comparison
   ambiguous, 88
   illogical, 87–88
   incomplete, 87
   problems, 86–88
   sentence connectives, 40
*Complacent* versus *complaisant,* 172
*Compliment* versus *complement,* 172
Compound sentence
   coordinating conjunctions in, 60
   predicate in, 60
   subject in, 60
Compound words, hyphenation of, 157–159
Compound–complex sentence
   independent clauses in, 61
   structure, 61
   subordinated structure in, 61
Computers, impact of data from, 3
Conciseness through consistent use of active voice, 70–73
Conclusion of a written communication, 32
Conjunctions, coordinating (*and, but, for, or,* and *nor*)
   in compound sentence, 60
   preceded by a comma, 147, 153
   in subject, 65
Conjunctions, correlative
   list of, 80
   parallelism with, 80–82
Connotation
   formal, words with Latin origins having, 108
   informal, words with Germanic or Celtic origins having, 108
   as social interpretation of meaning, 92–94
*Contemptible* versus *contemptuous,* 172–173
Content
   form and, relationship of, 31–52
   loss of, vii
*Continually* versus *continuously,* 173
Contractions
   apostrophe to indicate, 160
   out of place in formal writing, 188–189
Contrast topic sentence, 33
*Contrast* versus *compare,* 185
*Convince* versus *persuade,* 179

*Council* versus *counsel*, 173
Creative writing versus professional communication, 22

Dash to signal interruption or change of thought, 154
Database sources, 221–223
Definition paper, 195–196
Definition topic sentence, 33
Demonstrative pronouns, 124–125
Denotation as dictionary meaning of word, 93–94
Dependent clause
  adverbial transition subordinators in, 60–61
  in complex sentence, 60
  in compound–complex sentence, 61
  noun and verb contained in, 53
  relative pronouns to relate structures to nouns and pronouns in, 61–65
  sentence pattern using initial, 66
  subordinator preceded by, 45
Dialogue, commas and quotation marks used for, 152
Diction, appropriateness of, vii
Dictionaries
  English language, 231–232
  subject, 226–227
*Different from*, 185
*Disinterested* versus *uninterested*, 179
Distortion probability, 11
*Diverse* versus *divers*, 173
Documentation for scientific research, 23
Documents, professional, 193–205
*Dosage* versus *dose*, 179
Double negative positives, 93
Dropped D's, 177
Drucker, Peter F., 5

Economics sources, 230
Editing written communications, 21, 26
  examples of, 99–103
  sensitivity in, 105
*Effect* versus *affect*, 170
*Elicit* versus *illicit*, 173
*Eminent*, *imminent*, and *immanent*, 174
Emphasis, italics for, 160
Encyclopedias, subject, 224–225
English language dictionaries, 231–232
*Ensure*, *assure*, and *insure*, 174
Enumeration sentence connectives, 40
*Equally as* as awkward, 189

*Erratic* versus *sporadic*, 179
*Etc.*, 179
Euphemisms, samples of how to correct, 101, 109–110
*Everyone* used in comparison with *else*, 185
Evidence to support message, 14
Example sentence connectives, 40
*Except* versus *accept*, 169
Exclamation points, placement of, 157
Executive summary, 207, 214–215
Executives, communications of, 5
*Expect* versus *suspect*, 179

False elegance, samples of how to correct, 101, 108
*Famous* versus *notorious*, 181
*Farther* versus *further*, 186
*Feel* versus *think*, 179–180
*Fewer* versus *less*, 186
Film reviews and film review indexes, 241
Fine arts sources, 233
First draft of a written communication
  composing, 21, 25
  cooling or distancing writer from, 21, 25
  editing or revising, 21, 26
Focus of communication, 27
Foreign terms
  italicizing, 159
  plural of words derived from, 186–187
Form and content, relationship of, 31–52
Fractions, 158
Fragment. See Sentence fragment
*further* versus *farther*, 186

Geographical names, dates, and places, commas to list, 152
Geography sources, 233–234
Gibbon, Edward, 13
Good
  not an adverbial intensifier, 136
  versus *well*, 57

*Hanged* versus *hung*, 180
*Have* versus *of*, 180
Hierarchy of company or institution
  communicating horizontally in, 16–17
  communicating radially (diagonally) in, 16–17
  communicating vertically in (throughout), 15–17
History sources, 234
*Hopefully*, 180

*Hung* versus *hanged*, 180
Hyphenation rules, 157–159
Hyphens
  to indicate dash in typewritten work, 154
  "suspended," 159
  word division with, 159
*Hypothesis* versus *theory*, 180

*I*, *me*, and *myself*, 181
Ideas
  as part of body of communication, 31–32
  as proof, 24
  researching a communication's, 21, 23
  sequencing, 50
*If* versus *whether*, 183
*Illicit* versus *elicit*, 173
*Illusion* versus *allusion*, 170–171
Illustrations
  for long report, 24
  to supplement writing, 14
*Imminent*, *immanent*, and *eminent*, 174
Imperative mood, 77
Impersonal pronoun (*one*), 125
*Imply* versus *infer*, 180
*In* versus *into*, 180
Indefinite pronouns, 126–127, 184
  subject–verb agreement for, 130
Independent clauses, 45–46
  in complex sentence, 60
  in compound sentence, 60
  in compound–complex sentence, 61
  noun and verb contained in, 53
Indexes
  to scholarly journals, 223
  social sciences, 228–229
Indicative mood, 77
*Infer* versus *imply*, 180
Infinitives, parallelism with, 79
Information sources, 221–242
*Insure*, *ensure*, and *assure*, 174
Interpretation, limiting professional writing to single, 22
Interrogative sentence, *who* or *whom* in, 64–65
*Into* versus *in*, 180
Introduction of a communication, 31–32
*Irregardless* as double negative, 180
*Irritate* versus *aggravate*, 177
*Is when* or *is because* as awkward, 189
Italics
  for emphasis, 160
  for foreign words, 159

245

for name of magazine, newspaper, or book, 157, 159
for name of plays, works of art, and music, 159
*It's* versus *its*, 124, 180
*-ize* as trite suffix, 183–184

Jargon, samples of how to correct, 102, 112–113
Journal(s)
indexes to scholarly, 223
learning preferred format for submissions to, 26
name listed in italic type or underlined in typed material, 157

Key points, summarizing, 13
Key word or idea, coherence aided by repeating, 41

Language usage
appropriateness of, 31
assertive, 99–103
bureaucratic, 107
concrete, 100, 103–104
Law sources, 235–236
*Lay* versus *lie*, 174
*Led* versus *lead*, 174–175
*Lend* versus *loan*, 181
*Less* versus *fewer*, 186
Letter
of application, 203
"breathing" time for, 25
cost of producing business, 2
of inquiry, 201–203
length of, 13
purpose of, 9
responsibility for content of, 15
of transmittal, 26, 207, 209–210
*Liable, apt,* and *likely,* 178
*Lie* versus *lay,* 174
*Like for instance* as redundant, 189
*Like* versus *as,* 178
*Likely, liable,* and *apt,* 178
Lists, parallelling of ideas in, 82–83
*Loan* versus *lend,* 181
Loose sentence, 65
*Loose* versus *lose,* 175

*Mad* acceptable in informal usage, 181
Main issue stated first in paragraph, 27
Malapropisms, samples of how to correct, 101, 110

Marketing
cycle of written communication for, 3–4
role of communication in, 7–8
*May* versus *can,* 188
*Maybe* versus *may be,* 184
*Me, myself,* and *I,* 181
Mechanics of communication, "noise" in message as result of careless, 11
Memorandum
assignments, 200–201
"breathing" time for, 25
by executive, 5
length of, 13
pattern, 200
purpose of, 9
responsibility for content of, 15
sample organization of, 39
Message
conclusive, 14
distortion probability due to "noise" in, 11
geared to audience, 9–10, 15, 31
generative, 14
good writing to express well-focused, 1
horizontal and vertical directions of, 16–17
substantive, 14
wordiness of, 14
Michener, James, 25
Mills, John Stuart, 3
Misconceptions, correcting, 99–118
Mixed metaphors, samples of how to correct, 102, 111–112
Modifiers
meaningless, samples of how to correct, 101, 109
misplaced, 83–84
relative pronouns as, 61–65
squinting, 85–86
*Momentarily* versus *temporarily,* 181
Mood, shifts in, 77
*Moral* versus *morale,* 175
*Most* versus *almost,* 181
Music, italics for names of works of, 159
*Myself, me,* and *I,* 181

*Nauseate* versus *nauseous,* 181
Negative–positive problems, 93–94
Newspaper
article names in quotations, 157
indexes, 240–241
title in italic type of underlined in typed work, 157

"Noise" entering communication, 11, 17
Nonrestrictive clause, 61–62, 151
*Not only . . . but also,* 185
*Notorious* versus *famous,* 181
Noun clause, 120
Noun complement to linking verb, 56
Noun phrase
gerund, 119, 122, 124
infinitive, 119
used with verb "to be," 56, 83
Nouns
collective, 119, 130
common, 119
compound, 152–153
ending in *-ics,* 130
ending in *-s,* 130
forming plural of, 120–121
parallelism with, 77–78
proper, 119
transform structures using, 119–120
used as adjectives, 91
*Number* versus *amount,* 186

Object of preposition, *whom* or *whomever* as, 64–65
Object of verb, *whom* or *whomever* as, 64–65
*Of* versus *have,* 180
*One* as impersonal pronoun, 125
*Only,* misplacement of, 91–92
Organization of a written work, planning, 21, 23–24
*Other* used with *any,* 185
Outline, developing formal, 24
*Over with,* 182

Paragraph
announcing main idea of, 34
defined, 32
function of, 32
inductive, 35
introductory, 37–38, 49
main issue stated first in, 27
structure, 34
summary, 37–38, 49
transitions to tie sentences together within, 50–51
Parallelism, 77–83
with adjectives, 78
with adverbs, 79–80
with clauses, 79
and coordination, 80–82
defined, 77
with infinitives, 79
in listing, 82–83
with nouns, 77–78

with participles, 78–79
with prepositions, 80
of thoughts and constructions, 42
Paraphrasing, 193–194
Parentheses to enclose interrupting or supplementary structures, 154
Participial phrase
comma to set off beginning, 152
dangling, 84–85
Participles, parallelism with, 78–79
*Passed* versus *past*, 175
Passive transformation of transitive verbs, 55
Passive voice
overuse of, 69
proper use of, 73
unnecessary shifts between active and, 69–73
*Past* versus *passed*, 175
Period
at end of sentence, 147
not used in acronyms, 161
placed inside quotation marks, 156
Periodic sentence, 65
Periodicals, sources for, 240. *See also* Journal *and* Newspaper
Personal data sheet, 204–205
Personal pronouns
antecedents of, 121
list of forms and uses of, 122
nominative form, 121–122
objective form, 121–123
possessive form, 122–124
*Personal* versus *personnel*, 175
*Persuade* versus *convince*, 179
Philosophy sources, 236
Place sentence connectives, 40
Point of view problem, 73–75
Political science sources, 237
Possessive case
apostrophe to indicate, 160–161
to indicate possession, 122–124
*Precede* versus *proceed*, 175–176
Predicate
compound, 59
of compound sentence, 60
of simple sentence, 59
subject noun separated incorrectly from, 153
Prefixes, hyphenation rules for, 158
Prepositional phrase
to start sentence, 66
used as an adjective, 136
Prepositions
parallelism with, 80
sentence subordinators as, 47–51
*Prescribe* versus *proscribe*, 176
*Present* versus *presently*, 182

*Principal* versus *principle*, 176
*Proceed* versus *precede*, 175–176
Process paper, 196–197
Product marketing. *See* Marketing
Production, role of communication in, 7–8
Professional documents, 193–205
Pronoun. *See also* individual types
agreement, 125–126
point of view, consistent, 73–75
references, clear, 42–43
Proofreading, objective, 105
Proposal
assignment, 199
by executive, 5
format, 199
length of, 13
purpose of, 9
*Proscribe* versus *prescribe*, 176
*Proved* versus *proven*, 182
Psychology sources, 238
Publishers, specifications for submission printed by, 26
Punctuation, 145–167
Purpose of writing
isolating, 21–22
tied to submission step, 28

Quantitative differences, 186
Question marks, placement with quotation marks of, 157
Question–answer topic sentence, 34
Quotation marks, 155–156
and commas used in dialogue, 152
to enclose name of periodical article, newspaper headline, or section or chapter of book, 157
end punctuation with, 156–157
to indicate speaker's words, 155
single, 155–156
Quotation sources, 241
*Quotation* versus *quote*, 182
Quotations, block or poetry, 156

*Raise* versus *rise*, 182
*Rational, rationalize,* and *rationale*, 182
Reaction paper, 194–195
Readers. *See also* Audiences
sensitivity of writers to, 17, 113
*Real* misused as adverbial intensifier, 136, 182
Receiver's responsibility in communication, 13
Reflexive pronouns, 125
Relative pronouns and modification, 61–65
Religion sources, 238–239

Report
derivation of, 14
formal, 23, 207–219
illustrations for, 24
length of, 13
letter of transmittal for long, 26
as product of industry, 3
to provide information, 208
purpose of, 9
to report investigations, 208
for research and development, 3
sample, 214–219
scientific, ordering of, 9–10
structure, 207–208
style, 2
trip, 201
Research for a written communication, 21, 23
*Respectfully* versus *respectively*, 182
Restrictive clauses, commas not used to set off, 151
Résumés, 204–205
*Reverend* as adjective, 189
*Rise* versus *raise*, 182
Roosevelt, Franklin D., 1

Scientific writing, quotation marks in, 157
*Semi* versus *bi*, 178
Semicolon, 149–150
placed outside quotation marks, 156
for series when one or more elements contain commas, 149
to show relationship between sentences, 147, 149
with transition adverb for chunking, 147, 149
Sender–Message–Receiver
for communication situation, vii
diagram, 11
Sense words, 57–58
Sentence, 53–67
balance, 83
complexity not measure of good writing, 1
connectives, 40–41, 47
role of a paragraph's final, 34–35
run–on, 149–150
subordinators, 43–51
topic. *See* Topic sentence
types, 58–61. *See also* individual types
variety of patterns in, 65–66
Sentence fragment
defined, 53
subordinator preceded by, 45

247

Sentence structure, 69–98
   "noise" as result of jumbled or wordy, 11
Sequence sentence connectives, 40
*Set* versus *sit*, 183
Sexist references, samples of how to correct, 102, 114–115
Shifts in level of usage, 75–76
Shifts in mood, 77
Shifts in structure of sentences, 69–77
*Sight, site,* and *cite*, 172
Simple sentence, 58–59
   defined, 58
   imperative form of, 59
   indicative form of, 59
   predicate in, 59
   subject in, 58–59
*Sit* versus *set*, 183
*Site, sight,* and *cite*, 172
Skill level, appropriateness of, 31
"Smoke" talk, 100–101, 107
"Snow" jobs, samples of how to correct, 102, 113–114
*So . . . that*, 185
Sound–alike words, 169–177
Sources list, sample of, 219
Specifications for submission for periodical, 26
Speech compared to written communication, 2
Split infinitives
   avoiding, 90
   awkward, 185
Split–verb phrase problem, 89–90
*Sporadic* versus *erratic*, 179
Statement–support deductive topic sentence, 33
*Stationary* versus *stationery*, 176
Steps in the writing process, 21–29. *See also* Written communication
Structure of written communication
   paradigm of, 36–39
   planning, 21, 23–24
Style
   apologists, 1
   appropriateness of, vii
   artificially weighty, 105–106
   copying inappropriate, 99
   lapses, 69
Style guides, 242
Subject(s). *See also* Subject–verb agreement
   alternative, 129
   compound, 128
   of compound sentence, 60
   dependent clause, 62–63
   interrogative sentence, 64
   position changes, 129
   separated incorrectly from predicate, 153
   simple sentence, 58–59
Subject line
   meaningful, 31, 39
   repeating in text the topic from, 27–28
Subject sources, specific, 229–239
Subject–verb agreement, 127–131
   alternative subjects and, 129
   basic subject used to determine, 127
   collective nouns and, 130
   for compound subjects, 128
   effect of intervening phrases on, 129
   effect of subject position changes on, 129
   indefinite pronouns and, 130
   words ending in –*s* and, 130–131
Subjunctive mood, 77
Subordinators
   adverbial, 54
   in complex sentences, 60–61
   in compound–complex sentences, 61
   sentence, 43–51, 147–148
Summary
   final sentence in paragraph as, 34–35
   paragraph, 37–38
   sample report, 216–217
Superlative degree, *most, –est,* or *–iest* used with, 137–138
Supporting information, placement of, 24, 31–32, 49
*Sure* misused as adverbial intensifier, 136
*Suspect* versus *expect*, 179

*Take* versus *bring*, 178–179
Tautology, samples of how to correct, 101, 108–109
Technical data presented for varying audiences, 9–10
Technical writing, quotation marks in, 157
*Temporarily* versus *momentarily*, 181
*That*
   as demonstrative pronoun, 124, 183
   misuse of *where* as substitute for, 92–93
   as restrictive modifier in essential dependent clause, 62, 183
   versus *which*, 183
*Their, there,* and *they're*, 176

*Themselfs* incorrect reflexive form of *themselves*, 183
Theory of communication, 7–20
*Theory* versus *hypothesis*, 180
*These* as demonstrative pronoun, 124–125, 183
*They're, their,* and *there*, 176
*Think* versus *feel*, 179–180
*This* as demonstrative pronoun, 124–125, 183
*Those* as demonstrative pronoun, 124, 183
*Thusly* as archaic form, 183
Time
   budgeting, 24
   estimating reader's, 13
   for good writing, 69
   sentence connectives, 40
   writer's project, 24
Title line
   meaningful, 31, 39
   repeating in text the topic from, 27–28
*To, too,* and *two*, 176–177
Tone
   appropriateness of, vii, 31
   connotation versus denotation and the effect on, 93–94
*Too, to,* and *two*, 176–177
Topic
   divided into parts, 37
   explicit statement of, 27–28
Topic sentence
   defined, 32
   placement in paragraph of, 34–36
   relation of final sentence in paragraph and, 34–35
   types of, 33–34
Transform structures
   noun, 119–120
   to start sentence, 66
Transition
   devices, 40–41
   techniques, 50–51, 147
Transmittal for long report, 26, 207, 209–210
Trite phrases, 76
   samples of how to correct, 102, 111–112
*Two, to,* and *too*, 176–177
Typewriter, composing first draft at, 25

*Uninterested* versus *disinterested*, 179
Unity of communication, 32, 37
Usage, shift in level of, 75–76

Vagueness, sentence
   ambiguity of referent cause of, 88–89
   squinting modifier a cause of, 85–86
Verb phrases
   in compound predicate, 59
   split, 89–90
Verb tense(s), 131–135
   future, 134–135
   future perfect, 134–135
   infinitive, 132–133
   of irregular verbs, list of, 133
   past, 131–135
   past participle, 131–134
   past perfect, 134–135
   present, 131–135
   present participle, 131–133
   present perfect, 134
   of regular verbs, list of, 132
Verbs, 54–58, 127–135. *See also* Subject–verb agreement
   active, 70–73
   Be ("to be"), 56, 70, 83, 123, 127–128
   compound, 152–153
   gerund form of, 124
   intransitive, 55–56
   irregular, 128–131, 133
   linking, 56–58
   matched to "person," 73–75
   passive, 69–73
   regular, 131–132
   of the senses, 57, 136
   "to have," 55
   transitive, 54–55

Waste words, 105
*Well* versus *good*, 57
*Where*, misuse as substitute for *that* of, 92–93
*Whether* versus *if*, 183

*Which*
   clause, misplaced, 86
   as nonrestrictive modifier in nonessential dependent clause, 61–62, 183
   versus *that*, 183
*While*, misuse as coordinator of, 92
*Who*
   as relative pronoun to relate adjective clauses to nouns, 62–63, 121
   versus *whom*, 62–65
*Whoever*, 63
*Whom*
   as relative pronoun, 123
   versus who, 62–65
*Whomever*, 64
*Whose*
   as possessive case for *who* or *whom*, 123–124
   versus *who's*, 183
–*wise* as trite suffix, 183–184
Word confusion, samples of how to correct, 102, 110–111
Word processor
   composing first draft at, 25
   impact of data from, 3
Word usage, 169–191
   adjusted to audience, 108
   interpretation influenced by, 93–94
   "noise" in message as result of careless, 11
Wordiness
   gobbledegook, 106
   of message, 14
   passive voice cause of, 70–73
   samples of how to correct, 100, 104–107
   of sentence structure, 11
Working summary, 23
Working title, 23–24

Writer
   communication as personal emissary of, 25
   overspecialization problem of, 16
   self–perception of role, 12
   sensitivity to reader of, 17
   training, experience, and research for, 4
"Writer's fallacy," 27
Writing
   connected to clarity of thought, 1–2
   measuring success of, 17
   personal advancement through good, 5
   starting, 21–29
   symptoms of bad, 1–2
Written communication
   compared to speech, 2
   cooling first draft of, 21, 25
   cycle and product marketing, 3–4
   editing first draft of, 21, 26
   format considerations, 31
   isolating the purpose of, 21–22
   organization of, 21, 23–24, 31–32
   preparing first draft of, 21, 25
   research required for, 21, 23
   submitting the completed, 21, 26–28

*Your* versus *you're*, 177